HUMAN RESOURCE DEVELOPMENT

Dr. LALITHA BALAKRISHNAN
PG Department of Business Administration
MOP Vaishnav College for Women
Chennai.

Ms. S. SRIVIDHYA
PG Department of Business Administration
MOP Vaishnav College for Women
Chennai.

Himalaya Publishing House
ISO 9001:2008 CERTIFIED

First Edition : 2007
Second Edition : 2011
Edition : 2015
Edition : 2017
Edition : 2019

Published by : Mrs. Meena Pandey for **Himalaya Publishing House Pvt. Ltd.,**
Ramdoot, Dr. Bhalerao Marg, Girgaon, Mumbai - 400 004
Phone: 022-23860170/23863863; **Fax:** 022-23877178
E-mail: himpub@bharatmail.co.in; **Website:** www.himpub.com

Branch Offices :

New Delhi : Pooja Apartments, 4-B, Murari Lal Street, Ansari Road, Darya Ganj, New Delhi - 110 002. Phone: 011-23270392, 23278631; Fax: 011-23256286

Nagpur : Kundanlal Chandak Industrial Estate, Ghat Road, Nagpur - 440 018. Phone: 0712-2738731, 3296733; Telefax: 0712-2721216

Bengaluru : Plot No. 91-33, 2nd Main Road, Seshadripuram, Behind Nataraja Theatre, Bengaluru - 560 020. Phone: 080-41138821; Mobile: 09379847017, 09379847005

Hyderabad : No. 3-4-184, Lingampally, Besides Raghavendra Swamy Matham, Kachiguda, Hyderabad - 500 027. Phone: 040-27560041, 27550139

Chennai : New No. 48/2, Old No. 28/2, Ground Floor, Sarangapani Street, T. Nagar, Chennai-600 017. Mobile: 09380460419

Pune : First Floor, Laksha Apartment, No. 527, Mehunpura, Shaniwarpeth (Near Prabhat Theatre), Pune - 411 030. Phone: 020-24496323, 24496333; Mobile: 09370579333

Lucknow : House No. 731, Shekhupura Colony, Near B.D. Convent School, Aliganj, Lucknow - 226 022. Phone: 0522-4012353; Mobile: 09307501549

Ahmedabad : 114, SHAIL, 1st Floor, Opp. Madhu Sudan House, C.G. Road, Navrang Pura, Ahmedabad - 380 009. Phone: 079-26560126; Mobile: 09377088847

Ernakulam : 39/176 (New No. 60/251), 1st Floor, Karikkamuri Road, Ernakulam, Kochi - 682011. Phone: 0484-2378012, 2378016; Mobile: 09387122121

Cuttack : New LIC Colony, Behind Kamala Mandap, Badambadi, Cuttack - 753 012, Odisha. Mobile: 9338746007

Kolkata : 108/4, Beliaghata Main Road, Near ID Hospital, Opp. SBI Bank, Kolkata - 700 010, Phone: 033-32449649; Mobile: 07439040301

DTP by : **Sri Siddhi Softtek** (Bengaluru).

Printed at : M/s. Sri Sai Art Printer Hyderabad. On behalf of HPH.

Preface

The corporate world is in the process of transformation driven by human resources and globalisation. We all do business today in a highly networked world. Organisations have started considering their employees as an inevitable asset — "The Human Capital" Corporations across the world are taking coherent and integrated efforts to develop their human assets. They intend to create contemporary HR practices that focuses or developing their human resources. Human Resource Development functions are more strategically structured as a way to compete in the market by ensuring that their HRD efforts are linked with their business strategies.

This book is an endeavour to develop the conceptual skills of students to be able to integrate the contemporary practices in Human Resource Development. We have emphasized on the concepts that have proven to be most useful in understanding the human resource development practices and its potential impact in the business activities.

The chapters in this book critically analyses the concepts and issues to acquaint the student with the literature of this area. Through a series of special comprehensive cases, it provides the student with an opportunity to apply concepts and techniques to the real world corporate problems. We have kept up a strong commitment to the philosophy of linking theory with practice all through his book. The emerging field of Human Resource Development is analysed with conceptual fundamentals to be able to link it with business strategies.

Dr.Lalitha Balakrishnan

Ms.S.Srividhya

CONTENTS

Chapter 1

AN INTRODUCTION TO HRD

Learning Objectives

1. *To Understand the Meaning and Definitions of HRD*
2. *To Understand the Approaches and Scope of HRD in Organizations*
3. *To Understand the Relationship Between HRM & HRD*
4. *To Understand the Functions of Human Resource Development in Organizations.*

Earlier, productivity was the focus, but now retention of human resources is equally important. The labour welfare myth is over. The workers' liberation of the 60s and 70s have been replaced by a new profit oriented, quality conscious pragmatism with calls for linking human resources to corporate strategy. In short, contemporary global focus is on integrating human resource development with organization growth to achieve corporate excellence.

Organizations find themselves dealing with competitive market with up-to-date technologies. The business environment today is global, customer-centric, information based, highly dynamic, and technologically up-to-date; possess high capital inflows, fast decision-making and continuous learning. With this scenario, organizations need to grapple with acquisitions, recruit and develop human resources, increase quality consciousness, build appropriate culture for excellence.

Given all this, Human Resource Development (HRD) is the fundamental idea, which drives the organizations across the globe today. Human Resource Development help organizations to assess mistakes, manage change better to retain talent to grow towards the achievement of organizational goals.

Meaning of HRD

Human Resource Development can be defined as a set of systematic and planned activities designed by an organization to provide its members with opportunities to learn necessary skills to meet current and future job requirements. Learning is the fundamental principle that drives organizations towards higher concentration on Human Resource Development. HRD activities should begin when an employee joins an organization and continue throughout his or her career, irrespective of the authority and responsibility level that the person holds. HRD programs are focused on integrating long terms plans and strategies of the organization with the requirements of changes in the job to ensure the efficient and effective use of all the resources available to the organization.

The definitions of Human Resource Development cannot be distinct and disjointed any more as more organizations are taking efforts to go global. Slowly, the whole globe is emerging as one single economic market.

- "Human Resource Development (HRD) is organized learning experiences provided by employees to bring about possibility of performance growth or personal growth within the specified period of time." – *(Giley and Eggland, 1989)*

- "Human Resource Development is a process of developing and unleashing human expertise through personal training and organizational development for the purpose of improving performance." – *(Swanson and Holton, 2001)*

- " Human Resource Development is a process in which the employees of an organization is continuously helped in a planned way to —

1. Acquire or sharpen their capabilities required to perform various tasks and functions associated with their present and future expected roles;
2. Develop their general enabling capabilities as individuals so that they are able to discover and exploit their own inner potential for their own and /or organizational development purposes and develop an organizational culture where superior-subordinate relationships, teamwork and collaboration among different sub-units are strong and contribute to the organizational health, dynamism and pride of employees." – *(T.V. Rao, 1985)*

Therefore, Human Resource Development in any organization aims at the following:

- To develop the competence of its human resources
- To create an environment of commitment and motivation among employees of the organization
- To develop a conducive organizational culture to achieve its mission for existence

- To create policies, procedures and systems to train people for better performance that is based on trust, commitment, loyalty and growth.

Approaches to Human Resource Development

Being a central part of the all the activities aimed and creating a culture of commitment and morale, Human Resource Development plays a vital role in making the employees grow vertically or horizontally in the organization through motivation and education.

There are several models developed by various experts after the evolution of Human Resource Development as a discipline of study. The few models are discussed below.

1. The Strategic HR Framework Approach (1990)

This framework was developed by Ulrich and Lake. Human resource development procedures and practices, business strategies and organizational capabilities are the three important elements of this framework. This framework basically aims at leveraging human resource development practices that would help the organizational capabilities. These capabilities would help companies to formulate business strategies for the achievement of organizational goals. Ulrich and Lake have offered tools and paths that are specific to identify and leverage effective human resource development practices of the organization.

2. The Integrative Framework (1997)

This framework was contributed by Yeung and Berman that focus on changing the priorities of the organization to maximize organizational capabilities towards the achievement of organizational goals. Yeung and Berman have given three basic routes for the successful business performance through human resource development practices.

It is a step-by-step approach to leverage on human resource development practices. Building organizational capabilities can lead to employee satisfaction and thereby customer and shareholder satisfaction. i.e.,

Build organizational capabilities

↓

Improve employee satisfaction

↓

Shape customer and shareholder satisfaction

They advocated that the human resource development measures should be business driven rather than human resource development driven; impact driven rather than activity driven; forward looking and innovative, rather than backward looking; and instead of concentrating on human resource development practices, should focus more on the entire human resource development system. This approach is widely accepted by many practitioners who intend to leverage on human resource development practices for the growth of the organization.

3. Human Capital Appraisal Approach (1998)

Friedman of Arthur Anderson Consulting Company gave this approach to the world. He believes that there are five stages in the management of human capital in any organization. They are clarification stage, assessment stage, design stage, implementation stage and monitoring stages. On the other hand, they are five areas in the management of human capital in organizations. They are recruitment, retention and retirement; rewards and performance management; career development, succession planning and training; development of organizational structure; and human capital enablers. A 5×5 matrix using all these five stages and five areas of human capital managements can be used to manage human resource development function of any organization.

Human Capital Management

Stages of HCM	*Areas of HCM*
Clarification stage	Recruitment, retention and retirement
Assessment stage	Rewards and performance management
Design stage	Career development, succession planning and training
Implementation Stage	Development of organizational structure
Monitoring Stage	Human capital enablers

4. HRD Score Card Approach (1999)

T.V. Rao outlined this framework. According to him, any human resource development practice should be mature in terms of systems, culture, competencies and business linkages in order to create the right business impact. It is an approach, which believes that a well developed human resource system would lead proper impact of business. It is the maturity level of the human resource development intervention that would lead the organization to create an impact in the market through its strategies.

5. PCMM Approach (1995)

This is approach that is basically developed for software companies by Curtis and team. The People Capability Maturity Model (PCMM) assumes that the organizations attain maturity in five stages. They are initial, repeatable, defined, managed and optimizing. Each stage has several Key Process Areas (KPAs) that would help in identifying group of work practices.

These KPAs leads to discontinuation of inconsistently performed practices and enhance the possibility of using consistently proven practices. The PCMM includes practices such as work environment, communication, staffing, managing performance, training, competency development, team building, development of organizational culture and compensation. All this would lead to continuous development of human resource capabilities in terms of the level of competence. The PCMM approach to human resource development is a widely accepted approach by the software industry.

6. Integrated Systems Approach

The integrated systems approach advocated a separate human resource development department for effective designing and implementation of human resource development systems. It believes that HRD function would evolve over a period of continuous practice of all HRD practices. This approach presumes that development of strategy is the starting point for developing the level of satisfaction among employees and achieving the goals of the organization.

Relationship between Human Resource Management and Human Resource Development (HRM and HRD)

Human Resource Management (HRM) can be defined as the effective selection and utilization of employees to best achieve the goals and strategies of the organization, as well as the goals and needs of employees. In most of the large organizations, training or human resource development is a separate department or a stand-alone function. In most small organizations, human resource development or training is a part of a human resource management department. The functioning of HRM functions in any organization is very unique in its own style and culture. However, in some organizations, HRM is a separate centralized department with highly specialized staff while in some other organizations, it is decentralized and managed by the various functional heads of the organization.

The relationship between the human resource management and human resource development can be explained as given below:

1. HRM is a large system in an organization. HRD is a sub-system of a large system and human resource development activities cannot be performed in isolation.
2. HRM functions are largely maintenance oriented and a function of management. HRD is an ongoing function and it is development oriented. HRD cares for human resources in the organization and aims at enhancing both their personal and professional growth.
3. HRM believes that an increase in the business results would lead to increase in performance or productivity level. HRD believes that it is improvement in the performance, which would result in continuous increase in business results.

4. HRM is more of a result-oriented function, whereas HRD is more of process-oriented function.

5. HRM focuses more on the improvement in performance and HRD focuses on improvement in the capabilities of employees for productivity.

6. HRM provides a narrower view towards retention of human resources in the organization. It believes that the compensation patterns which would decide on the satisfaction levels of the employees. HRD provides a broader view towards increase in the morale and commitment levels of the employees of the organization. It advocates the care of the organization in the growth of the employees that decides the levels of satisfaction of the employees.

7. HRM aims at creating organization of successful business results through performance and HRD aims at creating learning organizations for improving the organizational capabilities and thereby successful business results.

Scope for Human Resource Development

Human Resource development helps the organizations in developing systems and structure, planning and organizing the manpower, employee development, developing performance management systems, management of career path of the employees and consulting and organizational development. In fact, human resource development focuses on 'care and concern' on the part of the organization towards their employees which would lead to achievement of the organizational goals.

Human resource development empowers an organization to be adaptable to the changes in the environment. It enables an organization to be more dynamic which is of primary importance today for its successful existence. HRD, by creating organizations that are continuously learning and adapting to the environment creates competent organizations. Successful enterprises are more often enterprises that possess a very high degree of competitiveness. Creating competent organizations is a function of three important phases, which are inter linked with each other. The important phases are achieving organizational capabilities, integrating human resources into business and achieving corporate excellence. Each phase has two important functions to be focused on, to achieve the results. At each of three phases, the HRD practices of an organisations focuses on certain important activities to achieve the organisational goals. They are:

1. Enhancing organizational capabilities
   - HRD practices for enhancing quality consciousness among employees
   - Continuous improvement in the performance of employees

3. Achieving corporate excellence
   - HRD programs to facilitate group communication in the organization
   - Achieving organizational effectiveness in terms of performance and communication.

The three phases are inter-linked with each other and do not happen in isolation. A continuous concentration on the human resource development will definitely increase the competitiveness of any organization. Competitiveness can also be measured in terms of communication, performance and level of commitment of employees. Human resource development does not limit itself to just improvement of performance among employees but extends itself to continuous improvement in the level of performance. HRD basically believes that this continuous improvement is direct function of integrating human resources into business through excellence in communication.

Importance of Human Resource Development

Excellence of any organization cannot be confined to the pillars of productivity alone. Managing human resources has much more challenges today. Human resource development practices provide a broader perspective for any organization to grow more dynamic, adaptable and thereby improve performance continuously.

The importance of human resource development are discussed below:

1. HRD facilitates the complete utilization of human capital of the organization. Talent can be retained by the organization only by providing opportunities for growth and rewarding the innovativeness and performance. Effective practices on human resources development would ensure retention of the top talent of the organization.
2. Human resource development offers a nurturing environment for higher quality of work life through job satisfaction, career growth and development.
3. Human resource development facilitates more open communication among the employees and management in any organization.
4. Human resource development ensures increased job satisfaction, commitment and morale of employees.
5. Human resource development ensures smooth functioning of all functions of human resource management from recruitment, selection, compensation till handling attrition and retirement of employees.
6. Human resource development practices provide an organizational culture that vibrates positive synergy for excellence.
7. Human resource development facilitates better understanding of organizational goals and also helps to synchronize the same with the personal goals of the employees of the organization.

8. Human resource development helps in framing systems, policies and procedures that are dynamic in nature.
9. Human resource development function of any organization makes the organization more adaptable to changes in the environment.
10. On the whole, it is human resource development practices of any organization which helps employees to understand the organizational goals better, improve performance for achieving those goals and also ensures the relationship between the management and employees is sharpened to be more focused towards the achievement of goals in a stimulating and nurturing environment.

Functions of Human Resource Development

An ASTD (American Society for Training and Development) sponsored study by Pat MCLagan sought to identify roles of HRD function and competencies required for an effective HRD function. The study identified four trends affecting HRD.

1. Greater diversity in the work force
2. More people involved in knowledge work, which requires judgement, flexibility and personal commitment rather than submission to procedures
3. Greater expectations of meaningful work and employee involvement
4. A shift in the nature of the contract between organizations and their employees.

The ASTD study documented a shift from the more traditional training and development topic to a function that included career development and organization development as well. The study depicted the relationship between HRM and HRD functions as a 'human resource wheel'. (*source:* www.astd.org)

The human resource wheel identifies three functions as the primary functions of HRD and others are to be considered as the secondary functions of HRD. The primary functions are training and development, organization development and career development. Let us discuss the functions of HRD in detail.

1. Training and Development

Training and development focuses on changing or improving the knowledge, skills and attitude of individuals. Training primarily focuses on providing the knowledge and skill required to perform the job and change in the attitude, if required is also attempted the conduct of training. Development has a long-term perspective. Development concentrates on preparing employees to perform current jobs and also prepare them for future job requirements. HRD activities should focus more on training initially and once the employees are proficient in their jobs, should focus more on development to prepare employees for the responsibilities of tomorrow.

Organization Development

Organization Development (OD) is the process of enhancing the effectiveness of an organization through planned interventions that apply behavioural science concepts. OD focuses more preparing the organization for changes and help them to adapt change smoothly. Organization Development applies various interventions to facilitate such kind of smooth transition or change. It emphasizes both on organizational changes and changes in the individual employees.

Career Development

Career development is an "ongoing process by which individuals progress through series of stages, each of which is characterized by a relatively unique set of issues, themes and tasks". Career development includes both career planning and management. Career planning helps the individuals to identify their career path by analyzing their individual skills and abilities. Career management is concerned with moving in the career path chosen that would foster career development.

The three primary functions of human resource development are linked with each other. For example, career development programs may give inputs of the kind of training required for the employees or inputs from OD interventions would facilitate some career development programs in the organization.

Secondary functions of Human Resource Development

Performance Management Systems

Performance management helps in aligning employees' work and behaviour towards the achievement of organizational goals. Performance Management systems includes all the functions related to the performance of employees. It includes performance planning, analysis, performance appraisal and potential appraisal. Human resource development facilitates effective performance management systems by integrating the resources and processes with people to enhance the level of productivity.

Organizational Learning

Another important function of human resource development is to create 'learning organizations'. HRD initiates and stimulates a culture of learning in the organization. The HRD programs help the employees to identify the relationship between work and learning and HRD insists on continuous learning. The efforts for human resource development in an organization helps in cultivating a culture for continuous learning and drives the employees towards a new or enhanced behaviour of creativity, innovation and knowledge generation for the benefit of the organization as a whole.

Employee Mentoring

"The process of building a beneficial partnership to help develop the skills, behaviours and insights to reach one's leadership goals. Importantly, the mentor may have no stake in the outcome" – Kate Mckee, Anita Champion and Amy Davis Kruize.

Mentoring is a voluntary collaborative and mutually beneficial partnership between a person of group of people who possesses the knowledge, skill and experience and a person or group of people who are looking for that knowledge, skill and experience. HRD practices in an organization facilitate the employees of the organization to benefit from such kind of beneficial relationships to enhance the quality of the work life.

Strategic Human Resource Development

The approach of strategic human resource development lies at the organization as an entire system. All the divisional parts of the organization need to work with the goals of the organization. A strategic human resource management need to check on the viability of achieving the goals of the organization through its employees. A strategic human resource development system focuses largely on the high performance work system i.e., improved performance, increased quality and dynamism, customer delight and enhance quality of work life. The function of human resource development in any organization should ensure that the HRD strategies are consistent with overall strategy. To ensure the same, HRD activities in any organization need to ensure that —

1. The employees are directly or indirectly participating in the process of setting goals
2. To provide education and training for the employees to achieve the goals
3. The relationship between the employees and the management to sail in a smooth relationship to achieve the goals of the organization.

The HR systems in an organization need to look at the management practices, organizational structure, human resource systems and other work practices are in tune to achieve the objectives of the organization as a whole.

Review Questions

1. Define Human Resource Development. Explain the approaches to human resource development.
2. What are the functions of human resource development?
3. Explain the need, scope and importance of human resource development.
4. Strategic Human Resource Management is the order of the day. Comment for organisations.

✿ ✿ ✿

Chapter 2

A Role of a HRD Professional

Learning Objectives

1. *To Learn the Structure of HRD Function*
2. *To Understand the Roles and Qualities of HRD Professionals*
3. *To Trace the Evolution of HRD*

Organizations intending to have a good HRD system need to possess a high degree of top management philosophy towards human resource development. Making the employees and the management feel that HRD is an important component would be top priority for organizations that require a good HRD system in place. Human Resource Development is all about unleashing human capabilities for enhanced organizational performance and impact. It also requires the support and motivation for the line and staff managers with relevant HRD systems and tools in place. One important managerial responsibility would be to make sure that all managers and employees apply human resource development policies on a day-to-day basis and distribute tasks and responsibilities fairly and equitably among employees.

To ensure a proper wholesome coverage of human resource development practices for the organization, the most important task would be set up a human resource development department. In large organizations, HRD is considered to be a separate department. In India, most large organizations have set up a separate training and development department to take care of the functional responsibilities of HRD. In medium and small enterprises, HRD department or the Training and Development department functions under the human resource management department. In either case, it is important for organizations to possess well-trained and groomed professionals for managing the HRD functions of the organization.

Structure of the HRD Department

If the organizations decide to possess a separate HRD department, the organizational structure of the department decides the flow of authority and responsibilities. A Vice President will lead the function in very large organizations or Managers will head with the function in medium and small enterprises. But, whether HRD is a part of a HRM function or a separate department, it is important that it is managed by a group of well trained employees with a dynamic manager to lead the function.

The figure given below will depict the functional flow chart of the HRD department in the organization.

Structure of the HRD Department in Large Organizations

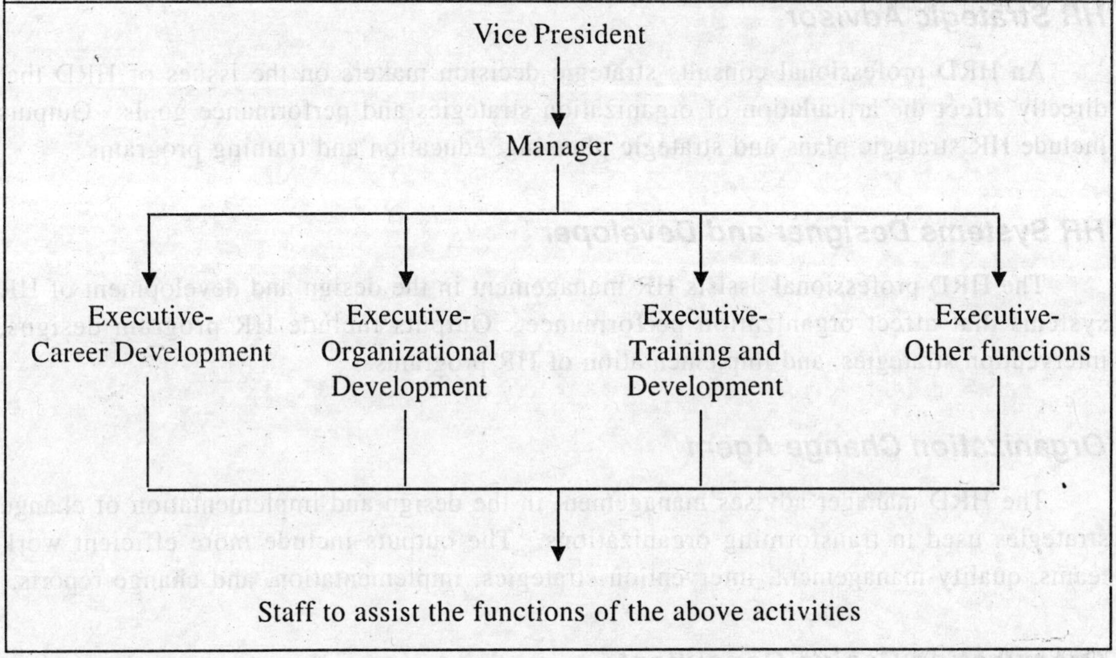

The HRD Professional

The manager of the HRD function has the responsibility to integrate the HRD programs and make arrangements to include long-range plans and strategies, policies and budget allocation schedules. The immediate challenge of any HRD profession would be to establish a clear relationship between the HRD expenditures and organizational effectiveness. It also becomes his responsibility to make the employees and management believe that human resource development is a valuable tool to organizational members for their current and future job requirements. More importantly, it is the responsibility of the human resource development manager to make organizations capable of working in a global economy from the perspective of the adequacy of the knowledge level of the organizational members. Often, it is the responsibility of the human resource development manager to make organizations, that are capable of managing change dynamically and need to redefine the new role of human resource development during the period of unprecedented change.

Roles of a HRD Professional

As organizations have adjusted to environmental challenges, the roles played by the HRD professional have changed. Based on the ASTD (American Society for Training and Development) study results, Pat McLagan states the contemporary HRD professionals perform nine distinct roles, which are discussed below. **(source:** www.astd.org)

HR Strategic Advisor

An HRD professional consults strategic decision makers on the issues of HRD that directly affect the articulation of organization strategies and performance goals. Outputs include HR strategic plans and strategic planning, education and training programs.

HR Systems Designer and Developer

The HRD professional assists HR management in the design and development of HR systems that affect organization performance. Outputs include HR program designs, intervention strategies, and implementation of HR programs.

Organization Change Agent

The HRD manager advises management in the design and implementation of change strategies used in transforming organizations. The outputs include more efficient work teams, quality management, intervention strategies, implementation, and change reports.

Organization Design Consultant

The role of the HRD manager also includes advising the management on work systems, design and the efficient use of human resources. Outputs include program objectives, lesson plans and intervention strategies.

The Instructor or Facilitator

The HRD professional presents materials and leads and facilitates structured learning experiences. Outputs include the selection of appropriate instructional methods and techniques and actual HRD program itself.

The Individual Development and Career Counsellor

The HRD professional assists individual employees in assessing their competencies and goals in order to develop a realistic career plan. Outputs include individual assessment sessions, workshop facilitation and career guidance.

The Performance Consultant

The HRD professional advises the line management on appropriate interventions designed to improve individual and group performance. Output includes intervention strategies, coaching, design and implementation.

The Researcher

The HRD professional assesses HRD practices and programs using appropriate statistical procedures, to determine the overall effectiveness and communicate the results to the organization. Outputs include research designs, research findings and recommendations and reports.

Therefore, the HRD professional is truly a change facilitator, who ensures smooth functioning of organizational strategies, systems and sub-systems for the achievement of organizational goals.

Qualities of a HRD Professional

Given the dynamic changes in the global economy, the roles of a HRD professional seem to encompass in it, the great need for facilitating organizational learning and organizational communication. It is important for enterprises to possess professionals, who are trained and groomed in the area of Human Resource Development. Apart from the basic managerial skills, that a true HRD professional need to possess, there are certain secondary skills, which will lift him up to the level of a global manager.

Qualities of a HRD Professional →

1. Training Skills
2. Leadership capabilities
3. Analytical skills
4. Interpersonal communication
5. Multi-cultural communication capabilities
6. Technical Skills

Training Skills

An important element of any good HRD manager is the capability to train people. He should be a person who can train organizational members both for the current and future job requirements. It also becomes his responsibility to convince the management and make them understand that HRD is a valuable tool for attaining the organizational goals with an emphasis on quality and increased productivity. His training skills will help employees to align their work planning and performance. It is his training skills that would help the employees more motivated towards work. He should be more of a 'people's person'.

Leadership Capabilities

A HRD professional should be capable of leading a team and also a person who can lead by example. Being a good leader would help him to align the employees' personal goals and principles with that of the organizational goals. A leader can motivate, support, encourage and guide the employees of the organization. Moreover, the activities of the HRD department will also be more focused and organized if the HRD professional is a good leader.

Analytical Skills

Often it becomes important for the HRD professional to be challenged with people who possess different kinds of personalities. Only the person working in HRD is logical and analytical, he will be in a position to resolve the issues around him. Also, it would help to be critical while there are opportunities and problems.

Technical Skills

Good knowledge about the organization and staying up-to-date in terms of technology seem to be a prerequisite to work for HRD in enterprises. A HRD professional need to possess sound technical abilities. This would help him to be a tchno-managerial person and more suitable to run the training programs.

Interpersonal skills

A HRD professional must be able to articulate in dealing with people issues. A good rapport with the people in the organization will help him to understand the background of the issues before he endeavours to resolve the same. A good rapport with people outside the organization will in turn help the organization to make use of the best opportunities that are available for training and development of the employees.

Multicultural Communication skills.

Businesses have gone beyond the walls of the domestic economy to a whole world shrinking itself into a global village. Therefore, organizations are challenged to handle different people from different cultures and background. To communicate very effectively to all the employees in the organization, a HRD professional need to expose himself to different cultures and understand the nuances of handling people from different cultures. It is also the moral responsibility of the HRD professional to be able to create a culture of global sensitivity among the employees.

Therefore, a proper combination of the Knowledge, Skill and Attitude (KSA) becomes vital for an HRD professional to manage the developmental operations of the whole organization.

Challenges faced by HRD Professionals

Since the whole world is economically shrinking to become one market economy, organizations are trying to unfold the challenges before them. In fact, since HRD professionals are in a position to create a bottom-line impact in the organization, they need to be more sensitized with these changes in the business environment. The major challenges faced by the HRD professionals are listed below.

1. A drastic change in the work force demographics in small, medium and large scale enterprises.
2. To handle employees who hail from multicultural background.
3. The HRD professionals are expected to prove in a short span of time that the expenditures in human resources development and the achievement of organizational goals are correlated.
4. To bridge the knowledge and the skill gap between the employees.
5. There is a clear need for the HRD professional to focus more on continuous learning and also facilitate organizational learning.
6. To innovate continuously on the HRD practices in the global economy.

The Evolution of Human Resource Development

Only after the 1980s, Human Resource Development has become an accepted phenomenon across the world. Earlier there existed only the apprenticeship training programs. These apprenticeship-training programs dates back to the eighteenth century. Basically, apprenticeship training served as a technical school, which helped the employees to tune the intricacies of the skills that they have already learnt.

Then, in the early 1800s, there were vocational education programs that would help the unskilled employees learn the techniques of doing a job of good quality. This concept gave room for 'early factory schools' after the industrial revolution. These are training programs that are tailor-made to do a particular job in a particular industry.

One of the by-products of the factory system was the frequent abuse of unskilled workers. The appalling conditions spurred a national anti-factory campaign. Led by Mary Parker Follet and Lillian Gilbreth, the campaign gave rise to the 'human relations movement' advocating more humane working conditions. With the outbreak of the Second World War, the industrial sector once again asked to retool its factories to support the war effort. Slowly, there was a need for formal education in HRD; hence universities and colleges started delivering a course in training and development.

In 1970s, the training professionals felt that there was a need to extend the training function beyond the classroom. The employees' involvement in organizational goal setting processes and strategy formulation processes was slowly increasing. Organizations started considering human resource as a great asset. In 1980s and 1990s, several organizations and government started conducting seminars and conferences on human resource development, organizations started believing that human resource development would be a valuable means to achieve the organizational objectives.

In the 21st century, with the advent IT and ITES industries, the need for human resource development is being largely felt by many organizations. Today, irrespective of the size of the companies, the organizational members are focusing more on the training and development not only in the classroom but also beyond it.

In India, in the late 1990s and the early 21st century saw an increase in the HRD activities almost in all the organizations. The top management of many companies has started showing commitment and interest in the development of their human resources. Some companies have transparent and explicit corporate policies towards the human resource development. Some of the early Indian establishers of a separate human resource development department in their organizations are Crompton Greaves, Steel Authority of India, BHEL, Larson and Turbo and others.

Review Questions

1. Describe the role of a HRD professional in an organization.
2. HRD professionals need to be multi-faceted personalities. Comment.
3. The global economy challenges the HRD professionals to a large extent. Trace the reasons.
4. Briefly trace the history of human resource development.

✿ ✿ ✿

Chapter 3

DEVELOPMENT OF HRD SYSTEM

Learning Objectives

1. *To Familiarize with the Concepts and Subsystems of HRD*
2. *To Understand the Process and Outcomes of HRD*
3. *To get Knowledge about HRD Planning*

The human resource development function in any organization needs to address various problems and issues. They help to induct new employees to the culture of the organization, to help individuals enhance their levels of productivity and understand what would be the future job requirements. In order to perform all these functions effectively, the function of human resource development in the organization needs to be more focused and stabilized. The professionals in the human resource development need to establish a process that is dynamic in nature in order to execute the tasks in hand. The achievement of the HRD goals in the organization largely depends on the design of HRD interventions. These HRD interventions can be designed successfully, if it undergoes a proper process. The process would be self-sufficient to eliminate mistakes at the stage of design itself. So, the implementation becomes less complicated and ensures a smooth transition.

Process of HRD

The below diagram explains the process of HRD

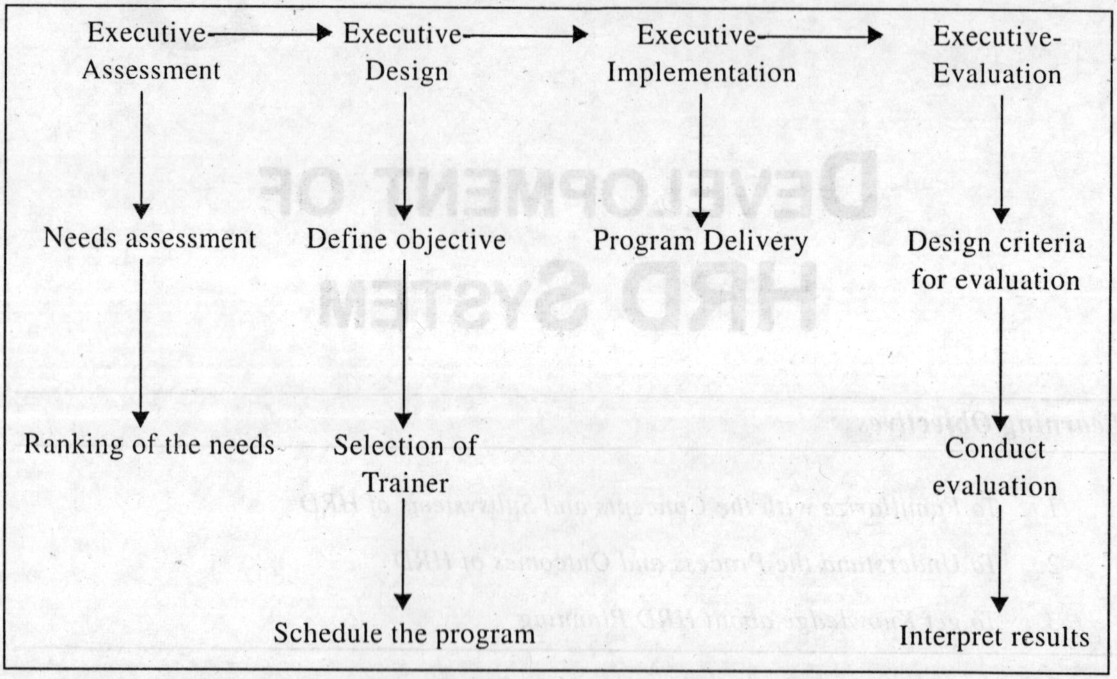

1. Assessment

This is the first stage of the assessment process. The needs of the training efforts need to identify by a training needs assessment done scientifically. When the assessment is being carried there would arise a list of needs, there would arise a need for many things. The HRD department needs to do a thorough analysis of the need. This analysis would provide data for prioritizing those needs. The prioritization would be based on increase in the immediate productivity levels of the employees, increase in the level of motivation, cost involved in that particular training etc. Based on these criteria, the needs have to be prioritized.

2. Design

The design includes the following:

(a) Development of the objectives of the training program

(b) Development of the lesson plan for the training program

(c) Design of the program

(d) Selection of the trainer

(e) Methods of training

(f) Choice of the techniques of training

(g) Schedule the program.

The schedule so developed will be circulated inside the organization for people to go through and make-work arrangements in case of outbound training programs. The selection of the trainer, content and preparation of the schedule forms the primary work during this phase. The design has to be done with proper care because it forms the primary data for the implementation of the same.

3. Implementation

Delivering HRD program has numerous challenges such as the delivering the program according to the schedule, creating an environment of learning, work adjustments and resolving the issues in implementation.

4. Evaluation

Evaluation is the stage where the HRD department is given an opportunity to assess the effectiveness of training. There can be numerous criteria based on which one can evaluate an HRD effort. The professionals need to make choice of the criteria and implement the same. Interpretation on the effectiveness of the HRD activity would provide data for deciding on the —

(a) Continuance on the usage of the same technique

(b) Deciding on the quality of the program

(c) The value for the effort and cost

(d) Offering the particular program in the future.

The Systems of HRD

There are various targets of HRD. They are the person, role, group, inter-group and organization. In other words, all the efforts of HRD are focused on improving these human units of the organization. These human units form one axis. On the other axis, we will find the HRD systems and activities. These two axes can be called as the HRD matrix. All the HRD efforts and activities should be focused on the human units. All the HRD efforts in enhancing the qualities of these human units will be categorized as the HRD systems. These systems are concerned with individual roles of the employees, their appraisal, the employees' development and growth, their management of work, which would help the organization to renew itself every day. The following diagram represents the HRD matrix:

HRD MATRIX

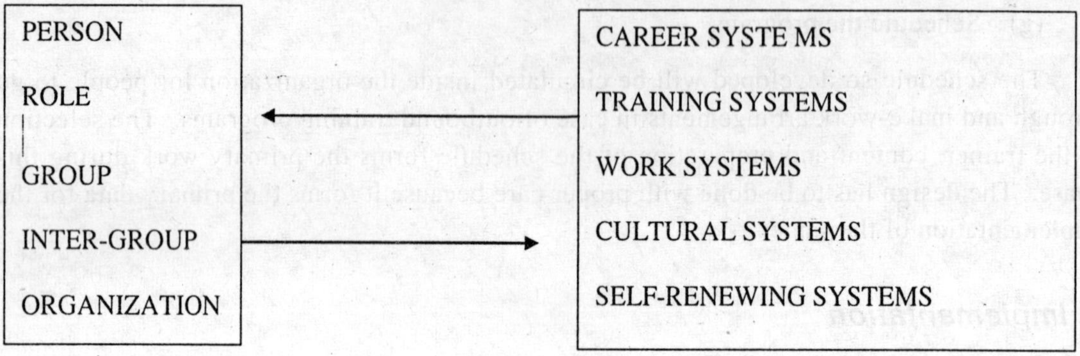

The above diagram illustrates that the first axis is a cluster of the beneficiaries of the system that exist in the organization. They provide the inputs for the formation of these systems and in turn the systems that are developed control the working pattern and functioning of all these units. The two axes are inter-related and the first cluster acts as the input for the development of other and the second cluster helps the first axis to function smoothly and efficiently. Let us discuss the HRD systems in detail.

1. Appraisal Systems

This system deals with everything pertaining to the performance of the individual. There are two appraisal systems that have gained much importance. They are performance appraisal and potential appraisal. This will be discussed in the later chapters.

2. Training Systems

This system works with the identification of training needs, design of the training program, implementation and delivery of the training program. This system is the oldest system of HRD.

3. Work Systems

This particular system deals with the improvement of the productivity levels in India and improvement in the quality consciousness among employees. Work systems help the employees to divide the work, prepare a job description manual and take efforts to manufacture quality products in a good quality of work life.

4. Cultural Systems

The cultural systems facilitate better communication inside the organization and develop a climate for open communication. This cultural system is also concerned with the development of culture, which facilitates a culture of learning and enhanced communication.

5. Self Renewing systems

This is the system that helps the organization to adapt itself with the changes in the environment. This system, through the organizational development interventions facilitates smooth transition of change. This system gives room for growth in terms of enhancing the research abilities and facilitating organizational learning.

The diagram below on the HRD matrix would discuss on some the examples of the HRD matrix.

HRD MATRIX

	Appraisal Systems	*Career Systems*	*Training Systems*	*Work Systems*	*Cultural Systems*	*Self-renewal Systems*
Person	Appraisal	Career planning	Identification of training needs	Role efficacy	Rewards	Involvement
Role	Developing key result areas	Job rotation	Job description	Job enrichment	Communication	
Group	Group appraisal		Training	Quality of work life	Communication	Team building
Inter-group	Policies and procedures		Training	Productivity	Communication	Team competitive-ness
Organization	Suitability of the person to the organization	Succession planning	Organizational effectiveness	Improved performance	Climate	Organizational learning

(**Source**: www. astd.com)

HRD Planning

Organizations find themselves dealing with strong competitive employees who demand some degree of efforts from the organization for the improvement of his performance. Hence, the HRD department is under the pressure to communicate to the employees the proper plan of their HRD activities. One important responsibility of the HRD department of the organization is to make sure that all the managers and employees apply the human resource development practices in the organization on a daily basis. Only when the system is implemented, it would strengthen the organization in terms of handling their human resources.

The HRD plan of the organization must include the following components.

a. HRD philosophy

b. HRD sub-systems

c. HRD objectives

d. HRD policies and procedures

e. Implementation of HRD efforts.

Let us discuss each component in detail.

HRD Philosophy

This forms the basic principle of forming a HRD department. It explains the beliefs, ideals and principles, which are held by the management towards the employees' growth and development. It gives rise to a particular style of management and how the organization intends to use the potential of the employees and help them grow with the organization. The organization needs to believe that the human resources are the most important assets to develop a good HRD philosophy. A good HRD philosophy will give room for the growth of positive organizational culture, which would motivate the employees. HRD philosophy also acts as a tool to communicate the goals of the organization to its employees' explicitly. Most often, it is only the philosophy of human resource development that guides the HRD efforts and programs that are being run in an organization. It is a set of fundamental principles of human resource development in the organization.

HRD Sub-systems

Sub-systems are various tools and interventions used to enforce the human resource development efforts in the organization. Some of the sub-systems of HRD are:

1. Concentration in career development
2. Good performance appraisal systems
3. Improved quality of work life
4. Training and development
5. OD interventions for change management
6. Employee counselling
7. Participatory devices etc.

Basically, sub-systems include all the tools that the organization is trying use under the system to enhance the quality of the human resource in the organization.

Objectives of HRD

These are the ends towards which all the activities are planned. The HRD objectives are to be set keeping in mind the goals of the organization in general and development of human resources in particular. Most often, the attainment of HRD objectives may not be verifiable in quantitative terms. Still, the organizations today need the prove that the HRD efforts have resulted in increased productivity to the management and a justification to the funds that they have used. Therefore, the HRD department need to set goals with an idea of the measurability of the achievement of the same. There need some kind of tangible criteria to measure whether these objectives are attained.

HRD Policies and Procedures

Policies are general statements that guide the actions of the HRD department and procedures are step-by-step process to implement these policies. The HRD policies may pertain to training, compensation, career management etc. There are ready-made documents available for ready reference.

Implementation of HRD Efforts

It is important that there are set action plans for implementing the HRD efforts of an organization. There are various tools such as organizational development and potential appraisal to facilitate a smooth implementation. For example, preparation of training calendar is one technique to implement the training plan of the organization. Every plan needs to be broken into different units for implementation purposes. A HRD plan that is not implemented will nullify all the efforts that are taken.

Organizational Outcomes of Human Resource Development

If the HRD plan were implemented in the required fashion, it would have various outcomes, which would benefit both the organization and the employees. A good HRD system would ensure the functioning all activities of human resource management. The organizational outcomes of good human resource development efforts in the organization are discussed below.

1. It would provide data that is required for manpower planning, training and development plans etc.

2. Since the communication system in the organization has become more transparent, the top management will be in a position to acquire more information and slowly it would lead for acceptance of idea openly.

3. Well-planned human resource development activities in the organization would help the employees become more competent with their work.

4. It would help the employees to develop trust with each other and towards the management. It also helps the organization to develop teamwork and mutual respect among the employees.

5. The top management can expect loyalty and commitment from the employees as they have taken conscious efforts to fulfill the needs of the employees.

6. It helps the employees to take more initiatives to solve the issues and improve performance.

7. Employees feel motivated to take challenges and bring creative ideas to meet those challenges. The top management becomes more sensitive to the problems and processes due to increased openness in communication.

These organizational outcomes will lead the organization to grow in size, revenues, profits and visibility in the market place. The success or failure of a good HRD system should be measured qualitatively and not in terms of the number of grievances handled or numbers of complaint received. The ideal situation would be when the balance sheets of the companies include the human element in the organization along with the financial data.

Review Questions

1. Discuss the HRD matrix with an example.

2. Explain about the HRD process in large organizations.

3. What are the organizational outcomes of HRD.

4. A good HRD planning will justify the expenditure made on the activities of human resource development. – Discuss.

✿ ✿ ✿

Chapter 4

PERFORMANCE MANAGEMENT SYSTEM

Learning Objectives

1. *The Concept and Process of Performance Appraisal*
2. *Effective Performance Evaluation*
3. *Methods of Performance Appraisal*
4. *Potential Appraisal*

Performance Management Systems constitute all the components of assessing the performance of employees in the organization. Performance Management System is the process of planning the expected performance level of the employees, analyze the performance, appraise and actions taken to improve the productivity of the employees. Performance Management is a tool for continuous improvement of performance of the employees of the organization at all levels. A good performance management system will be highly individualized and based on evidence. The most important component of performance management systems is performance appraisal. It is a tool to assess the employees' performance with already set standards of performance. Performance Appraisal is basically the process of analyzing the performance of the employees in comparison with the standards already set for performance of that particular job.

Performance Appraisal can be defined as follows:

" Performance appraisal is a process of systematically evaluating performance and providing feedback upon which performance adjustments can be made" – Schermerhorn, Hunt and Osborn.

Objectives of Performance Appraisal

The objectives of performance appraisal system can de depicted with the diagram given below.

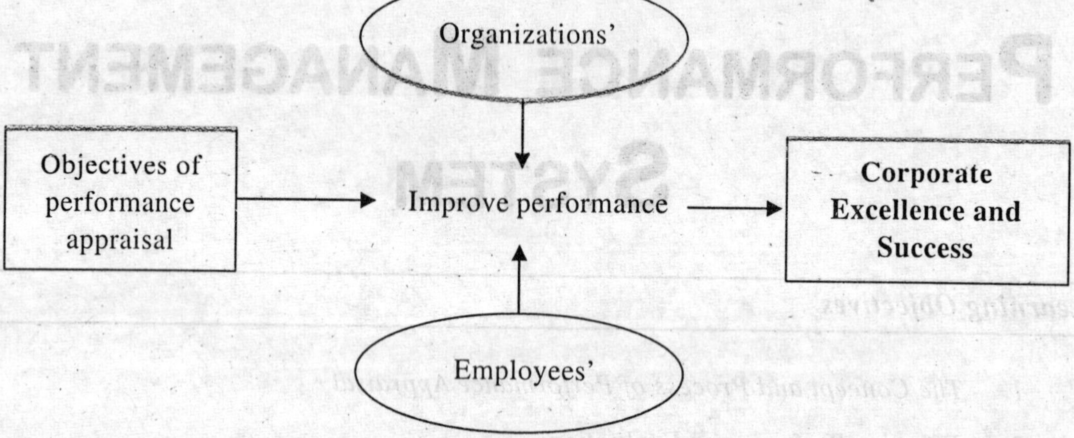

The elements of performance appraisal include goal setting, performance rating and individual pay to be decided with the rating of the performance. Primarily, the performance appraisal intends to do the following:

- Evaluate the performance of the employees
- Develop the employees for better performance
- Design a performance related pay.

The basic objective of the performance appraisal is to enhance the performance of the employees' and thereby the organization. (Figure above). This would help the organization to gain corporate excellence and success in the due course of time. To attain excellence in the industry, the performance appraisal needs to focus on the following points also.

They are:

- Increased motivation and productivity
- Enhance transparency
- Increase commitment towards work
- Establish meritocracy among the employees
- Retain top talents
- Develop employees (job and career)
- Improve collaboration between the employees
- Ensure accountability and ownership.

Once the organization has successfully implemented a performance appraisal system, it would lead to corporate excellence automatically.

Process of Performance Appraisal

The process of performance appraisal has various steps in it. The understanding of the process would give a clear picture about the issues that are concerned with the preparation and application of the assessment system

The picture given below would give a clear idea about the process of performance appraisal.

Organizational goals

↓

Job analysis

↓

Determination and setting performance standards

↓

Determination of the measurement methods

↓

Identification of appraisers

↓

Conduct performance appraisal

↓

Evaluate the results

The above diagram illustrates that the step one of the whole process would give clear understanding of the organizational goals. Given the understanding of the organizational goals, there would be clear description of the duties and responsibilities of the employee's of the organization. The duties, functions and responsibilities pertaining to the particular job need to be described appropriately.

The next step would be setting the performance standards for the employees. These performance standards that are set should possess the following:

a. The standard of performance set should be linked to the organizational goals.

b. The criteria would be the parameters based on which the parameters of performance need to be assessed should also be mentioned.

c. There are certain aspects of the actual performance that would be left out from measurement are called as the criteria deficiency.

d. Any standards that are being set should have some reliability in terms of consistent measures across appraisers over a period of time.

The standards of performance that are set need to possess the above requirements. Since setting of standards form the base with which the actual performance is being compared with, care should be taken to determine the standards of performance.

The next step would be determination of measurement methods. There are various choices for companies to implement the appraisal system such as the ranking method, comparison methods and objective methods. There is no single solution or choice of the method. The suitability of the method of evaluation largely depends on the dynamics of the organization. Sometimes, a combination of many methods can also be used for the same.

The further step would be the choice of the appraiser to conduct the appraisal. The appraiser needs to be very analytical and logical who has a thorough knowledge of the organization. The appraiser needs to be unbiased towards the whole organization. Generally, the appraisers are good managers chosen by the organization and sometimes, organization would prefer a third party appraiser to conduct the appraisal. He should not only administer the appraisal but also, capable of training the manager to administer the same. The next step would be to conduct the appraisal with strong determination to conduct smoothly and finish on time. It is important to keep in mind that there should not be any lapse in time for the same.

The last step is the evaluation and interpretation of results. This would form the base data for ranking purposes and in some organizations; the results would also be used for deciding the incentives and annual increments. Most often, comparing the performance and determining the deviation of the same from the standard performance interpret the results. The last and final step would be the conduct of appraisal interview. Performance appraisal interview is the process of initiating the performance dialogue with an objective to improve the performance. It includes performance review discussions, appraisal meetings and performance appraisal discussions etc.

The process of performance appraisal can be altered from time to time depending on the organization's philosophy and ideals. Also, it is important that the performance appraisal is conducted scientifically so as to understand where the employees stand and where they need to proceed for the attainment of organizational objectives.

Types of Performance Appraisal

Depending on the size and nature of business the organization is into; the methods of performance appraisal would differ.

Basically, there are four types of performance appraisal. They are behavioural methods, comparative methods, rating methods and narrative methods.

Methods of Performance Appraisal
• **Comparative Methods** — Ranking Methods — Paired Comparison Methods — Grading Methods — Forced Distribution Methods — Forced Choice Methods • **Rating Methods** — Graphic Rating Scale — Checklist Methods • **Narrative Methods** — Periodic Report Methods — Field Review Methods — Critical Incidents Methods • **Behavioural Methods** — MBO/Results Methods — BARs Methods — Assessment Centre Technique — 360 Degree Feedback — Balance Score Card

They are explained as follows:

• *Comparative Methods*

These methods basically intend to measure the employee's performance in comparison with the employees of the same organization of employees in the same industry.

These methods give us the data on the relative difference in the performance of the employees. The companies also conduct a 'benchmarking of the performance; that is the companies try to standardise with an ideal performance and a standard with which the performance of the employees are compared with. The following are the different kinds of comparative methods.

1. Ranking Method

Under this method, a ranking of the employees of the team or department is being conducted. The appraiser tries to identify the performance of only employees with the relative performance of the other employees. This process will help the organization to identify the 'most valuable employees' and the 'least valuable employees' of the organization and it is a simple inexpensive method of appraisal.

2. Paired Comparison Method

This is basically a multiple ranking method. That is, if there are employees X.Y,Z and W, the performance of the employee X will be compared with Y,Z W. Sameway, the performance of Y will be compared with Z,W and X. Likewise, all the permutations and combinations of the comparison of the performance of the employees will be conducted. This method is regarded to be time consuming and cumbersome if there are large number of employees.

3. Grading Method

There are different grades of the performance level that is to be fixed. The appraisers need to fit the performance of different employees in different grades. This is the simplest and the easiest method of all.

4. Forced Distribution method

The appraisers have a tendency to rate most of the employees around high points. To avoid this, the appraisers are forced to mark the performance of the employees in a normal curve (bell shaped curve). This method assumes that there are excellent, good and poor performers in any organisation. This is a grouping technique of performance evaluation.

5. Forced choice method

Under this method of appraisal, the appraiser has a questionnaire that contains certain statements about the performance of the employees. The supervisors need to choose one statement that best describes the performance of the employees. This method forces the supervisors to choose one, which indirectly reveals whether the employee is an excellent, average or a poor performer.

• Rating Methods

The rating methods are methods, which help us to assess the employees' performance with a certain pre-defined assessment scale. There are two methods.

1. Graphic Rating Scale

The performance of the employees is placed in a graph. That is assessed for the amount of work that he has performed with the level of quality of that particular job. These graphs serve a good document to assess the performance of employees over a period of time.

2. Checklist Method

Under this method, the appraisers need to check certain statements. If the statements are true of the employee or false about the performance of the employee needs to be marked. This method is narrowed to the level or mentioning one-word statements of the employees' performance. This method is easy to conduct but has lot of problems in analyzing and weighing data.

• Narrative Methods

In various narrative methods, the appraiser is given an opportunity to write descriptively in detail about the performance of the employees. This method gives an opportunity to describe in detail about the performance of the employees instead of just choosing or rating the employees' performance. Often, the supervisors tend to concentrate on their writing abilities instead of describing the performance of their employees. The various narrative methods are:

1. Confidential Reports Method

Under this method, the supervisor or the appraiser is expected to judge the performance of the employees and submit a report, which would be kept confidential. This method does not give an opportunity to check whether the supervisor is unbiased.

2. Field Review Method

This is group review technique, which reduces the room for bias. A group of raters join together to rate the performance of the employees. They set the standards together and also review the performance together. The HR employee goes with the raters at the time of appraisal and tries to analyze the conduct of performance appraisal.

3. Critical Incidents Method

Under this method, the supervisors are expected to maintain a book of the critical incidents that was caused or managed by the employees. These incidents would have produced positive outcomes or negative outcomes. The book serves as the record of the performance of the employees over a period of time. Finally, the manager needs to verify the book for the work behaviour of the employees during the period and make a report of the same.

• Behavioural Methods

The behavioural methods lay more focus on the behavioural aspects of the employee's performance. If the performance evaluations were conducted for the purpose of incentives and promotions, this method would be of great use. It also includes and work aspects of the employee along with the behavioural aspects at large.

The various behavioural methods of performance appraisal are as follows:

1. Management by Objectives or Results Method

Valentine and Humble as an appraisal technique gave this method to the organisations to follow. Under this method the superiors and subordinates jointly set the objectives that are verifiable in nature. The superiors and subordinates decide together to describe each role and the areas of results and determine the KRA (key result areas). Key Result Areas refer to the core areas on which the performance of the employees of the organization would be measured. The appraisal is also conducted together by the superiors and subordinates where they would discuss the employees' actual performance in comparison with the KRAs that are already set in the beginning of the period. During the period in which the employees' performance is being assessed. there would be some interim assessment where changes are made with the objectives, if required and new inputs for KRAs would get added on. Interestingly, the final review that take place may give data pertaining to the organizational performance which would help the organization to modify or add to the organizational goals some information for the organization towards its goals and objectives. The steps are described in the diagram below.

This is considered to be a participatory approach. Since both the superiors and subordinates try to set goals together, this increases the commitment level of the employees to perform the task completely. But, this method may not suit all the leadership styles of the superiors. A comparative or a relative analysis of the performance of employees is difficult to be measured under this method.

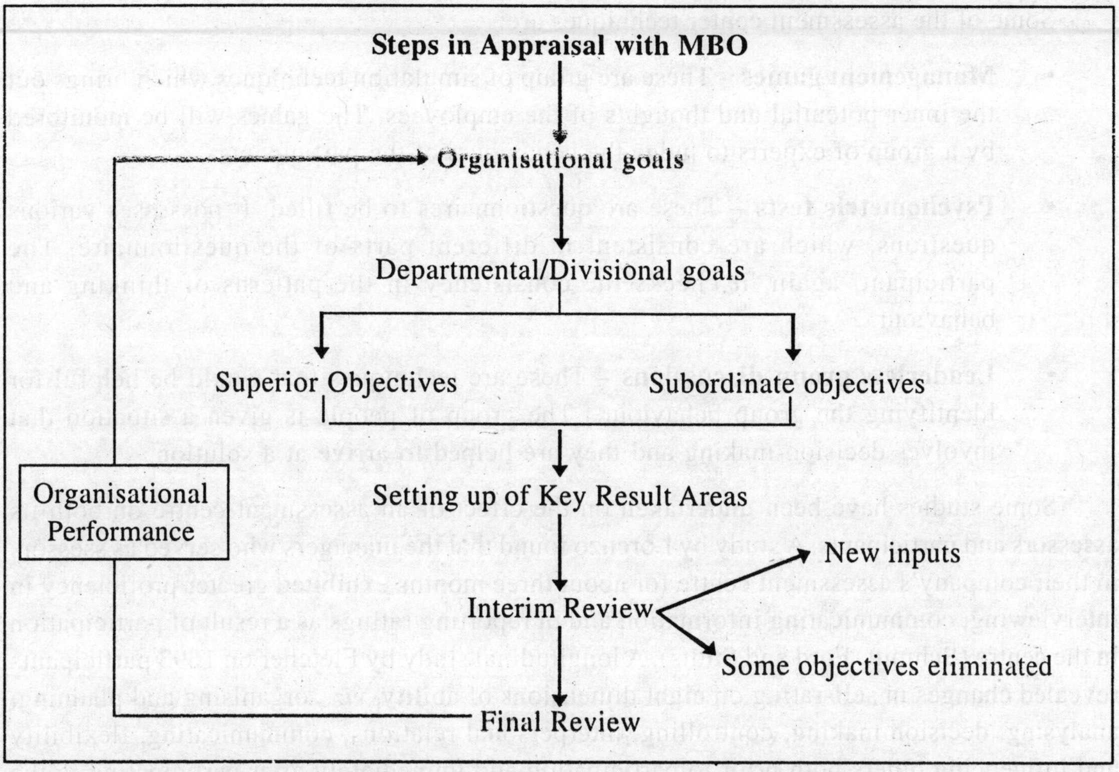

2. BARS Method (Behaviourally Anchored Rating Scales)

Performance appraisal through the BARS method is a combination of rating scale method and critical incidents method. The first step in the process is to identify the measure of performance for each role. Then, the behaviours that are essential for performing the job is identified. These are termed as critical behaviours and they are assigned some numerical values depending on the importance of the same to perform that particular job. Now each critical behaviour is placed on a scale depending on the mean value. This scale would be used for the performance appraisal. This method will be helpful to identify the effective and ineffective behaviours and would be helpful to increase the effective behaviours of performance.

3. Assessment Centre Technique

Assessment Centre technique was in use in British army since 1960. It is a combination of various techniques and involves experts to assess the performance of every employee. Generally, multiple assessors are employed and evaluation is done using difference assessment techniques. Any conclusions about the assessment of the employee are to be made by a group of assessors.

Some of the assessment center techniques are:

- **Management games** – These are group of simulation techniques which brings out the inner potential and thoughts of the employees. The games will be monitored by a group of experts to judge the behaviours of the participants.

- **Psychometric tests** – These are questionnaires to be filled. It possesses various questions, which are consistent in different parts of the questionnaire. The participant, again, it checks the consistency in the patterns of thinking and behaviour.

- **Leaderless group discussions** – These are techniques that would be helpful for identifying the group behaviour. The group of people is given a situation that involves decision-making and they are helped to arrive at a solution.

Some studies have been undertaken on the effect of an assessment centre on both its assessors and participants. A study by Lorenzo found that the managers who served as ssessors in their company's assessment centre for about three months exhibited greater proficiency in interviewing, communicating information and in reporting ratings as a result of participation in the centre (Schmitt, Ford and Stults). A longitudinal study by Fletcher on 1693 participants revealed changes in self-rating on eight dimensions of ability, *viz.*, organising and planning, analysing, decision making, controlling, interpersonal relations, communicating, flexibility and influencing others both prior to participation and immediately after participating in the assessment centre.

Despite the positive contributions of the assessment centre mentioned above, some negative research findings have also been reported showing a positive correlation between the colour of the assessor and the participants of the assessment centre with the same colour. But such studies are few and far between. However, a number of studies have supported the view that 'assessment centre' is a strong predictor of future job performance.

Pre-requisites for Assessment Centre

In planning the assessment process, the following three factors are prerequisites for undergoing the process:

(a) list of competencies or other qualities to be assessed and the procedure for scoring and rating;

(b) the weightage to be assigned to each element and exercise; and

(c) the various forms of assessments for a competency to ensure consistency of judgement and the prevention of any bias.

Figure below presents the steps involved in an assessment centre.

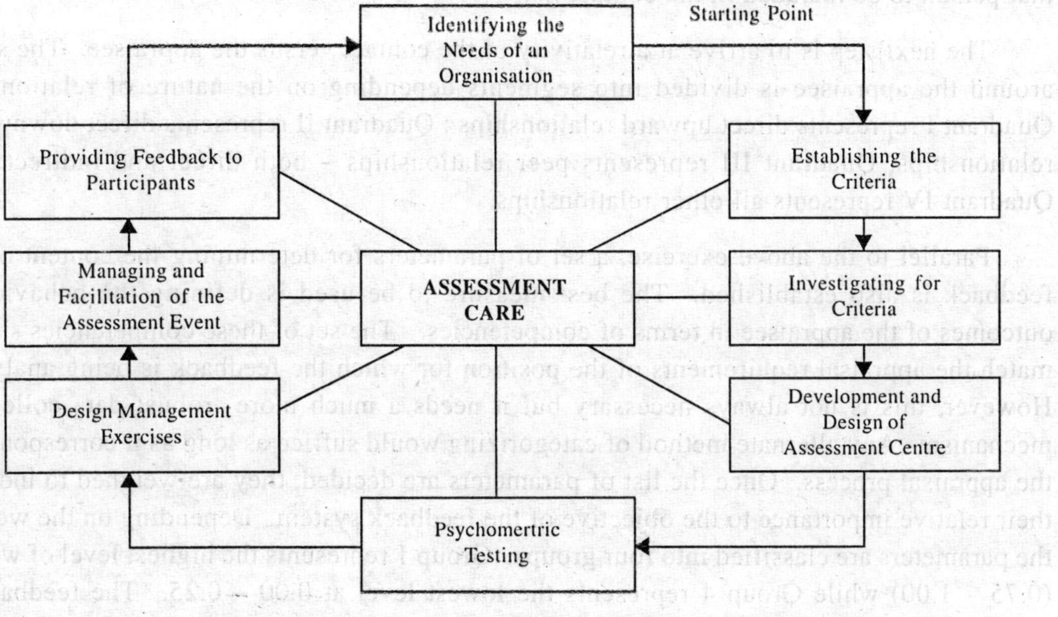

Fig.4.1 Steps involved in assessment centre

Assessment centres need to be properly designed and implemented to achieve the desired results without any bias. These need proper staffing; if the organisation does not have the expertise, a consultant may be hired initially to train the staff and to undertake the responsibility of running the assessment centre till the expiry of the contract. Further, if the organisation is not willing to allocate a large amount of resources for the assessment centre, it may focus on factors/competencies that have proven links with business.

Having identified the need for having an assessment centre and also for establishing the criteria of competencies, weights need to be assigned for various parameters. One can give even equal weight to all. The assessment centre will add value if it can identify and select people who demonstrate competencies that drive outstanding performance. Details regarding competency-based assessment have been discussed later in this chapter. Psychometric tests of ability and personality are frequently used but these do not constitute an essential element in an assessment centre and many organisations do not use them.

4. 360-Degree Feedback

The term 360 degree is taken from geometry to mean "all around". The model first establishes the contact points for any appraisee. Therefore, in any given appraisal cycle, it is first determined who would the employees (the appraisee) come into contact with. Next, a cut off point is established to determine which of the contacts are likely to be meaningful. In general, the higher the number of contacts, the higher is the degree of contact necessary for that person to be included in the contact list.

The next step is to arrive at a relativity of the contact versus the appraisee. The space around the appraisee is divided into segments depending on the nature of relationship. Quadrant I represents direct upward relationships ; Quadrant II represents direct downwards relationships, Quadrant III represents peer relationships – both direct and indirect; and Quadrant IV represents all other relationships.

Parallel to the above exercise, a set of parameters for determining the content of the feedback is also established. The best measure to be used is defining the behavioural outcomes of the appraisee in terms of competencies. The set of these competencies should match the appraisal requirements of the position for which the feedback is being analyzed. However, this is not always necessary but it needs a much more robust data collection mechanism. Any alternate method of categorizing would suffice as long as it corresponds to the appraisal process. Once the list of parameters are decided, they are weighed to indicate their relative importance to the objective of the feedback system. Depending on the weight, the parameters are classified into four groups. Group 1 represents the highest level of weight (0.75 – 1.00) while Group 4 represents the lowest level at 0.00 – 0.25. The feedback is classified in terms of the four groups and are represented by four concentric circles of varying radii. The circle closest to the centre has the highest weight. It is represented in the following figure.

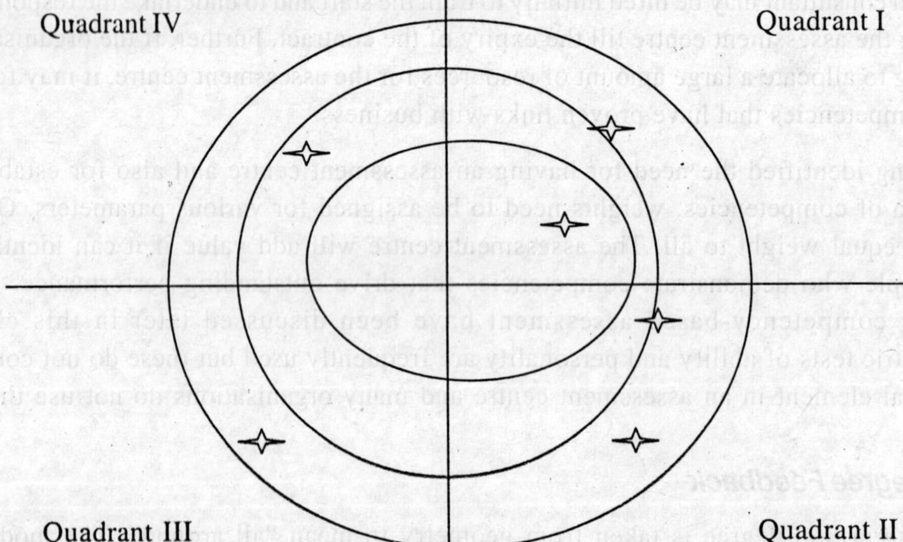

- **The internal points represents the source of the feedback. Feedback from the supervisor, subordinates etc.**

Moving from a 360 degree feedback to a 360 degree appraisal is not just a matter of extending the concept. If we incorporate a 360 degree appraisal system, we are building on at least one more critical element., i.e., the element of standards of performance expectation. This means that the standards which the appraiser is using for judging the performance of the appraisee must be seamlessly integrated with the measures of performance used by the organisation as well as those understood by the appraisee. Any 360 degree appraisal system should be based on competencies. A good 360 degree feedback of appraisal is never perfect from the starting day. Most organizations go through a period wherein they keep on refining the process, till they take it to a workable status.

APPLICATION OF 360 DEGREE FEEDBACK

Personal Development of Employees

- Improving perception of the individual about oneself by understanding how others perceive him/her;
- Helping an individual manage one's performance better; and
- Facilitating learning process for the employee.

Team Development

- Increase in inter-personal communication among team members; and
- Improved customer service as customer feedback is included in the 360 degree feedback.

Human Resource Management

- Personnel selection and employee coaching;
- General personnel decisions–promotions, pay increases, probationary status or termination;
- Training and Development–employee training, management development, and organisational development;
- Planning for development centres, identification of development needs like the potential for leadership, development and honing of competencies, career planning and development.

How 360 Degree Feedback System Adds Value

"Being the best way to produce an accurate picture of how people are perceived by the people with whom they work, be it their manager, co-workers, direct reports, clients or customers," 360 degree feedback enables an organisation to focus on developmental efforts, at the individual and group levels, in the present business environment where the success of the company depends on continuous revolution, which is possible through organisational development interventions involving changes in the culture of an organisational system. Once introduced, 360 degree feedback facilitates the alignment of individual capabilities and behaviours with organisational strategies. How it adds value to the organisation has been summarised below:

- The multi-rater feedback gives a comprehensive view of an individual's performance;
- It captures unique information, which other methods usually cannot;
- It serves to complement supervisory feedback as the only source for performance standards;
- It promotes a new psychological contract and increases the understanding about one's role expectations;
- It focuses on competency framework in various roles;
- For top level executives, it can serve as a useful source of feedback;
- It promotes self-directed learning and provides a road-map for employees' development planning;
- It builds in action-orientation around the self-monitoring of gaps in performance between others' expectations and a person's perceived performance;
- It helps everyone to work for a common standard and institutionalises performance management;
- It promotes commitment to good work among people;
- It acts as a key relationship-building tool to enhance team processes and work relationships;
- It is an important monitoring and regulatory device;
- It empowers individuals to obtain a realistic assessment of their strengths and areas of improvement;
- It helps in the strategic integration and alignment of performance management, keeping in view the new organisational complexities;

- It creates mechanisms for integrating multiple constituencies and inputs and facilitates the development of an appropriate culture for competitive advantage; and
- It facilitates organisational transformation.

Why Should An Organisation Use 360 Degree Feedback?

If an organisation is not clear about the benefits of 360 degree feedback, it needs to ask itself the following questions:

- Is the company in a position to meet the new challenges and the increasing competition with the existing competencies of its employees?
- Are the people in the organisation aware of the organisation's future behavioural needs to ensure its success?
- Does the changing environment call for a change in people's behaviour?
- Does the training and development system reflect and is it equipped to cater to current and future requirements of jobs/positions/roles?
- Is there an alignment in the behaviour of people with the organisation's vision, mission and values?
- Do people in the organisation receive feedback on their behaviour and performance from more than one source?

Assessing Readiness of the Organisation for Implementing 360 Degree Feedback

The most significant aspect of the introduction of the 360 degree feedback system is assessing the readiness of the organisation which has been found to be a critical process. In the words of Tom Sullivan, "The process of preparing for 360 degree assessment is a development journey in itself." An organisation may have any of the following reasons for the introduction of 360 degree feedback: dissatisfaction with traditional performance appraisal by a single manager; promoting participation and empowerment by giving feedback, flattening of the organisational structure, promoting team work, focus on customers, performance development and improvement both at the individual and group levels, and in some cases, performance appraisal and compensation or organisational development. These may be classified into the following four categories:

1. Employee development and career planning;
2. Performance appraisal and succession planning;
3. Team development; and
4. Organisational development with strategic goals.

The first and foremost consideration for an organisation in deciding for 360 degree feedback is whether its objective is to use it as "feedback" or "appraisal". Once this decision is taken, the design and preparation for 360 degree feedback would fall in place. The problem then needs to be diagnosed and the processes worked out. An important factor in the readiness aspect is that those who will be rated in the 360 degree process perceive it as constructive, and as a tool to help people improve. An open communication system and employee empowerment are also desired values in the organisation. Communication is a key element in the 360 degree approach and is therefore, critical to its success.

The following steps may be taken to gauge the readiness of an organisation for 360 degree feedback:

(a) Identification of the problem;

(b) Analysis of the organisational context for finding a solution to the problem;

(c) Allocation of resources for the purpose in terms of time and finances;

(d) A detailed plan of implementation; and

(e) Follow-up.

The above steps will ensure a systematic implementation of the 360 degree feedback system. But the willing participation of people is very important in making this tool effective. Therefore, steps need to be taken to ensure that the behaviours that are being measured should be seen by people as important and relevant to their job. Also "people need clarification about what is expected of them after they receive the feedback, as well as ongoing support, if what they have achieved is going to lead to action or change" (Lepsinger, 1997). Other imperatives for the readiness of organisations are:

Support from Top Management

Overt support from top management is necessary for the success of this approach, as without it the approach will remain only on paper.

Trust among People Regarding the Objective

If the employees believe that the 360 degree feedback system introduced by the organisation is intended to facilitate their development, they will be interested in the tool and will trust the multi-rating processes. On the other hand, a feeling that the management is trying to identify their weaknesses and penalise them would foster resistance and a negative attitude among them.

Developing Competency Models

The organisation also needs to develop competency models detailing the requirement of various types of competencies, *viz.*, knowledge, skills and attitudes required for successful and superior performance. 360 degree feedback will focus on the employee's competencies and will enable him to enhance these.

Clarifying Role and Performance Expectations

The individual's role expectations must be agreed with the manager. The performance planning process should take into consideration competencies and behaviour, and employees should be made aware of these for successful performance so that when the 360 degree feedback process is introduced, there are no surprises.

Building a Psychologically Safe Environment

In this era of restructuring, downsizing and right-sizing, it is difficult to build a psychologically safe environment. However, if the employees are convinced about the value addition and the need for introducing multi-source feedback at an early stage of change in the organisation, it helps in focusing on priorities and facilitates employee development.

Validity of the Tool

One of the common concerns of organisations regarding 360 degree feedback is the validity of the tool. The face validity of the questionnaire can be established by conducting a pilot study on a representative group of people who would be giving and receiving feedback on the questionnaire. Questions can also be asked about the ambiguity and relevance of the questions contained in the questionnaire. Only a valid tool will give the correct results.

Formal and Informal Training

The organisation needs to carry out formal and informal training to use this tool. The allocation of funds alone is not sufficient, the training has to be a continuous process. Initially, the training would be required to generate awareness about the tool, then the employees need to be familiarised with the instrument and the process. Follow-up activities are also essential for which training would be necessary for the individual and his supervisors.

Steps Involved in the Comprehensive 360 Degree Feedback Process

The following steps need to be taken to implement the 360 degree feedback system:

(i) Determining organisational readiness for 360 degree feedback;

(ii) Developing an appropriate survey and process keeping in view the organisational needs;

(iii) Motivating key decision makers and participants;

(iv) Ensuring skill requirements among participants and managers to handle the process;

(v) Organising orientation briefing;

(vi) Administering the survey;

(vii) Coaching the participants in one-on-one meetings;

(viii) Providing organisational summary data; and

(ix) Re-conducting the survey in four to six months.

Pitfalls of 360 Degree Feedback

Following are the drawbacks entailed in 360 degree feedback:

- Many organisations treat 360 degree feedback as a special event, consequently the process does not go beyond one-time feedback.
- Failure in follow-up may bring the organisation back to square one and may cause more harm than good.
- If action is not taken for the development of skills identified through multi-rater feedback, people will resent participating in this exercise again.
- The behaviour and performance for which people would be held responsible need to be unambiguous, clear, specific, and observable and quantifiable.
- Most organisations send the feedback forms to an outsourced agency for the sake of confidentiality. This makes the process time-consuming and expensive.
- The process involves a lot of paper work and monitoring of the return of the completed questionnaire by the due date.
- Many organisations and consultants who have used the multi-rater system advise that it should be used as a development tool for several years before it is used as an appraisal tool.
- It should not be used as a means to support someone's promotion or termination (Bascal, 1999).
- The tool will lose its integrity if it is used for downsizing.
- Participation in 360 degree feedback may be voluntary to start with, but when confidence is gained, it could be extended to other levels as well.

Success of 360 Degree Feedback

The success of 360 degree feedback would, to a large extent, depend on the readiness of the organisations for this initiative. Besides, the following conditions have also been recommended (Karl):

- Intervention is business-driven.
- The organisation clearly needs the measured behaviours to support a corporate strategy.
- The survey instrument and administration process are reliable.
- Conditions for learning new skills exist.

Further, success would depend on the imperatives mentioned above and the effectiveness of the steps that have been adopted by the organisation. Finally, people in the organisation have to play a major role in making the 360 degree feedback process effective.

Balance Score Card

Balance Score card was a concept developed by Dr. Robert Kaplan and David Norton of the Harvard Business School, USA. In the words of Robert and David, inventors of Balance Scorecard —

" The Balance scorecard retains traditional financial measures. But, financial measures tell the story of past events, an adequate story for industrial age companies for which investment in long-term capabilities and customer relationships were not critical for success. These financial measures are inadequate, however, for guiding and evaluating the journey that information age companies must make to create future value through investment in customer, suppliers, processes, employees, technology and innovation".

Balance Score Card basically tries to translate the organizational goals into organizational performance indicators. In the process of achieving the organizational goals, there exist some indicators of performance focused on the objectives. The indicators can possess four perspectives to it.

1. Customer
2. Financial
3. Internal Business Processes (IBP)
4. Learning and Growth (L&G)

The inputs on these indicators with respect to the organization will help the organisation to understand its current performance levels and use the four perspectives as long term drivers for success. The organisation need to assess the performance indicators and —

- Link strategy to quantifiable and measurable metrics
- Provide enterprise-wide deployment capabilities
- Create rapid prototyping.

The four perspectives of the balance score card can be explained with a diagram given below.

Perspectives of Balance Scorecard

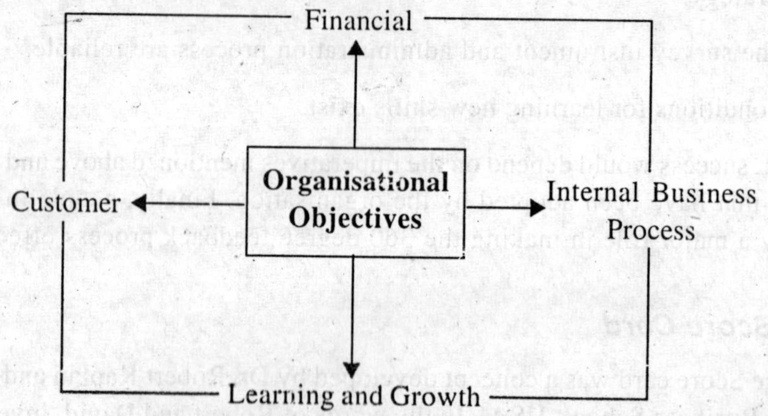

The above diagram clearly illustrates the organizational objectives and give inputs to the four important perspectives of the performance indicators.

The Customer Perspective

The most important goal of any organisation today is achieving customer satisfaction and thereby customer loyalty. The organisation should take initiatives to satisfy the customer, set targets to reach customers and measure the performance with regard to satisfying the customer.

The Financial Perspective

The financial perspective would be assessment of data available for a project, the assessment or risk and cost –benefit analysis etc., to identify whether the financial objectives are attained.

The Internal Business Process

Metrics based on this perspective will allow the managers to know how well their business is running, and whether it products and services confirm the customer requirement. This perspective intends to identify the performance level with respect to the satisfaction of shareholders and customers, with excellent processes in business.

The Learning and Growth Perspective

This perspective intends to measure the learning, knowledge levels and cultural attributes of the organization. Robert and David believe that the learning and growth perspectives would lead the organization to become more of 'learning organisations' to achieve its objectives completely. Robert and David emphasize more on 'learning' than 'training. Learning in terms of knowledge, innovation, technology, change and culture. Robert and David believe that this perpective would help organizations improve continuously.

The above mentioned four perspectives to balance score card is the key indicators of business as well as organizational performance. Interestingly, this assessment method aims at evaluating the organizational performance both in terms of finance and revenues and in terms of productivity and culture. The four perspectives would give inputs for the organisation to —

1. Link strategy to quantifiable metrics
2. Provide enterprise-wide deployment capabilities
3. Create rapid prototyping.

This method of assessment is critized by some experts that the organizational performance should not be measured in the metrics of finance but should be measured in terms of the progress made in productivity, customer satisfaction, innovation etc.

Therefore, a formal appraisal system becomes mandatory for organizations to perform successfully. Performance appraisal enables the organization to link strategy to management actions thereby attainment of organizational objectives.

The Concept of Potential Appraisal

A performance appraisal would give data about the current level of performance of the employees. A potential appraisal intends to go beyond measuring the current level of performance. Potential appraisal is concerned with assessing career enhancement possibilities of an employee in relation to his capabilities. The potential appraisal first tries to analyse the capabilities and competencies of an employee. Then, it is concerned with the career development possibilities of the same person. Many times, the current level of performance is not taken into account in a potential appraisal. But, some organizations intend to analyze even the current level of performance and assess his career development possibilities. Generally, the supervisor does the potential appraisal. The supervisor tries to observe the concerned employee for some period of time in terms of work, behaviour and his capabilities. Some organizations like Maruthi Udyog, Bajaj and Ranbaxy have included potential appraisal as a component of their performance appraisal itself. The last part of the performance appraisal exercise would be potential appraisal. It is not only an opportunity to understand the capabilities of the employee but also concerned with the training needs identification. It gives data for identifying the training needs of the employees.

Effective Performance Evaluation

Today, organizations are slowly moving away from the concept of performance appraisal to the concept of performance evaluation. A performance appraisal is a process of assessing the performance level of the employees in the organization. A performance evaluation is a process of understanding the level of performance of the employees and includes all the actions that are to be taken to improvise the same. Strategies are to be developed to monitor and evaluate employees' performance periodically instead of conducting it once in a year. A performance evaluation can be of two types. They are evaluative system and developmental system of performance evaluation. An evaluative system stops with understanding the level of performance of the employees in comparison with the standards already set. A developmental performance evaluation aims at identifying the level of performance and help the employees to improve the performance in terms of the behavioural aspects of performance and the work aspects of performance.

The following points are to be kept in mind to develop an effective performance evaluation system:

1. A good performance evaluation system in any organization should be developed synchronizing with the business plans of the organization.
2. A good performance evaluation system also requires a good internal communication system. That is, the parameters for good performance and the need for the measurement of the same are to be well communicated to the employees.
3. It is important on the part of the management to inform employees as to what is expected out of them in terms of their performance and monitoring the whole system is also important.
4. The performance objectives or the standards of performance expected are also to be communicated to the employees.
5. A performance evaluation system needs to be a continuous process all through the year.

Review Questions

1. What is performance appraisal? Explain the process of performance appraisal.
2. Discuss the different methods of performance appraisal.
3. Write short notes on:
   - Objectives of performance appraisal
   - Performance evaluation system
   - Potential appraisal.

✿ ✿ ✿

Chapter 5

CAREER GROWTH AND DEVELOPMENT

Learning Objectives

1. *The Concepts of Career*
2. *Career Planning and Process*
3. *Career Development and Models*
4. *Career Management Models*
5. *Succession Planning*

Introduction

Traditionally, many employees believed that if they joined an organisation became competent, worked hard and stayed out of trouble, they would have a job for as long as they would want it. Keeping this in mind, many employers, tried to offer job security and stability in exchange of the employees' loyalty. Career development was seen primarily as a concern of the enterprise the employees' are associated with. The objective was to ensure that the advanced and management ranks would be filled with individuals who were prepared for the kind of career development and growth would fit into the organizational culture. Individuals often viewed career management within the confines of this approach. They would engage in career planning to the extent that they had vertical aspirations and were selected for or volunteered to participate in the organizations' development activities. Most often the kind of long-term relationship that the employers and employees enjoyed were predictable and stable.

But, when the external environment forced the enterprises to slowly downsize and outsource, the relationship between the employers and employees started changing. The promise of a long-term security for any job has become questionable. Employees started realizing the responsibility of their own future lay with them and not with the organization. Facing the realization that they are responsible for their own continued employability has created uncertainty and fear for many people.

The work many organizations must do to achieve their goals changes over time. Even organizations that use contingent workers, outsourcing, partnership arrangements to get the work done need to maintain a core of employees with whom they have long term relationships. Often, organizations were able to retain the employees who were ready for changes every now and then. The organizational career development should be designed to fit the responsibilities and needs of both individuals and organizations, providing the opportunities and both need to prosper in a dynamic environment.

The study of careers and how they develop is one o the most active areas for educators, psychologists, sociologists and management scholars. Understanding and finding ways to influence the careers of employees is an integral part of HRD in any organisation. Career development provides a future orientation towards all developmental activities in relation to human resources in the organisation. If organizations can assist its employees in making decisions about future work, they can better prepare employees for new responsibilities within the organization and when appropriate enhance the employability of the employees. Therefore, the understanding of the concepts of career and the organizational endeavour and individual efforts would improve the quality of the jobs in the organisation.

Concepts of Career

The basic understanding of concepts in 'career' is important for us to understand career management. The concepts of career include defining career, career development, career planning and career management.

Career

According to Greenhaus and Schein the underlying several themes is the meaning of careeer.

- *The property of an occupation or organization*: When used in this way, career describes the occupation itself, or an employee's tenure within an organisation.
- *Advancement:* In this sense, career denotes one's progression and increasing success within an occupation or organisation.
- *Status of a profession:* Some use the term career to separate the ' professions' such as law or engineering, from other occupations, such as plumbing, carpentry or

general office work. In this view, the lawyer is said to have a career, while the carpenter does not.

- *Involvement in one's work:* Sometimes career is used in a negative sense to describe being extremely involved in the task or job one is doing , as in "Don't make a career out of it."
- *Stablility of a person's work pattern:* A sequence of related jobs is said to describe a career, while a sequence of unrelated jobs does not

This definition of career takes the focus away from the stereotypical idea of a career, as a stable, long term, predictable, organisation-driven sequence of vertical moves, It is broad enough to encompass many of the recent ideas that have offered in the concept of career development.

Career Development

Career development in a continuous process in the career graph of a person. The career development process can be defined as "an ongoing process by which individuals progress through a series of stages, of which is characterized by a relatively unique set of issues, themes and tasks".

Career Planning

Career planning is defined as "a deliberate process of —

1. becoming aware of self, opportunities, constraints, choices and consequences
2. identifying career related goals
3. programming work, education and related developmental experiences to provide the direction, timing and sequence of steps to attain a specific career goal."

Career planning is an activity performed by the individual to understand and attempt to control his own work life. The person can seek assistance from the counsellors, supervisors and others to do the planning but it is an individual effort.

Career Management

Career management is defined as "an ongoing process of preparing, implementing and monitoring career plans undertaken by the individual alone or in concert with the organization's career systems". Career management may include activities that help the individual develop and carry out career plans, but the focus is on taking actions that increase the chances that the organization's anticipated HR needs will be met. Career management is largely activity carried out by the organization. An example of such an activity is succession planning, which is typically carried out by senior management in secret, to determine which employees can and should be prepared to replace people of greater responsibility.

The spectrum of career management activities ranges from deciding on the career goals, planning for a career, working out the strategic career plan and achieving them. Thus, Career management includes a gamut of activities from gaining self awareness to setting goals and finding out the means of achieving them.

Let us discuss the different phases of career management in detail.

Career Planning

As discussed earlier, career planning is a deliberate process of becoming aware of self, opportunities, constraints, choices and consequences, identifying career related goals, programming work, education and related developmental experiences to provide the direction, timing and sequence of steps to attain a specific career goal. A career plan is basically an individual's choice of occupation and organisation. "Career planning is a process of systematically matching career goals and individual capabilities with opportunities for their fulfillment" (Schermerhorn, Hunt and Osborn).

Objectives of Career Planning

- Career helps the individual to become more aware of individual capabilities and strengths.
- It also helps the individual to understand his areas of weaknesses both in terms of the skill and attitude.
- Career planning facilitates him to understand his " best fit job."
- Career planning helps an individual to hone his skills and capabilities to get the kind of occupation he wanted.
- It helps the employees work with high degree of motivation and initiative.
- It helps to enhance the value system in the organisation.
- Career planning helps the organisation to empower its employees, in turn reduce the attrition rates.

Career Planning Process

The process of career planning involves a lot of exploration to understand his own skills and attitude levels. In turn, it gives an opportunity to accomplish in the organisation associated with or in the organization that the individual intends to work with. The process of career planning is given below.

Self-assessment

↓

Career Exploration

↓

Goal Setting

↓

Preparation

↓

Action

As and when the individual decides to plan his career, he tries to assess himself thoroughly. This understanding of his own skills, attitude and capabilities will help him to explore the various career opportunities that lie before him. He can try to do a SWOT analysis (Strengths, Weaknesses, opportunities and Threats) keeping in mind his capabilities and growth opportunities. That is the second step 'career exploration'. After exploring to a satisfactory extent, the individual tries to set goals for his career. The goals can be short-term or long-term goals. The most important point to be remembered is that the achievement of goals should be measurable. The goals should not be vague. It should have some cut-off points where the individual can stop and measure the achievement of the same. These goals can be short-term goals and long-term goals. These short-term goals act as check points for the individual to check whether the individual is in the right track towards the achievement of long-term goals. After setting the goals, the individual tries to prepare himself for action towards the achievement of these goals.

Career Development

Career development is an on-going process that occurs over the life span; includes home,school and community experiences (Pietrofesa and Splete). Career development is all about going through life and work, about learning , experiencing and creating the pathway for the individual to live the way he wants in life.

Career development provides an opportunity to understand the interrelationship between work, family, ambitions and all other roles in life. As a founding philosophy of human resource development, planning for the career development of its employees is the fundamental responsibility of the organisation. A strong concern for the career growth and development of employees in the organisation would help in retaining scarce talent and the morale of the employees. It also helps in succession planning in the organisaition. The concept of succession planning would be discussed later in this chapter.

Theories of Career Development

There are two models of career development, traditional models of career development and the contemporary models of career development.

Traditional Models of Career Development

These models have been offered to understand the age of the person with the progress in his career. Each of the models emphasizes the notion of orderly series of career stages linked to age. Given the similarities in the models, Greenhaus combined all the approaches into five stage model of career development. That is

They are depicted in the diagram below

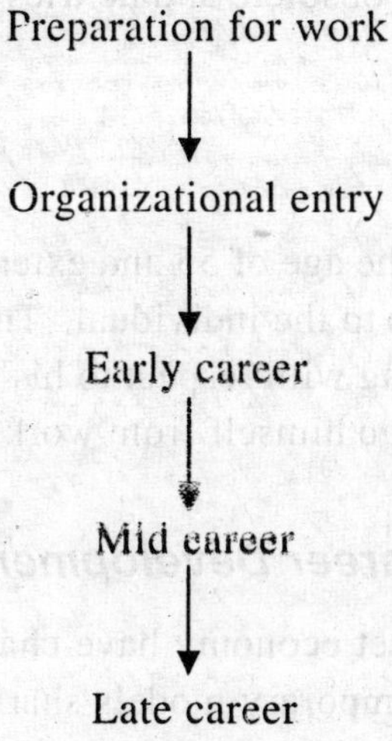

Stage 1

The task during the stage 1 which is preparation of work would be defining the idea of occupation, identifying his area of occupation and making necessary preparations to take up that career. This generally happens within the age of 0-25 in a person. A person tries to make his occupational choice during this phase.

Stage 2

The stage begins at the age of 18 and ends at the age of 25. During this phase, he tries to make a organizational choice . The person decides where to begin his career and starts picking up challenges. Depending on whether the career path he has chosen initially satisfies him, he tries to move to the early part of the career or decides to jump to a different career with his capabilities.

Stage 3

This is a early career between 25-40. At this stage, the individual tries to stabilize himself to focus more on growth. His challenges become very specific and he becomes aware of what he is into. Slowly, he enters the stage to find out whether the career he has chosen is fulfilling.

Stage 4

This is a mid career from 40-55. One of the challenges an individual faces in his mid career is a reexamination of the life structure and modify the dreams, making choices of the jobs and organisation and remain in mid career crisis. Certain skill sets he has developed over a period of time have become obsolete and he tries to unlearn the same to focus on the newer learning.

Stage 5

The late career life begins at the age of 55 and extends till the retirement.Basically, this stage throws a couple of challenges to the individual. The first one would be the continuous pressure the individual is undergoing with respect to his performance. The second would be the way the person tries to disengage himself from work and move towards retirement.

Contemporary Models of Career Development

The trends in the global market economy have changed the way the careers are being looked at considerably. The contemporary models share the view that individuals must be flexible and adaptable to succeed in a highly changeable and uncertain environment.

Hall and Mirvis brought the idea of protean career. The protean career concept (named for the Greek god Proteus, who could shape his will) is based on the notion that individuals reinvent their careers over time as needed. As individuals go through life, they are on a search for meaning and self-fulfillment and their careers are made up of their choices and experiences(work,educational, and otherwise). Each person's career will be unique. Instead of progressing through a series of discrete and predictable changes, the protean career "encompasses any kind of flexible, idiosyncratic career course, with peaks and valleys, moves and turns from one line of work to another and so forth."

Another contemporary career development model is termed as the multiple career concept model. This model suggests that there are four different patterns, or career concepts of career experiences. They four patterns are:

1. **Linear** – A progression of movement up in an organizational hierarchy to positions of greater responsibility and authority; motivated by desire for power and achievement.

2. **Expert** – A devotion to an occupation; focus on building knowledge and skill within a speciality; little upward movement in a traditional hierarchy, more from apprentice to master; motivated by desire for competence and stability.

3. **Spiral** – A life long progression of periodic moves across related occupations, disciplines or specialties; sufficient time to achieve a high level of competence in a given area before moving on; motives include creativity and personal growth.

4. **Transitory** – A progression of frequent moves across different or unrelated jobs; untraditional motives include variety and independence.

It is difficult to prescribe a model for career development. The connection of life stages and career provides a strong foundation for career development. The contemporary view gives an opportunity to think differently and untraditionally. The knowledge from both the theories would help organizations to develop strategies to manage the skills and experiences of their employees and develop career management systems that would meet the requirements of the individual and the organization as a whole.

Career Management

As discussed earlier in the chapter, career management involves both planning for career activities and putting those plans into action. There are two models to understand the concept of career management from different perspectives.

The Individually Oriented Career Management Model

This model was offered by Greenhaus. Greenhaus discusses about eight stages for career management. They are:

1. **Career exploration**: Career exploration involves gathering information about one's self and the environment.

2. **Awareness of self and environment**: Successful career exploration will lead the individual to a deeper self-awareness and an understanding of both opportunities and constraints present in the environment. This awareness of self and environment can lead the individual to set or revise career goals already set, it would lead to strategy development.

3. **Goal setting**: A career goal is an outcome the individual decides to try to obtain. Such goals may be specific or general.

4. **Strategy development:** A career strategy is an action plan for accomplishing the career goal. An effective strategy should include the actions that should be carried out and a timetable for performing them. Many of the HRD practices and programs presented can serve as a part of an individual's career strategy.

5. **Strategy implementation**: Strategy implementation involves carrying out the strategy the individual has developed. Following a realistic strategy as opposed to acting without a clearly defined plan increases the likelihood of attaining the career goal. It is easier to get where you want to go if you have the plan to follow.

6. **Progress towards the goal:** This is the extent to which the individual is nearing the career goal.

7. **Feedback from work and non-work sources:** Valuable information about the progress towards the career goal can be obtained from both work sources – such as co-workers, supervisors and specialists and non-work sources – such as family, friends, teachers, etc.

8. **Career appraisal:** Feedback and information on progress toward the career goal permit the individual to appraise his or her career . This appraisal leads to reengagement in career exploration and the career management process continues with another cycle of activities.

(*Source*: J.H. Greenhaus, G.A. Callanan, Career Management, 3rd edition).

Organizationally Oriented Career Management Models

Several authors have offered models that are more organizationally focused. These models believe that it is the responsibility of the organisation to provide opportunities for employees to manage their career.

The Pluralistic Approach

This model suggests that both the organization and the individual as a whole might benefit from a pluralistic approach that combines varied amounts and types of organizational structure with a array of quite different career experience opportunities. Organizations would retain sufficient structure to maintain certain core competencies and organizational leadership, while utilizing less structured arrangements to meet the demands of external change and flux.

Systems View of Career Management

Nicholson suggests this approach. He proposes three main elements for career management. They are:

1. *People system* – Activities involved in selecting, nurturing and motivating human resources.
2. *Job market system* – The structure for developmental opportunities.
3. *Management information system* – Facilitates exchange of ideas and information.

Nicholson suggests that the career management must link the people system and job market system through Management Information System (MIS).

Challenges in Career Management

There are some challenges in career management for the organisation even if the organization is willing to help employees for their career growth and development.

They are:

- Organisations sometimes find it difficult to motivate the employees towards the career. Career motivation affects how people choose their careers, how they view their careers, how hard they work in them and how long they stay in them.
- Organisations find it difficult to build career identities for every job title in the organization.
- To provide career resilence and career insights is also a challenge.
- To handle employees who are in their late career or who have reached a position in the organization beyond which it is difficult to grow in the organisation is also a great challenge for organizations.

The Concept of Succession Planning

The concept of succession planning lies in the fundamental principle of existence of continued business. Succession planning is a process of identifying and developing individuals to take up higher roles in the organisation in the future. Succession planning is a continuous process. The individuals chosen to be groomed for higher level positions can be internally sourced or externally sourced. It becomes easy for the organisation to identify human resources that are capable of occupying higher levels of job internally. At the same time, if there are enough number of people who are of the expected calibre, then organizations can choose to hire people externally and start grooming for the higher positions in the organisation. The organisation needs to undergo the below mentioned steps for effective succession planning.

- Analyse the demand for executives, managers and professionals, function and skill set.
- Analyse the possibility of sourcing people internally.
- After career counselling, plan individual career paths based on the goals of the organisation and objectives of the individual.
- Implement accelerated promotion schemes.
- Offer training and development programs for the executives who are to be uplifted or preparing to succeed.
- Planned recruitment drive.

Succession planning has started gaining importance in Indian industries. Indian industries have started believing that functional roles can be occupied by the professions with high degree of competency and attitude for performance.

Review Questions

1. Explain the concepts of career.
2. Explain the stages of Career Development Process.
3. "Career development is the responsibility of the individuals and career management is the responsibility of the organisation". – Comment.
4. Explain the concept of Succession Planning.
5. Explain the two approaches to career management.

✿ ✿ ✿

Chapter 6

Training and Development

Learning Objectives

1. *The Meaning and the Need for Training*
2. *Process of Training*
3. *Training Effectiveness*
4. *Methods of Training*
5. *The Concept of Management Development*
6. *Challenges in Training*

Introduction

Human resource development is based on faith in the inherent potential in every human that can be manifested by giving management direction and orientation. Human resource is an unpredictable resource but it has unlimited potential. HRD process maximizes the use of human resource by way of optimizing the competence of available human resource, improving the competence of future challenges and utilizing unemployed resource. The roles and activities of HRD will depend on the HRD needs of the organization, the HRD mechanism being used, and the facilities/opportunities provided. Thus, the role of HRD starts from the analysis of the organizational objectives/goals, characteristics of available resources and desired specification, manpower planning, recruitment, placement, performance appraisal, reward, punishments and maintenance of resource, organizational climate, etc.

Workplace training is a systematic approach to learning and development to improve individual, team or organizational effectiveness. A systematic approach refers to the idea that the training is intentional. It is being conducted to meet a perceived need. Learning and Development concern the building of expertise as a function of these systematic training efforts of the organisation.

Definition of Training

According to the British Manpower Services Commission, Training is a planned process to modify attitude, knowledge or skill behaviour through learning experience to achieve effective performance in an activity or range of activities. Its purpose, in the work situation, is to develop the abilities of the individual and to satisfy the current and future manpower needs of the organization.

According to Swanson, "Training and development is the process of developing expertise for the purpose of improving performance".

According to De Cenzo and Robbins, " Training is a learning experience, in that it seeks a relatively permanent change in an individual that will improve the ability to perform on the job. We typically say training can involve the changing skills, knowledge, attitudes or behaviour. It may mean changing what employees know, how they work, their attitudes towards their work, or their interaction with their co-workers or supervisor".

Therefore, training supports adaptive, productive workplaces that capitalize on investments in both technology and workforce skills to boost productivity. Training is organisation focused and is a key element of an orgnaisation's overall performance improvement plan.

Training and development efforts are required due to the following ground realities:

(a) The rapid rate of technological and social change in society has necessitated the training of managers, so that they may cope with these developments.

(b) The introduction of automation, intense market competition from foreign countries, the growth of new markets in developing countries, enlarged participation of labour in management, and greater interest by the public and the government in the action of business have all led to the need for the development of managerial personnel.

(c) Increased recognition by the organizations of the social and public responsibilities of management has necessitated the development of managerial personnel.

(d) The increased size and complexity of most organizations requires trained managers.

(e) Older personnel need refresher training to enable them to keep abreast of changing methods, techniques and use of sophisticated tools and equipments.

The primary objective of HRD is to prepare employees, for promotion to positions which require added skills and knowledge. It enables employees to develop and rise within the organization, and increase their 'market value', earning power, and job security. It moulds the employees' attitudes and helps them to achieve a better co-operation with the company and induce greater loyalty to it. Training heightens the morale of the employees, for it helps in reducing dissatisfaction, complaints, grievances, absenteeism, and employee turnover.

The objective of training is "to bridge the gap between existing performance ability and desired performance" and:

(a) To impart new entrants the basic knowledge and skill they need for an intelligent performance of defined tasks.

(b) To assist employees to function more effectively in their present positions by exposing them to latest concepts, information and techniques and developing the skills they will need in their future roles.

(c) To build up a second line of competence officers and prepare them to occupy more responsible positions.

(d) To broaden the minds of managers by providing them with opportunities for an interchange of experiences within and outside with a view to correct the narrowness of outlook that may arise from over-specialization.

The purpose of training can be:

(a) To increase quality, and productivity

(b) To help a company fulfil its future personnel needs

(c) To improve organizational climate

(d) To improve health and safety of personnel

(e) To address personal growth and prevent obsolescence

(f) To develop innovativeness and creativity

(g) To improve interpersonal communication, leadership, and team work.

Designing an HRD Programme

Training is a continuous process and not a one-shot affair. Since it consumes time and entails much expenditure, it is necessary that training programmes should be prepared with great thought and care, for it should serve the purpose of the organization as well as the need of employees. Moreover, it must guard against over training, use of poor instructors, too much training on skills which are unnecessary for a particular job, inadequate tools/equipment, etc.

As per the recommendations of the *National Industrial Conference Board,* the general principles to be considered while organizing a training and development programme are:

(a) The purpose of training and development should be to meet organizational objectives by providing opportunities for the employees at all hierarchical levels to acquire the requisite knowledge, skills and attitude

(b) Needs for training and development should be first identified

(c) Line management should be assisted in the determination of training needs

(d) Objectives and scope of training and development programmes should be defined

(e) Techniques and processes of training should be related to the training needs

(f) Principles of learning must be used.

Training and development programmes may be organized in the following steps:

(a) **Training Need Identification** Before the training programme is conducted, it is necessary that the training needs are identified. This means that we should know as to what training inputs are required to be given and to whom. Training need identification can be done through group problem analysis, interviews, survey through questionnaires, brain-storming, job analysis, performance appraisal, tests, records and reports, etc. Though, the responsibility of training need identification is that of line managers, HRD specialists have to play a greater role in facilitating this process.

(b) **Formulation of Training Objective** For successful training interventions, the objectives and scope of the course must be clearly defined. This will provide a basis for further development, common agreement and co-operative action on the part of all concerned.

(c) **Designing and Developing Programmes** This will include the course content, duration, timing, and method of training. The technique and process of training programmes should be related to the needs and objectives of the organization. The method adopted will depend upon the training objectives. They could be on-the-job-training, lecture method, apprenticeship, case studies, role playing, sensitivity training, business games depending upon what is the degree to which training has to be interactive. Some of these methods are shown in the figure.

(d) Conduct T&D Programme This is actual delivery of the product. The trainer should be well prepared to handle the session. The necessary training facilities including audio-visual aids should be available in operational state.

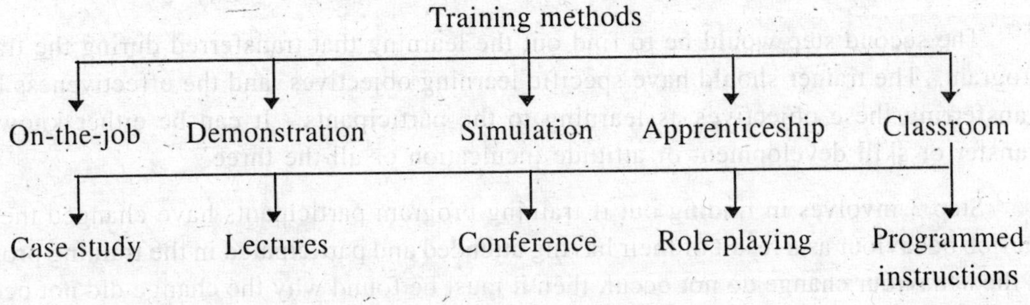

Classification of Training Methods

(e) Evaluation of Programme /Training Effectiveness The feedback or evaluation system should also be designed. It should relate to the desired output with the objective input. Sometimes programmes may be planned in parts or phases. The feedback of one phase then can be used as the input for the next phase. This is the most critical job of an expert to plan and design the feedback system in the programme. It must be appreciated that the changes in behaviour/performance as a result of training and development programmes cannot occur overnight. Therefore, the feedback taken at the end of the programme is not adequate. This evaluation should, therefore, be done in two stages, which are:

(i) On the concluding day—to know as to what is the reaction of the participants, relevance of the course content, techniques used, and also presentation effectiveness of the trainer.

(ii) After a lapse of certain period (say 3 to 6 months)—to know as to whether the performance of the trainee has improved on the job.

Steps in Training Effectiveness

The following attributes need to be measured to analyse the effectiveness of any training program:

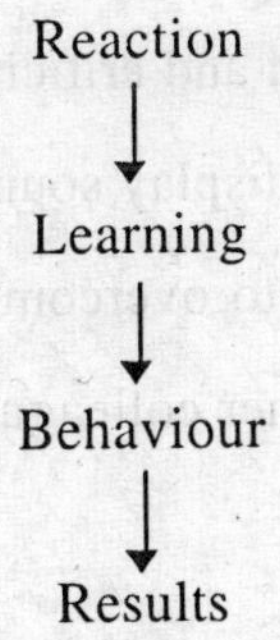

The goal in to find out the training effectiveness is to measure participants' reactions to the training program. The reaction of the participants immediately after the training programme is carefully observed and noted. This step speaks only about the reaction and not with respect to the learning of finding out how cost effective the training program was.

The second step would be to find out the learning that transferred during the training program. The trainer should have specific learning objectives and the effectiveness lies in transferring these objectives as learning to the participants. It can be either knowledge transfer or skill development or attitude inculcation or all the three.

Step 3 involves in finding out if training program participants have changed their on-the-job behaviour as a result of their having attended and participated in the training program. If the behaviour change do not occur, then it must be found why the change did not occur.

The last step would be with respect to the results achieved. It may be in the form of increased productivity or modified behaviour and development of work culture or increased profits. The results that are to be measured should be quantifiable in nature. It should not be vague.

Designing an Effective Supervisory T&D Programme

The training and development plans are aimed at developing talents to perform effectively in the present and future higher levels on more challenging work situations. The T&D activities are the techniques of enhancing on the human capital whose potential is much more than any other resources in the organization. The rapid increase in the size of the organization and the technological advancement have resulted in delegating the authorities and responsibilities to the supervisors. This has added new dimensions to the role profile of a supervisor.

The latest approach of supervisory development takes into account his foresight, sympathetic approach, ability to suggest improvements in methods, develop understanding between management and workforce, strive for improvement, etc. He has to organize the work and manage the operations. The success .of the department depends upon the supervisor. It calls for high standards of general ability, degree of intelligence, maturity of character and a temperament to control the shopfloor. A supervisor must be:

(a) Well equipped with technical processes and procedures

(b) Able to administer, recommend and criticize impartially

(c) Able to lead by examples and display sound judgement

(d) Able to demonstrate initiative to overcome obstacles

(e) Able to work amicably with other colleagues.

The main objectives of a supervisory T&D programme are:

(a) To help him improve knowledge, skill, and attitude for better performance

(b) To help him develop competence to increase productivity

(c) To help him prepare for greater responsibilities in higher levels of management

(d) To help him learn how to develop his subordinates

(e) To improve interpersonal relationship and communication skills

(f) To equip him with modern tools and techniques of management to harness the human resource and maintain industrial harmony.

A supervisor is to look after both the work situation and the worker to get maximum results.

The success of an organization depends on its ability to effect continuous improvement and provide quality products and services to its customer. This will require every personnel in the organization to possess the requisite knowledge, skill and attitude. For the purpose of determining training requirements, two levels of supervision could be identified. Each level of supervision should have a curriculum that addresses competencies required at that level.

(a) **First Level Supervisor:** An employee enters this level with little or no previous experience in supervision. First level supervisors have no subordinate supervisors. Typical duties include planning, setting performance standard, assigning and supervising work, and conducting performance appraisals.

(b) **Second Level Supervisor:** This level supervisors are senior people and are charged with the responsibility of co-ordinating the activities of one or more first level supervisors.

Every level requires inputs in three distinct core areas, namely—management development, administration, and technical. These have been described below:

(a) **Management Development:** Courses in this area will cover the competencies common to supervisors and managers. These will include organizational theory, planning, organizing, controlling and delegating work, leadership skills, counselling employees, conflict management, team building, interpersonal communication, etc. Specific course content could be:

(i) Introduction to supervision

(ii) Leadership skills for supervision

(iii) Art of delegation

(iv) Time Management

(b) **Administration:** This will cover administrative systems, procedures and regulatory requirements essential to functioning effectively on the shop floor. Some of the topics which could be addressed in this course are:

(i) Supervisors orientation—historical perspective, vision and mission statements, role, function and responsibilities of various divisions

(ii) Performance appraisal

(iii) Managing a diverse workforce

(iv) Financial management

(v) Material supply system

(vi) Management information system

(vii) Effective written communication

(viii) Safety aspects, hazardous material, etc.

(ix) Security of men and material.

(c) **Technical:** These are competencies that are specific to the technical occupation of the supervisor. There may be some competencies that are identified for all supervisors in general. This will remain an individualized case reflecting individual occupational requirements and departmental mission. Inputs required could be:

i. Technical topics related to the trade

ii. Statistical Process Control.

Framework for Developing an Effective Training Programme or Process of Training

The process of developing an effective training program is explained by a diagram given in the next page.

Development of Human Capacity

The American Society for Training and Development did a Human Performance Practices Survey of 540 organisations, provides lots of information about the types of training and individual specific training methods. The organisation has a moral responsibility to develop the 'individuals' in the organization. The development of human capacity would result in the development of the manpower in the organisation. The human resource development efforts of the organisation focuses primarily of improvement of the skills and knowledge, ability or the attitude, leadership etc. These are discussed below.

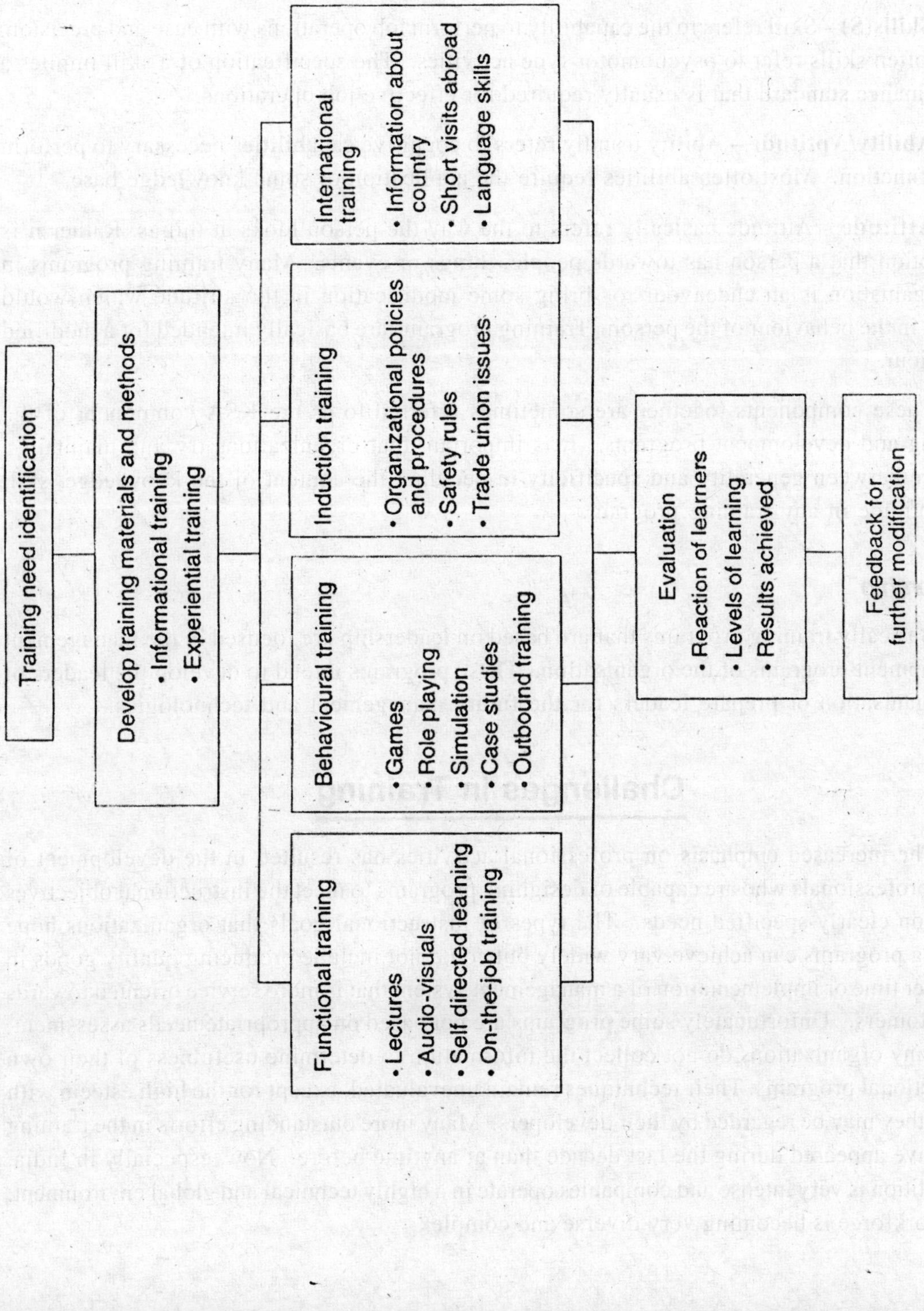
Training need identification
Develop training materials and methods
• Informational training
• Experiential training
Functional training
• Lectures
• Audio-visuals
• Self directed learning
• On-the-job training
Behavioural training
• Games
• Role playing
• Simulation
• Case studies
• Outbound training
Induction training
• Organizational policies and procedures
• Safety rules
• Trade union issues
International training
• Information about country
• Short visits abroad
• Language skills
Evaluation
• Reaction of learners
• Levels of learning
• Results achieved
Feedback for further modification

Knowledge(K) – Knowledge is the foundation on which the abilities and skills are built. Knowledge refers to an organized body of knowledge, usually of a factual or procedural nature, which , if applied, makes adequate job performance possible. It should be noted that possession of knowledge does not ensure that it will be used.

Skills(S) – Skill refers to the capability to perform job operations with ease and precision. Most often skills refer to psychomotor-type activities. The specification of a skill implies a performance standard that is usually required for effective job operations.

Ability/Aptitude – Ability usually refers to cognitive capabilities necessary to perform a job function. Most often abilities require the application of some knowledge base.

Attitude – Attitude basically refers to the way the person looks at things. Rather it is perception that a person has towards people, things or events. Many training programs in the organistion is an endeavour to bring some modification in the attitude which would reflect in the behaviour of the person. Training programs are basically intended for a modified behaviour.

These components together are sometimes referred to as the KSA component of the training and development programs. It is important that organizations try and maintain a balance between generality and specificity in deciding the content of the knowledge, skill and aptitude in any training program.

Leadership

Basically training programs that are based on leadership are focused in the management development programs of the organisation. These programs intend to develop the leaders of the organisation or prepare leaders for the future management and technologies.

Challenges in Training

The increased emphasis on professional activities has resulted in the development of many professionals who are capable of designing programs to meet the instructional objectives based on clearly specified needs. The types of instructional goals that organizations hope training programs can achieve vary widely but could not include producing quality goods in a shorter time or implementation of a management system that is more service oriented towards its customers. Unfortunately some programs are not based on appropriate needs assessment, and many organizations do not collect the information to determine usefulness of their own instructional programs. Their techniques remain unevaluated, except for the high esteem with which they may be regarded by their developers. Many more outstanding efforts in the training area have appeared during the last decade than at anytime before. Now, especially in India, competition is very intense and companies operate in a highly technical and global environment. The workforce is becoming very diverse and complex.

Training system are viewed by both organizations and individuals as a positive step in providing skills and opportunities. Changes in the industry and changes is the global market have affected the training at large. The challenges are

- ***Change Workforce Dynamics***

The composition of work force such as men and women, domestic nationals and foreign nationals, a large differences that existed between the technical work force and others, etc., have become a great challenge when it comes to the question of training them. They seem to be culturally very diverse with different backgrounds.

- ***Increasing Job Complexity***

There is a rush toward more highly technological, sophisticated systems. Industry has utilized the technology opportunities to establish advanced manufacturing techniques that permit the tailoring of products to the needs of a customer by simply reprogramming the machine. Peter Drucker believed that we are moving from an industrial to a knowledge society. This indirectly means that industry needs a lot of employees who are well trained with respect to the KSA part of their growth.

- ***Global Markets***

Companies try out many novel strategies today to make themselves very visible. The implication is that the companies not only train their own citizens but also employees across the globe. The domestic employees need to be trained for frequent changes and growing in a fast pace.

- ***Technological Impact***

There is tremendous amount of growth in terms of technology across the world. Organisations are forced to stand updated not only in terms of their work for preparing for the technologies of the future. Employees need to be trained for being global employees who would adapt and stand ahead in terms of technology.

The training implications of all the preceding issues are enormous, especially for managers who will be working with people. Kolb note that there is an increased emphasis on using training as a tool for coping with managing, and anticipating the rapid market changes occurring in work organizations today. Managers need to provide on the job training to integrate unskilled youth into the force, while working with job incumbents and other managers who previously may not have been a traditional part of the workforce.

Organisations are very complex systems and training programs are but one sub-system. Changes in the selection system, which can result in people with higher or lower job relevant skills and abilities, will have a dramatic effect on the level of training required. Changes in jobs as new technologies develop can have similar effects. More effective training programs can also affect all other systems in the work organisation. The dynamics of training systems must include the realisation that one of the first places to which many new employees are sent is a training program. Similarly, when individuals change positions as a result of changes in their career, many start undergoing a training program too. It is as important to understand the effects of training experiences as a part of the socialization process in entering organizations, as it is to evaluate specific training outcomes.

Review Questions

1. Define training. Why is it required for organizations?
2. If you are a training manager, how will you design a training program for 150 employees of a company which is indulged in selling business processes?
3. What are the challenges in training?
4. What is training effectiveness? How will you measure the same?
5. What is management development? Explain in detail.

✿ ✿ ✿

Chapter 7

EVALUATION OF HRD

Learning Objectives

1. *Concept of HRD Evaluation*
2. *Kirkpatrick's Framework of HRD Evaluation*
3. *Concept of HRD Accounting*
4. *Concept of HRD Audit*

Introduction

HRD evaluation is defined as "the systematic collection of descriptive and judgemental information necessary to make effective training decisions related to the selection, adoption, value, and modification of various instructional activities. This definition makes several important points. First, when conducting an evaluation, both descriptive and judgemental information may be collected. Descriptive information provides a picture of what is happening or has happened, whereas, judgemental information communicates some opinion or belief about what has happened. For example, the statement "25 percent of first-line supervisors attended a budgeting workshop in the last year" contains only descriptive information; it simply states the facts. Similarly, a statement that "20 percent fewer supervisors attended this workshop than in the previous twelve months" also contains descriptive information.

However, the statement, "The turnout for the – budgeting workshop over the last six months is disappointingly low compared to last year's turnout," provides judgemental information — someone's opinion based on the facts. Both descriptive and judgemental information are needed in an HRD evaluation. Some of the judgements are made by those involved in the program and others are made by those not involved in the program.

Second, evaluation also involves the systematic collection of information according to a predetermined plan or method to ensure that the information is appropriate and useful. Finally, evaluation is conducted to help managers, employees, and HRD professionals make informed decisions about particular programs and methods. For example, if part of a program is ineffective, it may need to be changed or discarded. Or, if a certain program proves valuable, it may be replicated in other parts of the organization.

Evaluation can serve a number of purposes within the organization. According to Phillips, evaluation can help to do the following:

- determine whether a program is accomplishing its objectives
- identify the strengths and weaknesses of HRD programs, which can lead to changes, as needed
- determine the cost-benefit ratio of an HRD program
- decide who should participate in future HRD programs
- identify which participants benefited the most or least from the program
- reinforce major points to be made to the participants
- gather data to assist in marketing future programs
- determine if the program was appropriate
- establish a database to assist management in making decisions.

Better and more informed decision making then, is an important benefit of conduct an HRD evaluation. But there are other benefits as well, Zenger and Hargis identified three additional reasons for conducting HRD evaluations:

1. HRD staff cannot substantiate its contribution to the organization, its funding and programs may be cut during the budgeting process, especially when the organization faces tough times.
2. Evaluation can build credibility with top managers and others in the organization.
3. Senior management often wants to know the benefits of HRD programs.

Building credibility is a key aspect of conducting an evaluation. After all, other functions performed within the organization are evaluated to determine their effectiveness. If the

HRD department fails to conform to this norm, it may not be taken seriously within the organization.

Thus, evaluation is a critical step in the HRD process. It is the only way one can know whether an HRD program has fulfilled its objectives.

Kirkpatrick`s Evaluation Framework

The most popular and influential framework for training evaluation was articulated by Kirkpatrick. Kirkpatrick argues that training efforts can be evaluated according to four criteria: reaction, learning, job behaviour, and results.

1. ***Reaction (Level 1):*** Did the trainees like the program and feel it was useful? At this level, the focus is on the trainees' perceptions about the program and its effectiveness. This is a useful information. Positive reactions to a training program may make it easier to encourage employees to attend future programs. But if trainees did not like the program or think they didn't learn anything (even if they did), they may discourage others from attending and may be reluctant to use the skills or knowledge obtained in the program. The main limitation of evaluating HRD programs at the reaction level is that this information cannot indicate whether the program met its objectives beyond ensuring participant satisfaction.

2. ***Learning (Level 2):*** Did the trainees learn what the HRD objectives said they should learn? This is an important criterion, many in the organization would expect an effective HRD program to satisfy. Measuring whether someone has learned something in training may involve a quiz or test — clearly a different method from assessing the participants' reaction to the program.

3. ***Job Behaviour (Level 3):*** Does the trainee use what was learned in training back on the job". This is also a critical measure of training success. We all know coworkers who have learned how to do something but choose not to. If learning does not transfer to the job, the training effort cannot have an impact on the employee's or organization's effectiveness. Measuring whether training has transferred to the job requires observation of the trainee's on-the-job behaviour or viewing organizational records (e.g., reduced customer complaints, a reduction in scrap rate.)

4. ***Results (Level 4):*** has the training or HRD effort improved the organization's effectiveness? Is the organization more efficient, more profitable, or better able to serve its clients or customers as a result of the training program? Meeting this criterion is considered to be the bottom line as far as most managers are concerned. It is also the most challenging level to assess, given that many things beyond employee performance can affect organizational performance. Typically at this

level, economic and operating data (such as sales or waste) are collected and analyzed.

Kirkpatrick's framework provides a useful way of looking at the possible consequences of training and reminds us the HRD efforts often have multiple objectives. It has sometimes been assumed that each succeeding level incorporates the one prior to it, finally culminating in what many people consider to be the ultimate contribution of any organizational activity: improving the organization's effectiveness. However, one of the more enduring and depressing findings about HRD evaluation is the extent to which most organizations do not collect information on all four types of evaluation outcomes. For instance, in the 2000 State of the Industry Report (ASTD), a survey of over 500 organizations reported the following: 77 percent collected reaction measures, 36 percent collected learning measures, 15 percent collected behaviour measures, and 8 percent collected results measures. Perhaps even more surprising, even the sub-group of organizations that ASTD highlighted as "training investment leaders" reported only slightly higher usage of these measures (80 percent, 43 percent, 16 percent and 9 percent). It does raise an important question as to why these usage rates are so low, particularly for behavioural and results measures, as these would seem to provide organizations with vital and even invaluable information.

While most discussions about training and HRD evaluation are organized about Kirkpatrick's four levels of criteria, Kirkpatrick's approach has increasingly been the target of criticism and modification. First, some authors point out that the framework evaluates only what happens after training, as opposed to the entire training process. A second line of criticism is that what Kirkpatrick proposed would be better described as a taxonomy of outcomes, rather than a model of training outcomes. For example, Holton states that Kirkpatrick failed to specify the casual relationships that exist among elements of the model. Kraiger, Ford, and Salas argue that Kirkpatrick's approach fails to specify what sort of changes can be expected as a result of learning and what assessment techniques should be used to measure learning at each level. Alliger and Janak question the validity of the assumptions that are implied by the framework (e.g., achieving the outcomes stated in higher levels of the model assumes achievement of outcomes at the lower levels). They suggest that it "may never have been meant to be more than a first, global heuristic for training evaluation." Kirkpatrick has responded to this criticism by stating that "I personally have never called my framework' a model and "I don't care whether my work is called a model or a taxonomy as long as it helps to clarify the meaning of evaluation in simple terms and offers guidelines and suggestions on how to accomplish an evaluation."

Human Resources Accounting

Traditional accountants do not recognize human assets in the balance sheet. The human being is considered as an economic factor of production. Costs incurred on human beings are treated as an expense like materials, power etc. Costs incurred on individual employees for their recruitment, training and development are partly charged along with the wages and salary bills and partly added to the general overhead charges of the organization. Similarly, the expenditure on human organization development gets merged with general overhead charges.

Traditional accounting practices have been designed to meet the needs of manufacturing firms where physical and financial assets predominate. Originally, balance sheets were intended to meet the needs of creditors. The creditors of an organization are concerned only with the security of their loans. So, the financial statements concentrated on physical assets and ignored human assets because human assets are not saleable. As such, the greatest asset, the loyalty and ability of the human resource are neglected and only non-human capital is recorded and reported.

On the other hand, people recruited today are not going to leave the organization tomorrow; the training that people receive today may not be totally valueless tomorrow. But the traditional accountants treat the human resources cost as expense and thus neglect their future benefit potentials. This violates the principle of matching periodic revenue with the corresponding expenses. Consequently, incomes are understated in periods of asset building and overstated in periods of the use of human resources. Because of this, management may lay emphasis on short-terms gains at the cost of long-term losses. Training and development may be postponed to improve current profitability. Alternatively, human resources may be stretched too far resulting in deterioration in their attitudes. This may lead to higher labour turnover and decline in long-term productivity. In absence of quantitative surveillance, productivity gains from technological improvements may well mask the deterioration in human performance. Managers who continue to squander human resources may be rewarded for such inefficiency and on the other hand, managers may be penalized for long-term development expenditure in the absence of information on the condition of the human resources. In absence of recognition of human resources as an asset, there is no provision in the traditional accounting practices to protect such asset against mismanagement.

When the costs on human resources are treated as expenses, the asset base of the organization includes only the physical and financial resources. As a result, the most important yardstick to measure the performance of a firm, namely, the return on investment may not be an effective guide to the managers in their decision making process.

Thus, the accepted practice of regarding all expenditure on human capital formation as an immediate charge against income is inconsistent with the treatment accorded to comparable outlay in physical capital. The omission of human resource from accounting would not only be misleading but some omissions to account for human resources are likely to cause uneasiness inside and outside the accounting profession.

People are different from expense items. Their goals, values and perceptions should be taken into account to build an efficient operating system. Human skills are the fundamental resource of an organization. So development of a set of skills is one of the most important organizational goals for long-term productivity improvement and employee satisfaction. So, 'an effective representation of the total resources of the organization requires that human assets also should be accounted for. However, human resources must fulfill certain criteria for being classified as assets. They are:

(i) An asset should possess future service potentials;

(ii) Its value should be measurable;

(iii) It should be acquired through a transaction;

(iv) It should be owned by an organization.

Future Service Potentials

The notion of future service potential is an essential criterion for classifying expenditure as a capital expenditure. The rights to such future economic benefits from the assets must accrue to the specific firm for recognition of the same as an asset in its balance sheet.

An organization incurs expenditure to recruit individuals and to train and develop them continuously with the expectation of future economic benefits from them by way of their services. This expectation of future service potential is the rationale behind such expenditure. So, these expenditures should constitute an asset rather than an expense. In addition to the potential to provide future economic benefits, such employment related cost might obviate the need to incur future cost. Like physical assets, human resources may also be insured to protect their potential and as such qualify as assets.

Future benefit potential is the main characteristic of an asset. So, the American Accounting Association has advocated that human resources may be considered as assets as they involve an element of future usefulness. To quantify the assets, expenditure on human resources needs to be analyzed. Expenditure pertaining to future benefits may be considered as assets and pertaining to current benefits as expense.

According to micro-economic theory, the value of human assets is zero in a perfect labour market under equilibrium condition. However, perfect market situation hardly exists in the real world. Accordingly, human resources will have value in the midst of permanent imperfection. Non-monetary compensation to employees may lead to marginal productivity of employees to be higher than their labour cost. This will result in the building of human asset. Expenditure on improving the working conditions may also create an asset.

The cost of training and development on a continuous basis constitutes the major part of the total expenditure incurred on the human resources of an organization. The existence of human assets and their corresponding value are based on the following things:

(i) Training should be effective. It should result in improvement of productivity. Then only, the expenditure on training and development can be considered as an asset. The extent of productivity improvement governs the size of the asset so created.

(ii) If the training is organisation specific, there is a low probability of employees leaving the organization. In such a case, differentials between wages and marginal revenue productivity may persist for a long lime. This leads to creation of an asset.

(iii) Skilled employees have the greatest opportunity to move laterally undermining the asset creation. Wages should tend towards marginal revenue productivity in course of time. Otherwise, employees may leave the organization, thereby reducing and negating the assets. Wages are usually revised upward with a view to protect the assets or to counter lateral mobility.

(iv) As the employees gain seniority and job security mobility is less feasible and less attractive. Greater the mobility restrictions, there is greater likelihood of asset creation.

(v) The organization may not fully invest for specific, training. Instead it may be a joint investment of both employer and employees. In such a situation, employees will be interested to continue with the organization to receive returns on their investment. This will avoid premature termination of the asset that has been created.

Thus, training may not necessarily lead to creation of human assets, the extent of asset creation may vary depending on the situation. However, the objective of any organization would be to ensure more and more asset creation from investments in organizational human resources.

Measurable Value

The value of any resource should be capable of being expressed in terms of money if it has to qualify an asset. The importance of human beings as the most valuable and the need for accounting of such a resource are accepted universally. However, unlike physical assets human resource is not traded in the market. So, the concept of exchange value may not be applicable for the value of human resources. Its value is to be assessed based on its relative contribution to the organisation *vis-a-vis* various physical and financial inputs.

The valuation of intangibles and invisible assets like human beings and reporting the same in the balance sheet is not readily acceptable to the conservative accountants. Most of the proposed approaches are subjective in valuing human resources. So, the objectivity criterion of traditional accounting makes it difficult for Human Resources' Accounting to gain recognition among the traditional accountants.

Acquisition Through Transaction

Organizations should acquire the rights to expected future benefits through transactions to qualify as assets. A transaction is measurable accounting event. The recruitment process of human resources by an organization does not constitute a transaction. The advance remuneration in terms of historical cost is a necessary condition for an acquisition to be identified as an asset. Asset recognition is based on definite commitment of resources to a course of action. In case of human beings, resource commitment does not take place at the time of acquisition unlike physical assets. So, no asset recognition can be accorded to the contemplated action. Only passage of time and continued employment binds the firm to a resource commitment, Contemplated fixed asset purchase or an intention to purchase a machine on credit cannot be recognized as an asset in the current year.

However, HR is acquired by an organization not for disposal but for continued services in the organization. Unlike physical assets they may not be remunerated on acquisition, but once individuals are recruited by an organization there is a definite commitment of the organization to pay appropriately for the services rendered. Even though the acquisition of human resource by an organization may not be considered as a transaction, a definite commitment to pay is associated with the acquisition.

Ownership

The items must be owned to qualify as assets. Human resource may be acquired and trained to create asset. However, they are not capable of being owned except cases of bonded labour. Legal ownership being a criterion for an asset, human resource may not be construed as an asset of an organization. Human assets are more volatile than physical assets and so, are not under control of the organization too. Organization acquires only contractual right to services from employees and the benefits of these services when they are performed.

However, American Accounting Association recommended that accounting is primarily concerned with events and objects that have economic significance and it does not necessarily involve legal ownership. Not the legal ownership but an operational right to continue to receive services from its human resources may be the criterion for asset status. It may not be necessary to presume absolute control over, the assets. Specific individual may leave the organization but the ever-present labour force is in some sense owned by the organization or controlled by the organization. As such they may be termed as quasi-assets. "The labour force as a whole is constantly associated with the firm. It can be constructively regarded as being owned by it. As long as employees can be replaced, it does not matter whether the labour force always contains the same persons or is a rapidly changing group. Thus, human resources are assets" [Lev and Schwartz]. Moreover, human resources *per se* are not considered as assets. It is only the services of people that are expected to be provided to an organization constitute the asset.

Human Resources Accounting may be viewed as a part of the process of managing people in the organization. The objective is to improve the way the people contribute to the organization in creating more and more assets. The conventional accountants may agree to consider them as assets if they are convinced that future benefits are associated with expenditures on human resources.

HRD Audit

In the last two decades a large number of organizations have established Human Resources Development departments, introduced new systems of human resource development, made structural changes in terms of differentiating the human resource development function and integrating it with HR function. A good number of CEOs saw a hope in human resource development for most of their problems, issues and challenges. Inspite of substantial investments, there is a widespread feeling that human resource development has not lived upto the expectations of either the top management or the line managers. There are also examples of corporations where human resource development has taken a driver's seat and has given a lot of benefits. In today's competitive world, employees are the only reliable source of sustained competitive advantage. To get the best out of employees, there should be a good alignment of the human resource development function, its strategies, structure, systems, and styles with business and its goals. It should be aligned both with the short goals and long-term strategies. The managers and the top management should synergise with the human resource development goals and strategies.

HRD audit is a comprehensive evaluation of the current human resource development strategies, structure, systems, styles and skills in the context of the short and long term business plans of an organization. HRD audit attempts to find out the future HRD needs of the organization after assessing the current human resource development activities and inputs available. Dr T. V Rao with his colleague Dr . Udai Par pioneered in India, a methodology for auditing human resource development function and implemented the same in a good number of Indian organizations successfully.

HRD audit starts with an understanding of the future business plans and corporate strategies. While HRD audit can be done even in organizations that lack well formulated future plans and strategies, it is most effective as a tool when the organization already has such long-term plans. The HRD audit starts with the following objectives:

1. To analyse the long-term future plans of the organization.
2. To examine the current skills and competencies of the employees *vis-a-vis* the long term plans of the organization.
3. To assess the available instruments and mechanisms of human resource development system in relation to their maturity and effectiveness.
4. To examine the capabilities of human resource development staff to handle the pressing and future human resource development needs of the organization.

These objectives form subsequently the basis of HRD audit strategies and methodology. The HRD audit normally attempts to assess the existing skills and the competency gaps in order to achieve the long-term business goals and short-term results of the organization. The competencies may deal with technical aspects, managerial aspects, and people related or conceptual. They may cover knowledge base, attitudes, values, skills and competencies.

Definition

"HRD audit is a comprehensive evaluation of human resource development encompassing strategies, systems, practices, structures, competencies, styles, culture and their appropriateness to achieve the short and long term business goals of the organization".

Objectives and Purposes of HRD Audit

The major objectives are:

1. Organizational Growth—expansion, diversification and entering into a fast growth phase.
2. Professional Endowment — for promoting more professionalism and professional management.
3. Benchmarking — for improving human resource development practices.
4. Coping with Dissatisfaction— with any component.
5. Leadership Change.

Methodology of HRD Audit

HRD audit is a tool to measure the maturity level of human resource development system of an organization and starts with an evaluation of human resource development strategy.

This is based on four metrics such as HRD competencies of the employees, human resource development systems, maturity of HRD culture and linkage of human resource development to business strategy of the organization.

HRD Audit starts with a close examination of the following organizational issues:

1. Examination of long term and short term plans and vision to assess competency requirements.
2. Identification of broad competency requirements for future business goals and objectives.
3. Examination of the existing human resource development strategies, systems and practices and assess their appropriateness to have the required competencies.
4. Examination of the adequacies and inadequacies of human resource development structure, staff and their competencies, line managers and their attitudes, top management and their support, unions and their role in competence building for future.

HRD audit requires the use of a number of methods, which can be used in combination for desired results. In order to validate HRD audit, following methods are adopted:

1. Interview Method

Top management and senior management (Line managers and HRD personnel) of the organization are interviewed by the HRD auditor to solicit information, thinking and perspectives on the future growth plans and goals of the organization. It involves understanding of the organizational culture, working style and work planning system of the organization. Also, the readiness of human resource development strategies to pursue future organizational goals is also analyzed.

Such interviews are generally structured and must be intelligently drafted to seek relevant information and insight.

Now, the employees of the organization are to be interviewed on same line, but the modus operandi will vary. Given large number of employees and constraints of time and resources, auditor uses sampling tools to interview representative employees about their perceptions on organization's vision, mission, values, culture, strengths and areas of improvement, various opportunities, SWOT analysis of human resource development function future prospects and their role in achieving the goals of the organization. This is essentially a vision making exercise where the employees have a free hand to air their views and concerns.

2. Questionnaire Method

Auditor designs, develops, and administers a questionnaire to asses various dimensions of human resource development including the competency of human resource development staff, line manager's styles, and implementation of various human resource development systems. It is a good practice to pilot the questionnaire before administering it to the employees to test its validity and reliability. The questionnaire should be carefully constructed and must be in commensuration with the objectives of the HRD audit. The questionnaire should be given to a representative sample of the employees and its size should be as large as time, cost and resources permit for greater dependability of the data collection.

3. Observation Method

HRD auditor should also observe the employees in their natural environment such as workplace, canteen, training centres, residential colony, etc. to assess the extent to which a human resource development conducive and supportive environment exists in the organization.

4. Analysis of Records and Secondary Data Method

Various secondary sources of the human resource development data such as training and development programmes conducted, frequency of the programmes, their duration, number of participation, evaluation and feedback of training, manner of assessment of training needs of employees and their business relevance, learning programmes and cultures to support learning, profile of human resources — biographic and professional credibility, etc., can provide the much needed insight into the organization's human resource development assets and liabilities.

5. Workshop Method

Large scale interactive process can be utilized to assess human resource development systems such as performance appraisal, potential appraisal, counselling, coaching and mentoring programmes, etc. A large number of employees are gathered in a single room and divided into small groups to conduct SWOT analysis on different dimensions of human resource development. Each group is then required to make a presentation to their theme and a representative presents it before all the groups for discussions and suggestions.

6. Task Forces Method

A task force can be constituted to identify, evaluate and recommend an appropriate solution to the identified human resource development issues, problems, strategies and concerns. HRD auditor can work on this for further development and insight. Audit plays a pivotal role in proving business of an organization as mentioned below:

1. Cost Effective — HRD audit is cost effective
2. Provide Insight — it can give many insights into an organization's affairs
3. Promotes Strategic Leverages — it could get the top management to think in terms of strategic and long-term business plans
4. Modify Style — changes in the style of top management
5. Role Clarity — of human resource development department
6. Improves human resource development systems
7. Developing Competencies — increased focus on human resources and human competencies
8. Effective Recruitment — better recruitment policies and more professional staff
9. Effective Training — more planning and more cost effective training
10. Enhancing Accountability — strengthening accountabilities through appraisal systems.

Benefits Of HRD Audit

HRD audit is cost-effective and can give many insights into an organization's affairs. HRD audit can lead to several benefits:

1. Fostering Strategic Business Plans

The HRD audit begins with such strategic plans, but wherever it is non-existent, HRD audit compels top management to think about such plans. Since the employees cannot participate in an HRD audit without some sharing of these plans, the audit forces the top management to share their plans, which increases employee's involvement and commitment to the achievement of the strategic business objectives of the organization.

2. Clarity of Role of HRD Function

HRD audit draws the attention of employees at various levels to the important role of the human resource development department, current as well as the future. Enhanced role clarity of human resource development function increases understanding of line managers about their human resource development role and increases their managerial and strategic support to the function. This helps in making human resource development activities more aligned to the business priorities of the organization.

3. Organizational Competency Analysis

HRD audit identifies the strengths and weaknesses in some of the management systems existing in the organization. It also points out to the absence of systems that can enhance human productivity and utilization of the existing competency base, which may have an effect on the work procedures, delegation of powers, clarification of roles and responsibilities, developing or streamlining of financial and accounting procedures and systems, strengthening the information systems, and sharing of information.

4. HRD Systems Analysis

An HRD audit points out to the competence base required. It sets the stage and gives direction for the competency requirements of employees at various levels and thus provides a base for recruitment policies and procedures, retention strategies, talent management programmes, leadership development, performance appraisal, induction training, job-rotation, career planning and promotion policies, mentoring, communication, and training, etc. The HRD audit has helped most of the organizations in taking stock of the effectiveness of their human resource development systems and in designing or re-designing the human resource development systems.

5. Changes in the Styles of Top Management

One of the objectives of human resource development is to create a learning organization. A learning culture can be created only if the top managers of the organizations exhibit an human resource development style of management. Such sty1e requires an empowering attitude, participative style of management, and an ability to convert and use mistakes, conflicts and problems as learning opportunities.

7. ROI Analysis

An HRD audit examines the return on investment (ROI) on various human resource development programmes and strategies such as training by looking into process of identifying training needs and utilization of training inputs and learning for organization's growth and development. As direct investments are made in training, any cost-benefit analysis draws the attention of the top management and HRD managers to review the training function with relative ease.

8. Increased Focus on Human Resources and Human Competencies

One of the results of an HRD audit is to focus on new knowledge, attitudes and skills required by the employees in the organization. Comments are made about the technical, managerial, human and conceptual competencies of the staff at various levels. This differentiation has been found to help organizations identify and focus sharply on the competency requirements and gaps. The audit establishes a system of role clarity and fixing of accountabilities. This can take place through separate role clarity exercises or through the development of an appropriate performance appraisal stem. In any case the attention of the organization gets focused on developing the competency base of the organization. More sensitivity is developed to the missing aspects of competencies.

9. Strengthening Performance Improvement Mechanisms

An HRD audit can give significant inputs about the existing state of the accountabilities of employees. This gets assessed through performance appraisals as well as through the work culture and other cultural dimensions. A number of organizations have introduced systems of performance planning, sharing of expectations and documenting the accountabilities of employees.

Review Questions

1. Define HRD evaluation. Why do you need to evaluate HRD?
2. What is HRD accounting? Explain the benefits of HRD accounting.
3. Discuss the importance of HRD audit.
4. Explain the various methods of performing HRD audit.

✿ ✿ ✿

Chapter 8

MANAGEMENT DEVELOPMENT

Learning Objectives

1. *The Changing Nature of Management Development*
2. *Evolution of Management Development*
3. *Objectives of Management Development*
4. *Techniques of Management Development*

Management Development is any attempt to improve managerial performance by imparting knowledge, changing attitudes, or increasing skills. It thus includes in-house programmes like courses, coaching, and rotational assignments; professional programmes like American Management Association Seminars; and university programs. It is estimated that well over 1 million U.S. managers participate in management development programs yearly for a cost to industry of several billion dollars a year.

The ultimate aim of such development programs is, of course, to enhance the future performance of the organization itself. For this reason, the general management development process consists of (1) assessing the company's needs (for instance, to fill future executive openings, or to make the firm more responsive), (2) appraising the managers performance, and then (3) developing the managers themselves.

Management development is important for several reasons. A survey of 84 employers reports that about 90% of supervisors, 73% of middle-level managers, and 51% of executives were promoted from within; virtually all these managers, in turn, required some development to prepare them for their new jobs. Similarly, management development facilitates organizational continuity by preparing employees and current managers to smoothly assume higher-level positions. It also helps to socialize management trainees by developing in them the right values and attitudes for working in the firm. And, it can foster organizational responsiveness by developing the skills that managers need to respond faster to change.

The Changing Nature of Management Development

Some management development programmes are company wide and involve all or most new (or potential) management recruits. Here the employees may be rotated through a preprogrammed series of departmental assignments and educational experiences; the aims are identifying their management potential, and at providing the breadth of experience (in, say, production and finance) that will make the new managers more valuable in their first "real" assignment as group product leaders. Then superior candidates may be slotted onto a "fast-track", a development program that prepares them more quickly to assume senior-level commands.

On the other hand, the management development programme may be aimed at filling a specific position, such as CEO, perhaps with one of two potential candidates. When it is an executive position to be filled, the process is usually called succession planning. Succession planning refers to the process through which senior-level openings are planned for and eventually filled.

Such a succession programme typically takes place in stages. First, an organization projection is made, here you anticipate your department's management needs based on factors like planned expansion or contraction. Next, the HR department reviews its management skills inventory to identify the management talent now employed. These inventories, you may recall, contain data on things like educational and work experience, career preferences, and performance appraisals. Next, management replacement charts are drawn. These summarise potential candidates for each of your management slots, as well as each person's development needs.

Evolution of Management Development

Efficient and loyal workers were promoted to the supervisory or management positions and it was soon realised that "Superior workers do not necessarily make superior managers. This realisation necessitated the need for planned programmes for the selection, training and development of managerial personnel".

Formal management development programmes started emerging in the late 1940s and 1950s. Several forces have operated to cause the expansion of management development activities. To name only a few —

1. Shift from owner managed to professionally managed enterprises.
2. Management has been recognised as a distinct kind of occupation consisting of acquired skills and a unified body of knowledge.

Objectives of Management Development

The management development programmes are organised with a view to achieving specific objectives. They are:

1. To overhaul the management machinery.
2. To improve the performance of the managers.
3. To give the specialist an overall view of the functions of an organisation and equip them to co-ordinate each other's efforts effectively.
4. To identify the persons with the required potential and prepare them for senior positions.
5. To increase the morale of the members of the management group.
6. To increase the versatility of the management group.
7. To keep the executives abreast with the changes and developments in their respective fields.
8. To create the management succession which can take over in case of contingencies.
9. To improve thought process and analytical ability.
10. To broaden the outlook of the executive regarding his role position and responsibilities.
11. To understand the conceptual issues relating to economic, social, and technical areas.
12. To understand the problems of human relations and improve human relations skills.
13. To stimulate creative thinking.

The Responsive Manager

For the past few years management development's focus has been shifting from preparing managers to fill higher-level slots to preparing them to meet the challenges of managing in a fast-paced environment. Increasingly, therefore, the emphasis is on developing a manager's ability to learn and make decisions under conditions of rapid change.

Two experts put it this way: 'As decision makers take on increasing responsibility across their career, their learning needs move from the arena of task learning to behavioural learning to conceptual or policy-level learning. For example, today's corporate managers are under enormous pressure to find the strategic opportunities their competitors have yet to find', means more emphasis on developing their conceptual ability to search for internal strategic opportunities to improve quality, service, and prices. Similarly, all managers — not just those to be posted overseas — have to be well schooled in global economics, foreign markets, and cross-cultural negotiating'. And to manage in flat tier, more empowered organizations the leader must increasingly become a teacher, coach, and consultant rather than a 'boss'.

This is causing a corresponding change in the techniques that are emphasized in management development programmes. Historically on-the-job experiences, including on-the-job training, coaching, and rotational assignments have been far and away from the most popular management development techniques. The problem is that these techniques tend to emphasize showing managers current procedures or getting them to think about how to 'do what we're doing today a little better'. Today there's a shift towards development techniques that teach managers how to learn and how to develop the competencies they need to cope with change, such as sizing up foreign markets and searching for new strategic opportunities.

Techniques of Management Development

There are mainly two types of techniques by which managers can acquire the knowledge, skills and attitudes and make themselves competent managers. One is through formal training and the other is through on-the-job experiences.

On-the-job training is of utmost importance as the real learning takes place only when the learner uses what he has learnt. But it should also be remembered that class room training or pedagogical techniques have also got their own importance in gaining new knowledge, and learning new techniques, and broader concepts. The below picture presents the concepts and areas of management development programme.

Concepts and Areas of Management Development Programme

General Administration

How to decide overall company strategy?

Corporate planning
Decision theory and decision trees
Games theory
Company model on computer.

How to evaluate capital expenditure proposals?

Discounted cash flow and net present value
Replacement theory
Decision theory and decision trees
Markovitz portfolio selection.

How to improve the flow of information needed to control the organization?

Costing systems
Reporting by responsibility
Organization and methods
Systems and analysis
Computers for data processing
Management by exception
Computers for data processing
Computers for information retrieval
Random observation studies
Information theory
Cybernetics.

How to launch a new project?

Critical path method including PERT
PERT/COST
Branching networks
Resource allocation
Using a computer with these techniques.

Marketing and Sales

How to forecast demand?

Exponential smoothing
Market research
Moving averages
Regression analysis
Box/Jenkins

Time series
Leontieff input-output tables
Use of computer with these techniques.

How to generate new product ideas?

Market research
Brainstorming
Value analysis.

How to launch a new product?

Critical path method including PERT
PERT/COST
Branching networks
Using a computer with these techniques.

How to determine the profitability of a product or product line?

Marginal costing
Contribution analysis
Profit volume ratio
Break-even charts
Linear programming.

How to improve product design?

Market research
Value analysis
Ergonomics.

Production

How to remove factory bottlenecks?

Production control by computer
Critical path methods including PERT
Branching networks
Resource allocation
Using a computer with these techniques
Simulation including Monte Carlo method
Queuing Theory.

How to improve product quality and reliability?

Statistical quality control
Process control by computer, including
Evolutionary operation, and
Adaptive control.

How to cope with complex mixes? such problems as: several factories, delivery to many customers, or several products from many raw materials available from many different sources, or several products profitability made by several process, etc. Mathematical programming by computer, including

Linear programming

Quadratic programming

Separable programming

Integer programming

Dynamic programming.

How to cut labour costs?

Method study
Incentive schemes
Ergonomics
Productivity bargaining.

How to improve labour relations?

Job relations programme.

HUMAN RESOURCE

How to improve training methods?

Teaching machines
Business games.

How to bring order and equity into wages and salary schemes?

Job description
Job evaluation
Merit rating
Salary progressing curves
Time-span discretion.

How to recruit the right number of the right type of people?

Manpower planning
Intelligence, personality and aptitude tests.

PURCHASING

How to check quality and reliability of raw materials?

Statistical quality control including quality protection
Statistical sampling methods including sequential stocks.

How to cut down the cost of purchasing and holding stocks?

Statistical stock control
Methods of forecasting demand (see under marketing)
Economic batch re-ordering quantities
Simulation by computer.

RESEARCH

How to reduce the time taken to complete research?

Method study
Critical path methods including PERT
PERT/COST
Branching networks
Research Allocation
Using a computer with these techniques
Statistical design of experiments
Scientific calculations by computer
Simulation by computers.

Learning is haphazard without background and, learning can never be called true learning if it is just theory without practice. When on-the-job training is properly balanced with the class-room training, the real learning takes place.

The following are some of the important on-the-job and off-the-job techniques of management development.

Important Techniques of Management Development

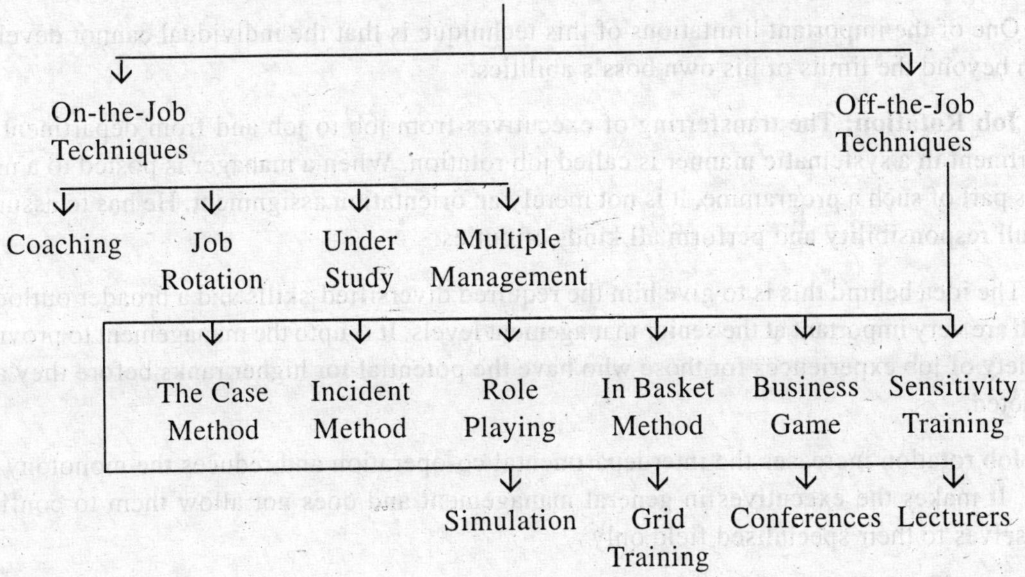

On-the-Job Techniques

These are the most widely used techniques. No other technique may interest the trainee so much as these do since the location of the learner is not an artificial one as the classroom. The success of these techniques depends on the immediate supervisor and how good a teacher he is. On-the-job techniques are especially useful for certain groups like scientific and technical personnel.

Though the costs of training initially appear to be low they may turn out to be high when wastages of all kinds are considered under this type of training.

This method of learning in isolation may prove to be inadequate but in combination with the other techniques will be excellent. The important on-the-job training techniques are: coaching, job rotation, under study, and multiple management.

Coaching: In coaching the trainee is placed under a particular supervisor who acts as an instructor and teaches job knowledge and skills to the trainee. He tells him what he wants him to do, how it can be done and follows up while it is being done and corrects errors. "Coaching should be distinguished from counselling.... Counselling.. involves a discussion between the boss and his subordinates of areas concerned with the man's hopes, fears, emotions, and aspirations. It reaches into very personal and delicate matters. To be done correctly, counselling demands considerable background and ability on the part of the counsellor. If carried out poorly, it may do considerable damage."

The act of coaching can be done in several ways. The executive apart from asking them to do the routine work, may ask them to tackle some complex problem by giving them chance to participate in decision-making.

One of the important limitations of this technique is that the individual cannot develop much beyond the limits of his own boss's abilities.

Job Rotation: The transferring of executives from job to job and from department to department in a systematic manner is called job rotation. When a manager is posted to a new job as part of such a programme, it is not merely an orientation assignment. He has to assume the full responsibility and perform all kinds of duties.

The idea behind this is to give him the required diversified-skills and a broader outlook, which are very important at the senior management levels. It is upto the management to provide a variety of job experiences for those who have the potential for higher ranks before they are promoted.

Job rotation increases the interdepartmental co-operation and reduces the monotony of work. It makes the executives in general management and does not allow them to confine themselves to their specialised field only.

Multiple Management: Multiple Management is a system in which permanent advisory committees of managers study problems of the company and make recommendations to higher management. It is also called Junior-board of executives system. These committees discuss the actual problems and different alternative solutions after which the decisions are taken.

The technique of multiple management has certain advantages over the other techniques. They are:

(i) Members have the opportunity to acquire the knowledge of various aspects of business;

(ii) It helps to identify the members who have the skills and capabilities of an effective manager;

(iii) Members have the opportunity to participate in the group interaction and thereby gain the practical experience of group decision-making;

(iv) It is relatively inexpensive method; and

(v) Considerable number of executives can be developed in a short span of time.

Off-the-Job Techniques

Because of the fact that on-the-job techniques have their own limitations, these off-the-job techniques are considered important to fill those gaps. The following are some of the important off-the-job techniques:

1. The case study
2. Incident method
3. Role playing
4. In basket method
5. Business game
6. Sensitivity training
7. Simulation
8. Grid training
9. Conferences
10. Lectures

1. The Case Study: Cases are prepared on the basis of actual business situations that happened in various organisations. The trainees are given cases for discussing and deciding upon the case. Then they are asked to identify the apparent and hidden problems for which they have to suggest solutions.

The situation is generally described in a comprehensive manner and the trainee has to distinguish the significant facts from the insignificant, analyse the facts, identify the different alternative solutions, select and suggest the best. This whole exercise improves the participant's decision-making skills by sharpening their analytical and judging abilities.

2. Incident Method: This method was developed by Paul Pigors. It aims to develop the trainee in the areas of intellectual ability, practical judgement and social awareness. Under this method each employee is developed in a group process.

Incidents are prepared on the basis of actual situations which happened in different organisations. Each employee in the training group is asked to study the incident and to make short-term decisions in the role of a person who has to cope with the incident in the actual situation. Later, the group studies and discusses the incident and takes decisions relating to that incident, based on the group interaction and decisions taken by each member. Thus, this method is similar to a combination of case method and in-basket method.

3. Role Playing: A problem situation is simulated by asking the participants to assume the role of particular person in the situation. The participant interacts with other participants assuming different roles. Mental set of the role is described but no dialogue is provided.

The whole play may be tape-recorded and the trainee may thus be given the opportunity to examine his or her own performance.

Role playing gives the participants vicarious experiences which are of much use to understand people better. This method teaches human relations skills through actual practice. The exemplary role playing situations are a grievance discussion, employment interview, a sales presentation etc.

4. In Basket Method: The trainees are first given background information about a simulated company, its products, key personnel, various memoranda, requests and all data pertaining to the firm. The trainee has to understand all this, make notes, delegate tasks and prepare memos within a specified amount of time. Abilities that this kind of exercise develops are: (i) situational judgement is being able to recall details, establish priorities, interrelate items and determine need for more information, (ii) social sensitivity in exhibiting courtesy in written notes, scheduling meetings with personnel involved and explaining reasons for actions taken, and (iii) willingness to make decision and take action."

5. Business Games: Under this method, the trainees are divided into groups or different teams. Each team has to discuss and arrive at decisions concerning such subjects as production, pricing, research expenditure, advertising etc., assuming itself to be the management of a simulated firm. The other teams assume themselves as competitors and react to the decision. This immediate feedback helps to know the relative performance of each team. The team's co-operative decision promotes greater interaction among participants and gives them the experience in co-operative group processes.

All this develops organisational ability, quickness of thinking, leadership qualities and the ability to adopt under stress.

6. Sensitivity Training: The main objective of sensitivity training is the "Development of awareness of and sensitivity of behavioural patterns of oneself and others." This development results in the (i) increased openness with others, (ii) greater concern for others, (iii) increased tolerance for individual differences, (iv) less ethnic prejudice, (v) understanding of group processes, (vi) enhanced listening skills, (vii) increased trust and support."

The role played by the trainee here is not a structured one as in role play. It is a laboratory situation where one gets a chance to know more about himself and the impact of his behaviour on others. It develops the managerial sensitivity, trust, and respect for others. One of the limitations of sensitivity training is that it exacts a huge emotional cost from the manager.

7. Simulation: Under this technique the situation is duplicated in such a way that it carries a closer resemblance to the actual job situation. The trainee experiences a feeling that he is actually encountering all those conditions. Then he is asked to assume a particular role in the circumstances and solve the problems by making a decision. He is immediately given a feedback of his performance.

One of the limitations of this method is that it is very difficult to duplicate the situation to the extent of making the trainee feel the pressures and realities of actual decision-making on the job. The very fact that the trainee knows that it is an artificial situation prevents him from experiencing all that he experiences in real job situation.

8. Managerial Grid: It is a six phase programme lasting from three to five years. It starts with upgrading managerial skills, continues to group improvement; improves inter group relations, goes into corporate planning, develops implementation method and ends with an evaluation phase. The grid represents several possible leadership styles. Each style represents a different combination of two basic orientations - concern for people and concern for production.

9. Conferences: A conference is a meeting of several people to discuss the subject of common interest. But contribution from members can be expected as each one builds upon ideas of other participants. This method is best suited when a problem has to be analysed and examined from different viewpoints.

It helps the members develop their ability to modify their attitudes. Participants enjoy their method of learning as they get an opportunity to express their views.

The success of the conference depends on the conference leader. In order to make the conference a success, the conference leader must be able to see that the discussion is thorough and concentrate on the central problem by encouraging all the participants to develop alternatives and present their viewpoints and by preventing domination by a few participants.

10. Lectures: It is the simplest of all techniques. This is the best technique to present and explains series of facts, concepts, and principles. The lecturer organises the material and gives it to a group of trainees in the form of talk. The main uses of lectures in executive development are:

(i) It is direct and can be used for a large group of trainees.

(ii) It presents the overview and scope of the subject clearly.

(iii) It presents the principles, concepts, policies and experiences in the shortest time. Thus, it is a time saving technique.

The lectures do not give scope for student participation and may sometimes be boring which in turn hinders learning. Skills can be learnt only by doing and therefore lectures are of no use for technical skills.

Management Development is of vital importance to any dynamic organisation today. Some organisation have hired professionals to take care of their management development activities.

Review Questions

1. Define 'Management development'.
2. Trace the evolution of management development.
3. What are the areas of management development programmes?
4. Discuss the important techniques of management development.

Chapter 9

ORGANISATIONAL DEVELOPMENT (OD)

Learning Objectives

1. *Meaning of OD*
2. *Nature of OD*
3. *Objectives of OD*
4. *OD Interventions*
5. *OD Models*
6. *Benefits from OD*

Introduction

Organizational development (OD) is an application of behavioural science to organizational change. It encompasses a wide array of theories, processes, and activities, all of which are oriented towards the goal of improving individual organizations. Generally speaking, however, OD differs from traditional organizational change techniques in that it typically embraces a more holistic approach that is aimed at transforming thought and behaviour throughout an entity.

OD has a fascinating history and has become a fundamental part of the drive for engineering change within business.

Organisational Development (OD) may be defined as a Behavioural Science approach to the improvement of organisational effectiveness. It constitutes long-range effort to:

- Improve the problem solving capacity of the organisation
- Foster effective management of the organisation culture
- Improve the effectiveness of work groups/teams. It is specifically concerned with
- The organisation climate, organisation culture –i.e.. norms, values, power structure
- Worker commitment
- Structure of roles in organisation - incorporating organisational structuring and organisational restructuring
- Inter-group collaboration
- The combination of the authority based in roles with the authority based in knowledge and skills
- The creation of an open system of communication –vertically, horizontally and diagonally
- Management development; the management of organisational change; and the management of conflict.

Definition

Definitions of OD abound, but they are all predicated on the notion of improving organizational performance through proactive activities and techniques. It is also worth noting that organizational development, though concerned with improving workforce performance, should not be mistaken for human resource development.

"Organization development is the planned process of developing an organization to be more effective in accomplishing its desired goals," wrote Rima Shaffer in *Principles of Organization Development.* "It is distinguished from human resource development, in that HRD focuses on the personal growth of individuals within organizations, while OD focuses on developing the structures, systems, and processes within the organization to improve organizational effectiveness."

Basics of Organizational Development

Although the field of OD is broad, it can be differentiated from other systems of organizational change by its emphasis on process rather than problems. Indeed, traditional group change systems have focused on identifying problems in an organization and then trying to alter the behaviour that creates the problem. Margaret Neale and Gregory Northcraft have observed that OD initiatives focus on identifying the behavioural interactions and patterns that cause and sustain problems. Then, rather than simply changing isolated behaviours, OD efforts are aimed at creating a behaviourally healthy organization that will naturally anticipate and prevent problems.

Objectives of OD

The objectives of OD may be stated as follows :

- Improved organizational performance as measured by profitability, market share, innovativeness, etc.
- Better adaptability of the organization to its environment
- Willingness of the members to face organizational problems and contribute creative solutions to these problems
- Improvement in internal behaviour patterns such as inter personal relations, inter group relations and involvement in planning for organizational development.

Characteristics of Organisational Development

OD programs usually share several basic characteristics.

- They are considered long-term efforts of at least one to three years in most cases.
- OD stresses collaborative management, whereby managers and employees at different levels of the hierarchy co-operate to solve problems.
- OD also recognizes that every organization is unique and that the same solutions cannot necessarily be applied at different companies—this assumption is reflected in an OD focus on research and feedback.
- In most OD programs there is an emphasis on the value of teamwork and small groups. In fact, most OD systems use small teams—or even individuals—as a vehicle to implement broad organizational changes.

The catalyst—whether a group or individual—that facilitates the OD process is known as the "change agent." Change agents are often outside consultants with experience managing OD programs, although companies sometimes utilize inside managers. The advantage of bringing in outside OD consultants is that they often provide a different perspective and have a less biased view of the organization's problems and needs. The primary drawback associated with outside change agents is that they may lack an in-depth understanding of key issues particular to the company. In addition, outside change agents may have trouble securing the trust and co-operation of key players in the organization. For these reasons, some companies employ an external-internal team approach, which seeks to combine the advantages of internal and external change agents while minimizing the drawbacks associated with the two approaches.

"Once we recognize that organizational development involves substantial changes in how individuals think, believe, and act, we can appreciate the necessity of someone to play the role of change agent. But who should play the role? Existing managers? New managers? Or individuals hired specifically for that purpose? Depending upon the situation, any of these can be called upon to orchestrate the organizational development process. The point is that the role of the change agent is necessary for organizational development to occur."

Models of Organizational Development

Three models of OD are popular- namely:

- Kurt Lewin's Unfreezing-Changing and Freezing Model
- Griener's – Equential Process and
- Leavitt's System Model

Kurt Lewin's Unfreezing-Changing and Freezing Model

According to Lewin, successful change requires *unfreezing* the status quo, *changing* to a new state, and *refreezing* the new change to make it permanent. The status quo can be considered an equilibrium state. Moving from this equilibrium requires unfreezing, which can be achieved in one of the three ways:

1. The *driving forces,* which direct behaviour away from the status quo, can be increased.
2. The *restraining forces,* which hinder movement from the existing equilibrium, can be decreased.
3. The two approaches can be *combined.*

Once unfreezing has been accomplished, the change itself can be implemented. However, the mere introduction of change does not ensure that it will take hold. The new situation therefore needs to be *refrozen* so it can be sustained over time. Unless this last step is attended to "there is a very strong chance the change will be short-lived and employees will revert to the previous equilibrium state. The objective of refreezing, then, is to stabilize the new situation by balancing the driving and restraining forces.

Lewin's Description of the Changing Process

Unfreezing ⟶ Changing ⟶ Refreezing

Lewin's three-step process treats change as a break in the organization's equilibrium state. The status quo has been disturbed, and change is necessary to establish a new equilibrium state. This view might have been appropriate to the relatively calm environment that most organizations faced 30 or 40 years ago. But one can argue that this is not the typical state current managers have to negotiate.

Griener's – Equential Process Model

Change according to this model is in terms of certain sequential stages. It is initiated by external pressure or stimulus on the top management and is motivated to take action. The succeeding stages of intervention by the change agent are: diagnosis of the problem, invention of a new solution, experimentation with that solution and reinforcement from positive results.

Leavitt's System Model

Leavitt's model focuses on the interactive nature of the various sub-systems in a change process. Organisation is a system of four interacting sub-systems – task, structure, people and technology. Change in any one of the sub-systems tends to have consequences for the other sub- systems. Hence, OD effort should not only focus on the intended change but also on the effects of change on the other sub-systems.

Managing Change Through Organizational Development

Organizational development initiatives do not automatically succeed. The benefits of effective OD programs are myriad, as many executives, managers, and business owners will attest. But OD interventions that are pursued in a sloppy, half-hearted, or otherwise faulty manner are far less likely to bring about meaningful change than those that have the full support of the people involved. Several conditions have to be present if an OD intervention could have any meaningful chance of bringing about the desired change:

- Ownership and all involved personnel needed to be genuinely and visibly committed to the effort.
- People involved in OD have to be informed in advance of the nature of the intervention and the nature of their involvement in it.
- The OD effort has to be connected to other parts of the organization; this is especially true of such areas as the evaluation and reward systems.

- The effort has to be directed by appropriate managers and guided by change agents (which, if used, must be competent).
- The intervention should be based on accurate diagnosis of organizational conditions.
- Owners and managers should show their commitment to OD at all stages of the effort, including the diagnosis, implementation, and evaluation.
- Evaluation is key to success, and should consist of more than asking people how they felt about the effort.
- Owners and managers need to show employees how the OD effort relates to the organization's goals and overriding mission.

Implementing OD Programs

OD efforts basically entail two groups of activities: "action research" and "interventions." Action research is a process of systematically collecting data on a specific organization, feeding it back for action planning, and evaluating results by collecting and reflecting on more data. Data gathering techniques include everything from surveys and questionnaires to interviews, collages, drawings, and tests. The data is often evaluated and interpreted using advanced statistical analysis techniques.

Action research can be thought of as the diagnostic component of the OD process. But it also encompasses the intervention component, whereby the change agent uses action plans to intervene in the organization and make changes, as discussed below. In a continuous process, the results of actions are measured and evaluated and new action plans are devised to effect new changes. Thus, the intervention process can be considered a facet of action research.

OD interventions are plans or programs comprised of specific activities designed to effect change in some facet of an organization. Numerous interventions have been developed over the years to address different problems or create various results. However, they all are geared toward the goal of improving the entire organization through change. In general, organizations that wish to achieve a high degree of organizational change will employ a full range of interventions, including those designed to transform individual and group behaviour and attitudes. Entities attempting smaller changes will stop short of those goals, applying interventions targeted primarily toward operating policies, management structures, worker skills, and personnel policies. Typically, organization development programs will simultaneously integrate more than one of these interventions. A few of the more popular interventions are briefly described below.

Interpersonal Interventions

Interpersonal interventions in an OD program are designed to enhance individual skills, knowledge, and effectiveness. This type of program utilizes group dynamics by gathering individuals together in loosely structured meetings. Subject matter is determined by the group, within the context of basic goals stipulated by a facilitator. As group members try to exert structure on fellow members, group members gain a greater awareness of their own and other's feelings, motivations, and behaviours. Other types of interpersonal interventions include those designed to improve the performance review process, create better training programs, help workers identify their true wants and set complementary career goals, and resolve conflict.

Group Interventions

OD group interventions are designed to help teams and groups within organizations become more effective. Such interventions usually assume that the most effective groups communicate well, facilitate a healthy balance between both personal and group needs, and function by consensus as opposed to autocracy or majority rule.

Group diagnostic interventions are simply meetings wherein members of a team analyze their unit's performance, ask questions about what the team needs to do to improve, and discuss potential solutions to problems. The benefit of such interventions is that members often communicate problems of which their co-workers were unaware. Ideally, such communication will spur problem-solving and improved group dynamics.

Role analysis technique (RAT) is used to help employees get a better grasp on their role in an organization. In the first step of a RAT intervention, people define their perception of their role and contribution to the overall company effort in front of a group of co-workers. Group members then provide feedback to more clearly define the role. In the second phase, the individual and the group examine ways in which the employee relies on others in the company, and how they define his or her expectations. RAT interventions help people to reduce role confusion, which can result in either conflict or the perception that some people are not doing their job. A popular intervention similar to RAT is responsibility charting, which utilizes a matrix system to assign decision and task responsibilities.

Intergroup Interventions

Intergroup interventions are integrated into OD programs to facilitate co-operation and efficiency between different groups within an organization. For instance, departmental interaction often deteriorates in larger organizations as different units battle for limited resources or become detached from the needs of other units.

Conflict resolution meetings are one common intergroup intervention. First, different group leaders are brought together to secure their commitment to the intervention. Next, the teams meet separately to make a list of their feelings about the other group(s). Then the groups meet and share their lists. Finally, the teams meet to discuss the problems and to try to develop solutions that will help both parties. This type of intervention, say supporters, helps to gradually diffuse tension between groups that has arisen because of faulty communication.

Rotating membership interventions are used by OD change agents to minimize the negative effects of intergroup rivalry that arise from employee allegiances to groups or divisions. The intervention basically entails temporarily putting group members into their rival groups. As more people interact in the different groups, greater understanding results.

OD joint activity interventions serve the same basic function as the rotating membership approach, but these involve melding members of different groups to work together toward a common goal. Similarly, common enemy interventions achieve the same results by finding an adversary common to two or more groups and then getting members of the groups to work together to overcome the threat. Examples of common enemies targeted in such programs include competitors, government regulation, and economic conditions.

Comprehensive Interventions

OD comprehensive interventions are used to directly create change throughout an entire organization, rather than focusing on organizational change through sub-group interventions. One of the most popular comprehensive interventions is survey feedback. This technique basically entails surveying employee attitudes at all levels of the company and then disseminating a report that details those findings. The employees then use the data in feedback sessions to create solutions to perceived problems. A number of questionnaires developed specifically for such interventions have been developed.

Structural change interventions are used by OD change agents to implement organizational alterations related to departmentalization, management hierarchy, work policies, compensation and benefit incentives programs, and other cornerstones of the business. Often, the implemented changes emanate from feedback from other interventions. One benefit of change interventions is that companies can often realize an immediate and very significant impact in productivity and profitability (provided the changes are warranted and implemented appropriately).

Sociotechnical system design interventions are similar to structural change techniques, but they typically emphasize the reorganization of work teams. The basic goal is to create independent groups throughout the company that supervise themselves. This administration may include such aspects as monitoring quality or disciplining team members. The theoretic benefit of sociotechnical system design interventions is that worker and group productivity and quality is increased because workers have more control over (and subsequent satisfaction from) the process in which they participate.

A fourth OD intervention that became extremely popular during the 1980s and early 1990s is total quality management (TQM). TQM interventions utilize established quality techniques and programs that emphasize quality processes, rather than achieving quality by inspecting products and services after processes have been completed. The important concept of continuous improvement embodied by TQM was carried over into other OD interventions.

Organisation Development and Consultancy Interventions

Organisation Development focuses on Human Behaviours, in turn by focusing on three underpinning factors:

- Performance Management
- Culture
- Practices

Consultancy Interventions

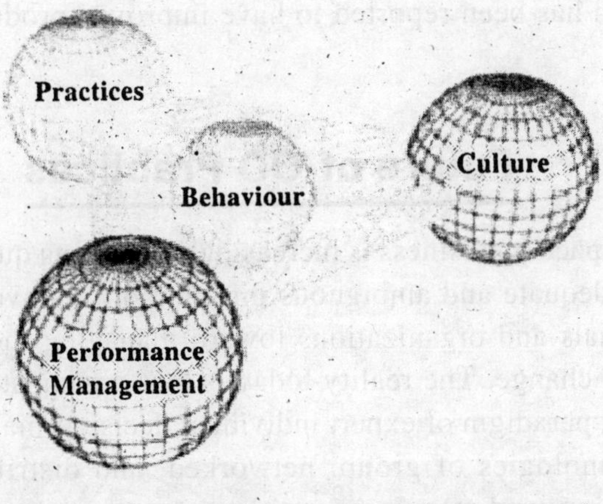

The OD Company™ Business Dependencies Model
© 2002 The OD Company

Steps in the consulting process:- DIAGNOSIS———ANALYSIS———DESIGN——— PLAN———IMPLEMENT———EVALUATE seem to be the trend in the current age.

Grid Training

Based upon the managerial grid of Blake and Mouton, Grid OD aims to achieve an ideal management style. This style, it is assumed is the one that integrates task completion and maintenance of good interpersonal relations. The Grid is used to clarify many complex roles and styles in the organization.

A programme starts with the focus on individual behaviour and then moves through a series of sequential steps involving work teams, relationships between groups and sub-units, and the total organizational management.

The Grid training is in six steps, namely:

- Grid seminar
- Team development
- Inter-group development
- Development of ideal strategic model
- Implementing ideal strategy, and
- Systematic critique.

Grid intervention has been reported to have improved productivity and organizational effectiveness.

Future of OD Practices

The accelerating pace of business is increasingly requiring quick decisions about critical matters, based on inadequate and ambiguous information. Innovative intervention methods must support individuals and organizations toward managing the exponentially increasing rate and magnitude of change. The reality today is that organizations have to be assisted to evolve from a limiting paradigm of expert individual decision-makers, toward new methods, assumptions and technologies of group, networked, and distributed nodes for decision-making, problem-solving, and meaning-creating.

Increasing economic interdependence and resulting chain reactions require OD professionals to use whole-systems perspectives and systems thinking tools with client organizations. Intervention designs must build capacity to think, make decisions, and take action systemically build in effective feedback loops; recognize or anticipate and adjust for unintended, delayed and counter-intuitive long-term consequences.

There is a need to work and understand the issues of working virtually in temporary teams, think systemically beyond the walls of the existing organization using concepts of value networks, and understand the principles of the knowledge economy.

OD can help organizations focus on moving from the old SWOT approach in strategic planning to a more Appreciative Inquiry based approach focused on Strengths and Opportunities. Focusing on Weaknesses and Threats is increasingly becoming a wasted activity in a world that is evolving at such an increasing pace that the future increasingly looks nothing like the past and the present is so transitory as to barely exist. It is important when we talk about AI to make sure that people understand that the term "appreciative" does not refer to "gratefulness" but rather to the accounting concept of "accrual" wherein we build on our assets.

Given economic interdependence, and chain reactions fuelled by bottom line criteria in making the business environment has become so complex. Traditional OD interventions are not adequate to deal with the size of the problem. Meta-organizational and multiple organizational techniques will have to be created.

OD needs to foster the capability to make collaborative decisions at the periphery of organizations based on consistency with organizational purpose and principles. This means helping develop a truly empowered environment and collaborative problem-identification and problem-solving skills. It also means training team members at all levels to become effective facilitators of the collaborative process.

Our clients are demanding that we develop ways to identify and monitor metrics that measure impact on intended results, rather than success of and satisfaction with tactical interventions. In the economy of today, businesses need proven and verifiable methods to increase efficiency (i.e., more and better alignment, precision and speed). OD can integrate methods that do this with our collaborative process methodologies to achieve sustainable progress and results.

If globalization and the concentration of wealth will tend to increase hatred and decrease mutual understanding around the World, OD practitioners should be joining global networks such as ODI and IODA, to stimulate global thinking. Alliances will need to be built that lead to OD involvement in global public policy groups as well.

Increased opportunities for OD to coach and support leaders looking to find meaning and purpose and to provide an environment that supports the whole person. We may need to more actively advocate our beliefs and values for individuals and workplaces.

OD professionals can assist companies in effectively building partnerships and share information with other companies by helping companies look at their organizational boundaries. First OD professionals need to assist organizations, break down boundaries within the traditional company structure, so sharing information is non-threatening. Concurrently,

OD interventions to increase the involvement of customers, supplies, and external stakeholders in developing and implementing business strategies will help shift the mental paradigm of today's definition of a "company".

New high-speed and wireless communication technologies may create a role for "virtual facilitators" with traditional facilitator skills plus high tech computer/internet knowledge. OD practitioners need first to learn how to do this themselves, and then how to teach it to others on a mass scale.

OD must implement effective ways to use the internet with virtual team. Just as this process uses Web council to create and refine new knowledge, clients' issues can be handled using this powerful tool. There are most likely numerous OD strategies and intervention models that can also be effectively implemented using this virtual team system. OD professionals will need to hone their knowledge and skills as virtual team guides and thought organizers, much as Saul is doing for this process; technologies such as Web council will need to continue to evolve as the interventions required increase in complexity.

Facilitation skills need to be recognized as a critical leadership competency versus an OD intervention.

Due to problems created by global business networks that they are not responsible to solve, and which governments increasingly do not have the power to solve, public-private partnerships involving government, business, and voluntary sectors could be a great growth industry for OD professionals. Here is the opportunity for initially pro-bono work to stimulate interest and awareness. This could lead to ongoing work as facilitators of the process of creating and operating public-private partnerships. Socio-economic-ecologic responsibility needs to be a part of basic Purpose and Principles of such activities.

If the prevailing "shareholder equity" and "short term returns" mental models make it difficult for managers to think in long term, systems global ways, OD can help to foster greater versatility in the mental models in use that are longer term, more creative, more inclusive, and more continuously learning.

If global companies continue to expand into developing countries, they need to more carefully factor into their approach aspects of diversity and multiculturalism. In addition to systems thinking, global level capability to work with diversity and multi-culturalism must be made an education requirement.

The ability to reach across our conceptual frames of "difference" will be necessary — mediation of conflict and appreciation for other ways of being are necessary skills. In addition to management of conflict (based on a presumption of misperceptions of mutual exclusivity of interests) it is going to be increasingly necessary to recognize the existence of polarities and genuinely mutually exclusive positions that need also to be dealt with on an effective basis; this may mean that OD practitioners are going to have to recognize that "idealized philosophies" are not always in consonance with the real world and that implementation of Dissonance Theory based activities may be necessary on a large scale... helping to educate people on such needs and facilitate implementation of such activities would be a definite role for future OD.

Diversity, conceptual frames and cultures need more prominence in global business decisions and the tendency to spread an ethnocentric model. We need more advanced work on relationships between groups and organizations, including more sensitivity and skill in diversity and conflict.

The need still exists for blending of competence in OD and business functions, e.g., HR, global operations, etc.

Effective OD interventions with "stickability" must reflect a whole systems perspective from a practical, results-oriented focus (vs. an academic, process-oriented focus) and strategies for identifying and sustainably effecting key leverage components. Knowledge and skill in applied systems thinking is critical for OD practitioners and organizational leaders.

An area for OD focus is achieving business results and leadership development simultaneously through action/reflection projects that use tools such as Webcouncil to support: virtual meetings; information exchange and knowledge creation; strategy identification, execution, and assessment; and increased leadership capacity from participation in and reflection on such projects.

Our view of hard-driving—and financially-driven—top executives as problems must change, along with our view of ourselves. To the extent that we operate from a polarized view of our role as consultants who must change our clients to our way of thinking, we add to their problems, or are simply irrelevant. Our interventions need to include and value the priorities of all organization participants, supporting holistic, inclusive integration at the level of core goals of people at all levels of hierarchy, as well as customers, suppliers, and other stakeholders.

Because culture needs to be understood as central to what OD is about, our intervention proposals, designs, and strategies must explicitly integrate culture awareness and culture work as a critical focus. We must articulate the relevance of culture work for the health and effectiveness of organizations and the people who staff them.

OD needs to focus on educating on the values of cultural diversity and processes that breed inclusiveness rather than exclusiveness. In particular, OD needs to facilitate a "diversity training" mentality that overcomes much of what has been done in the past under that rubric that has focused on difference awareness plus guilt and apology for the past, and that instead focuses on the present and future in terms of awareness, legitimization and usefulness of multiplicity in perspectives when approaching complex problems and situations.

The search for and engagement in partnerships as a means of enhancing business portfolios, means OD practitioners will have to not only assist organizations in understanding the importance of bringing different corporate cultures together, but also develop specific methods for creating "new" cultures.

Review Questions

1. Define OD. State the objectives of OD.
2. Examine the nature and scope of OD.
3. Explain the characteristic features of OD.
4. Examine some of the models of OD. Suggest the most suitable one for adoption by Indian industries.
5. What do you understand by OD intervention ? Discuss some of the techniques of OD intervention.

✿ ✿ ✿

Chapter 10

ORGANISATIONAL DEVELOPMENT PROCESS

Learning Objectives

1. *The Three Approaches to Planned Change*
2. *Strategies and Guidelines for Implementing Change*
3. *Seven Steps for Implementing Organisation Change*

THE OD PROCESS

Steps in the OD Process

1. Initial Diagnosis
2. Data collection
3. Data feedback and confrontation
4. Action planning and problem solving
5. Team building
6. Inter-group development
7. Evaluation and follow up.

1. Initial Diagnosis

Top management meets with the consultant to determine the types of the OD program that is required for the organization. During this phase, the consultant interviews various people in the organization to gather relevant information.

2. Data collection

The consultant gathers required information by circulating well structured questionnaires to people at various levels in the organization.

3. Data feedback and confrontation

Groups are formed to review the data collected. The group leaders identify areas of disagreement and set priority areas of change by mediating amongst themselves.

4. Action planning and problem solving

The next step is drafting the action plan. The plan has in-built time frame for completion as well as clearly fixed responsibilities.

5. Team building

Working together encourages the process of team building. The consultant helps the groups to see the value of open communication and trust.

6. Inter-group development

The process of working together helps development of groups and individuals *per se*.

7. Evaluation and follow up.

The consultant helps the organization to evaluate the results of the OD effort and develop additional programs where additional results are needed.

GAMING

Gaming is a laboratory method , put to limited use in OD. It has several similarities with Role playing but differs from it in the sense that gaming focuses more on administrative problems while role playing focuses on feelings between people. Gaming is essentially a group exercise in sequential decision making. Each group is further divided into sub-groups to compete with each other. Groups make decisions within a system model that has been created for them and is at least partly unknown to them. Decisions are processed through a computer according to the model thus providing feedback that will guide subsequent decisions.

A game can show how leadership evolves and how effective communication is. Further it indicates the effect of group conflicts on the market scenario as well as effect of success upon group cohesion. Games show effect of stress on participants as they undergo pressure of time and competition. It gives them an opportunity to unwind and react to stress in normal pattern. The learning process can be hastened through feedback and discussion with the Trainer at periodic intervals.

BENEFITS AND LIMITATIONS OF OD

Benefits	*Limitations*
Change throughout the organization	Major time requirements
Greater motivation	Expensive
Higher productivity	Delayed pay-off period
Better Quality of work	Possibility of failure
Higher job satisfaction	Possible invasion of privacy
Improved team work	Possible psychological harm
Better resolution of conflict	Potential conformity
Commitment to objectives	Emphasis not on performance
Willingness to change	Ambiguity in delivery of OD concepts

Survey Feedback

A questionnaire based analysis of organization to develop an understanding of problems within the organization and to identify areas or opportunities of change is the survey feedback method. The survey feedback is one of the earliest interventions of OD. It relies on larger participation by the client system. The data generated is perpetual and attitudinal in nature. A summary of results is prepared for group discussion. Generally, the feedback of results is given to the group that generated the data. Following the diagnosis steps are taken to devise measures for resolution of organizational problems. At times a second survey is necessitated to find measure of improvement in the situation.

Approaches to Planned Change

Harold J. Leavitt states that an organization can be changed by altering its structure, its technology, and/or its people. Changing the organization's *structure* involves rearranging its internal systems, such as its lines of communication, work flow, or managerial hierarchy. Changing the organisation's *technology* means altering its equipment, engineering processes, research techniques, or production methods. Changing the organization's *people* involves changing, training, relationships, attitudes, or roles of organization members. Here, main focus will be on change efforts aimed at the people in the organization; in particular, emphasize will be organizational development (OD) programmes, which attempt to change the ways people work together to achieve the organization's and their own objectives.

Interdependence of the Three Approaches

Organisations are made up of interacting, interdependent elements under the influence of common forces; that is, organizations are systems. The three elements mentioned above are structure, technology and people and therefore highly interdependent. A change in one is likely to affect the other elements as well.Thus, an effective change programme is likely to be one that acknowledges the interaction of these three elements and attempts to change all three, as necessary.

Normally, the greater the amount of change managers desire, the higher the likelihood that the change efforts will have to involve all three elements in order to be effective.

Interdependence Organisational Elements

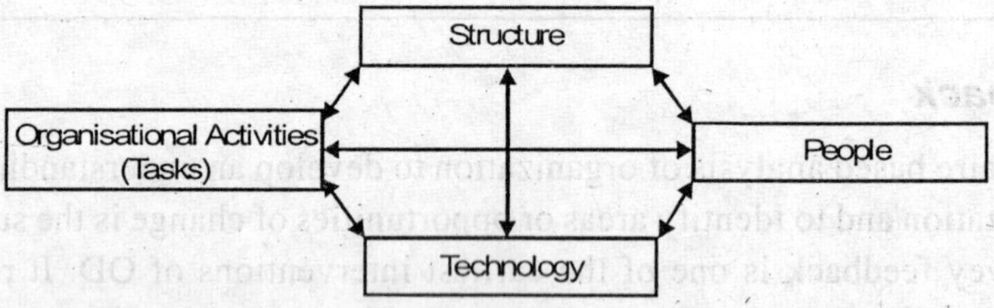

(Source: Adapted from Harold J. Leavitt, "Applied Organization Change in Industry: Structural, Technical, and Human Approaches", in W.W. Cooper, H.J. Leavitt, and M.W. Shelly II, eds., *New Perspectives in Organization Research,* (New York: Wiley, 1964, p. 56.)

For example, new computer programmes may have to be used to transfer the old marketing and sales information into more appropriate formats; or new sales techniques and procedures may be developed to increase the professionalism of the sales force. In addition, people changes are also likely to be required. Some new sales personnel may have to be hired and trained, and previously hired personnel will have to be retrained or reassigned. Individuals who are unable to adjust to the new circumstances may have to be transferred or even replaced.

Structural Approaches

Leavitt divides structural efforts to bring about organizational change into three areas. *Classical organisational design* seeks to improve organisational performance by carefully defining the job responsibilities of organization members and by creating appropriate divisions of labour and lines of authority. Managers can still improve the performance of their organizations by changing management spans, job descriptions, areas of responsibility, reporting relationships, and the like.

Decentralization creates smaller, self-contained organizational units that increase the motivation and performance of the members of those units and help them to focus their attention on the highest-priority activities. Decentralization also permits each unit to adapt its own structure and technology to the tasks it performs and to its external environment.

Modifying the *flow of work* in the organization and careful grouping of specialties may also lead directly to an improvement in productivity and to higher morale and work satisfaction.

Technological Approaches

Frederick Taylor, through "scientific management" attempted to utilise machines to increase efficiency in the workplace. Through time and motion studies, setting piece rates, and other efforts to redesign work operations and reward systems. Taylor and later industrial engineers tried to improve organisational performance.

Technological changes are often difficult to implement successfully and may prove incompatible with an organization's structure.

Combining Technological and Structural Approaches

Techno-structural approaches to change attempt to improve performance by changing some aspects of both an organisation's structure and its technology. Job enlargement and job enrichment programmes are examples of techno-structural approaches to change. In these programmes, the tasks that make up a job, the ways the tasks are performed, and employees relationships are altered to improve employee satisfaction and perhaps to increase productivity.

People Approaches

Both the technical and structural approaches attempt to improve organizational performance by *changing the work situation,* which should cause employee behaviour to become more productive. The people approaches, on the other hand, attempt to change the *behaviour of employees* directly by focusing on their skills, attitudes, perceptions, and expectations. Improvements in these may lead to more effective job performance and to employee-initiated changes in the organization's structure and technology.

Figure below summarizes the three approaches to change. Efforts to change people's behaviour and attitudes can be directed at individuals, groups, or the organization as a whole. Many, but not all such efforts are known as organizational development (OD) techniques. Non-OD approaches for changing people include management development behaviour modification and management by objectives.

The Three Change Approaches

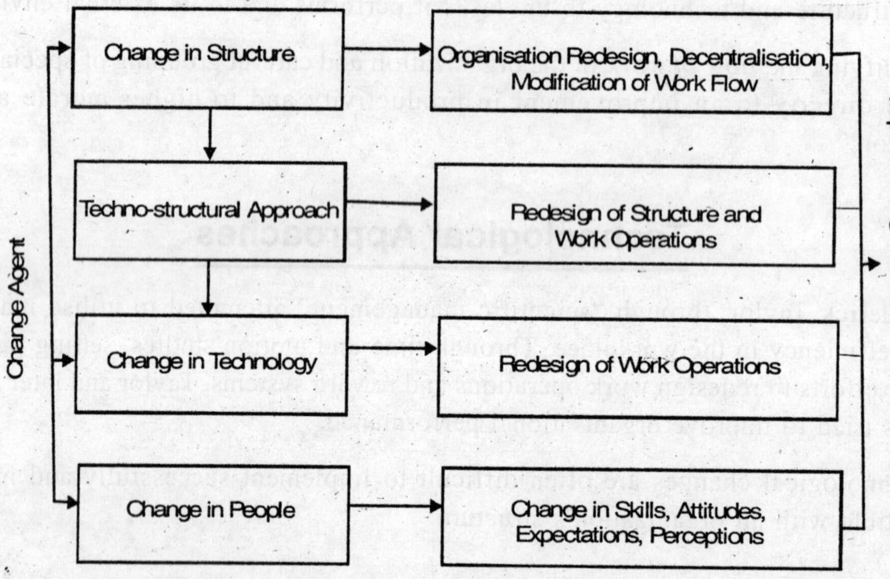

Organizational development is a longer-term, more encompassing change approach meant to cover the entire organization to a higher level of functioning while greatly improving the performance and satisfaction of organization members. Although OD frequently includes structural and technological changes, its primary focus is on changing people and the nature and quality of their working relationships is described in subsequent chapters.

Strategies and Guidelines for Implementing Change

There can be two types of philosophy for change.

(1) The top-down strategy, directions from top.

(2) The bottom-up strategy, more enlightened as it provides opportunity to contribute.

Which Strategy is Better?

Strategy of change depends upon the circumstances. It is a contingency approach:

(a) *Assess the situation* and depending upon your diagnosis of the situation, proceed to the task of implementing change.

(b) *Diagnosis of the situation,* such as time available, need for change or crisis, size of organisation, potential resistance, mangerial style and power base of the change agent. Need for involvement. Participation can help implementing change with reasonable success.

(c) Management may consider the *group as a basic unit* of change and group discussions are more effective in changing attitudes than other methods.

Steps for Implementing Change in Organisations

Steps for implementing changes in organisation are given in the following figure. Implementation starts from the time decision has been taken about the change programme. It is process of planning, arranging support and resources, action taking, monitoring, implementation, mid-term course correction and stabilisation of changes into culture of the organisation.

Guidelines for Change Agents

Some guiding points for change agents are:

1. Strategy for change should consider where success is better.

   (a) *Neutral forces:* This is the large category of employees. We can convert them into favourable force, by sharing information about the change programme. Change agent should discuss with them and create awareness and interest in the change.

   (b) *Dealing with resistance forces:* Change agent should convert these employees to favourable force. Some doubters will still be left and we should use interaction and dialogue; show respect and understanding, and at the same time learning from them the dangers and weaknesses seen by them.

Seven Steps for Implementing Organisation Change

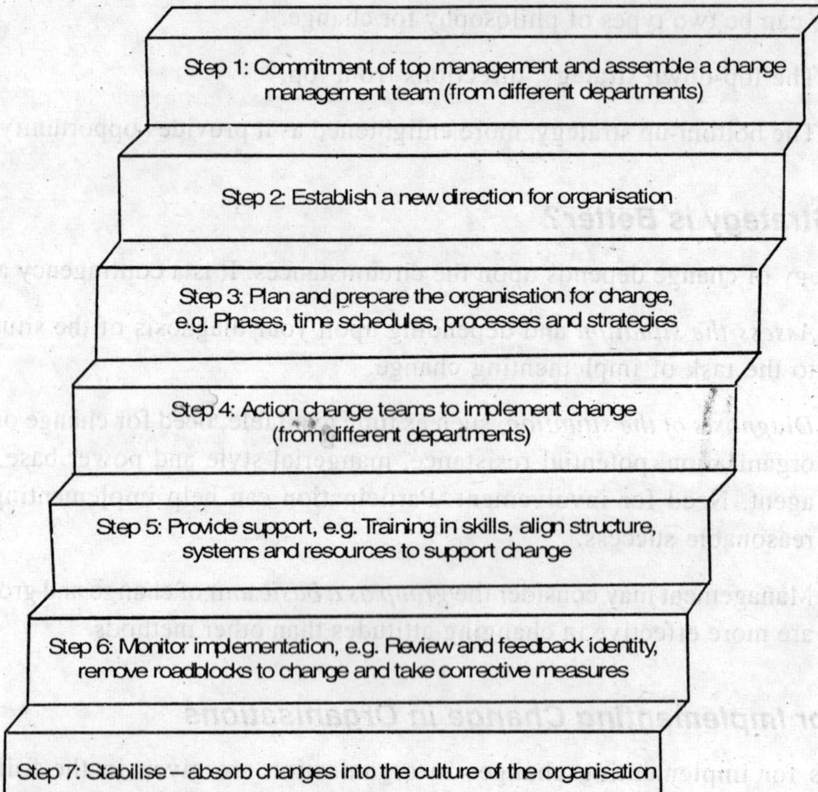

(c) *Dealing with favourable forces:* Change agent should restrain the over enthusiasm of this group of employees. Otherwise they may annoy resistance forces.

2. Change agent should *give up possessiveness* (it is his idea) of the change.

3. Allow scope for improvements in the *original change plan.*

4. *Support* other person's positive change programme going on simultaneously in the organisation.

5. Maintain *positive approach* at all times.

6. *Success in small changes* can reinforce further change. So design successive small changes in phases.

7. Do *not get perturbed* by ups and downs.

8. Managers who are *aware of change process* succeeding with planned change.

9. Success or failure of change rests on:

   (i) *Identification of problem,*

   (ii) Successful reduction of *resistance to change,* and

   (iii) Selection of appropriate *strategy for implementation.*

Principles for Change Agents

(i) Set a Clear Goal

1. Setting a goal involves a dialogue among the team, and the end users of the project.
2. The goal should be specific and measurable, and the team and the user should move in the same direction.

(ii) Determine the Objectives

- Objectives help to break the goal down into specific responsibilities for each team member.

(iii) Establish Check points, Activities, Relationships and Time Estimates

- Checkpoints help members monitor their own progress.

(iv) Direct People Individually and as a Project Team

- Change involves people from different departments who have different objectives, and have different types of training, yet must work together on a unique task.
- Appreciate the position of the other person; keep people informed on a regular and frequent basis.
- Be a good listener.

(v) Build Agreements that Vitalise Team Members

- Conflicts are inevitable; they serve to ensure interest and create energy. Use them as a force to unleash creativity.
- There are a host of possible approaches to conflict management depending on the nature of the problem (giving in; smoothing over; compromising; persuading; finding common ground). Use the appropriate method.

- Reaching agreement in conflict situations is not only a logical but also an emotional experience.

(vi) Empower Yourself and Others in the Team

- Influence without authority is the key. This is achieved through alliances, networks and exchanges. It is important to build personal power.
- What people want most from a change manager is credibility.

  Credibility = Competence + Honesty + Direction + Inspiration + Power.

(vii) Encourage Risk Taking and Creativity

(*Source:* Adapted from V. Nilakant and Ramnarayan, *Managing Organisation Change*, Response Books, a Division of Sage, 81-81.)

Qualities of Change Agents

Some qualities of change managers can be as analyser, implementer, collaborator and imaginator. These are illustrated through sketches in the figure on next page.

Ability to Adopt successfully to a changing environment is one of most important attribute of effective manager.

Organisation change must not be random or initiated merely for the sake of change. Managers have to *balance* the need for *adaptation* and innovation with equally important need for *stability* and *continuity.* Thus, management has to maintain dynamic equilibrium of the following:

(i) *Stability* to facilitate achievement of current goals.

(ii) *Continuity* to ensure orderly change in either ends or means.

(iii) *Adaptability* to react to external opportunities and changing internal conditions.

(iv) Innovativeness to allow organisation to be pro-active (initiate changes) when required.

Emphasis in managing the change process in such a way that organisation exists in a state of *continual renewal and effectiveness.*

Leadership Roles are Critical for Successful Change

1. *Articulating* a realistic, credible and attractive future for the organisation. Making dreams and visions apparent and meaningful to others, also reasons for change. To build strong committed team.
2. Effective *communication and involving* people in furthering shared vision and flood the information.

Sketches: Qualities of Change Managers

I. ANALYZER

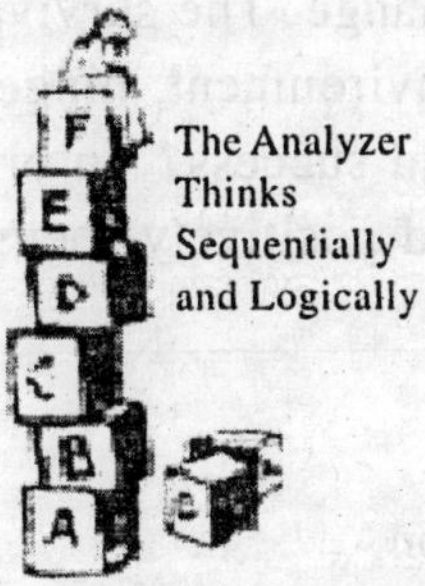

II. IMPLEMENTOR

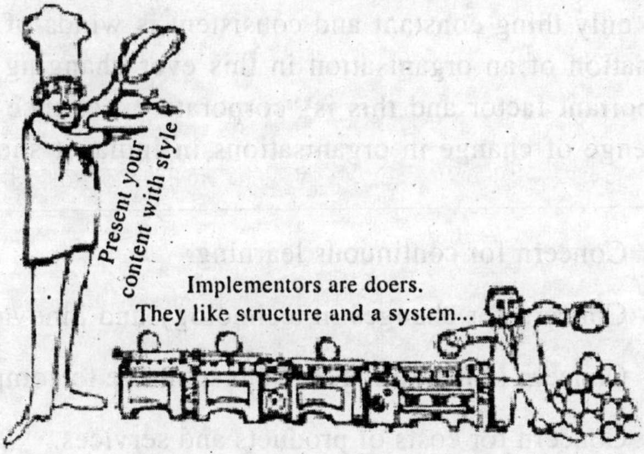

IV. IMAGINATOR

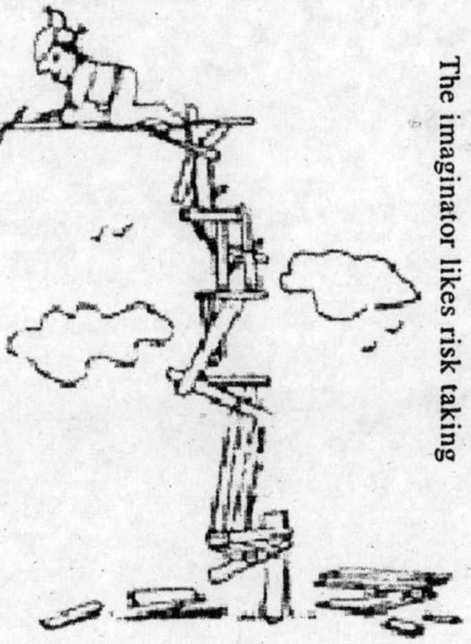

III. COLLABORATOR

Collaborators like gatherings

3. *Empowering* employees by changing practices so that they feel significant and work is exciting.

4. Creating a *trusting culture,* building credibility of change programme and nurturing openness to acknowledge mistakes and learn from one another.

5. *Channelising energy* to change and institutionalising the vision and action plans to all in the organisation.

6. Change to be addressed to all cultural components so as to achieve tangible results.

Focus Areas for Change in Organisations

The only thing constant and consistent is winds of change. The survival, growth and transformation of an organisation in this ever changing environment, hinges only on one most important factor and this is "corporate excellence and success." In order to address the challenge of change in organisations in India, it should positively focus on following areas:

(i) Concern for continuous learning.

(ii) Concern for changes in technology and innovation.

(iii) Concern in marketing, to be responsive to competitors and the community.

(iv) Concern for costs of products and services.

(v) Concern for quality in all aspects.

(vi) Core of all is value-based leadership, which establishes positive values of selflessness or service, compassion, justice fairness, tolerance, respect, integrity, trust and dharma.

(vii) Above all, concern for people centredness.

(viii) Success Mantra's

1970s	Production
1980s	Quality
1990s	Customer
2000s	Costs
2005s	Speed

Review Questions

1. What are the steps in OD process ? Explain briefly.
2. What are essential qualities of change agents ?
3. Explain the techno-structural approaches in change management.
4. Elaborate the role of leadership in change management.

✿ ✿ ✿

Chapter 11

QUALITY OF WORK LIFE

Learning Objectives

1. *Meaning of QWL*
2. *Objectives of QWL*
3. *Work Life Balance*
4. *Techniques of Improving QWL*
5. *Human Engineering*
6. *QWL – The Indian Scenario*

Introduction

Organization, in the past, gave more importance on innovative technology for higher productivity surpassing the needs and mental state of its employees. This created a negative impact on the working environment among the employees. Thus, it was realised that societal support goes hand in hand with technical innovations. This integration can only be made through quality of work life programmes. Quality of work life refers to all the organizational inputs that aim at the employee's satisfaction and enhancing organizational effectiveness.

Having concern with the life on the job is not new. The increased upheaval of union activities in the 30s and 40s, through collective bargaining and legislations, led to improved working conditions. Even before that, labour was vigorously protesting management attempts to change the work environment. A study by Professor Robert F.Hoxie, Chicago University in 1915, reported how the unions, particularly the machinists, were fighting scientific management techniques. In the late 1950s, the term QWL was used to stress the prevailing poor quality of life at workplace and it was first defined then in terms of people's reacting to work, particularly an individual's job satisfaction and mental health.

In the new economy, emphasis is placed upon the latest technology, most ground-breaking management practices, and state-of-the-art office buildings. However, these are of no worth without the talent, commitment, and contribution of a quality workforce. Every organization must do its best to provide a working environment that is inclusive, enriching and encouraging to all employees. This spirit must be visible in all work processes and benefits.

The focus on extrinsic or intrinsic rewards was contingent on the employees, for, some would place greater emphasis on the former than would others. The employee preferences could be predicted based on their education, occupation, and demographics.

Meaning and Concept of QWL

The term 'quality of work life (QWL) has different meanings of different people. Some consider it industrial democracy or co-determination with increased employee participation in the decision making process. For others, particularly managers and administrators, the term denotes improvement in the psychological aspects of work to improve productivity. Unions and workers interpret it as more equitable sharing of profits, job security and healthy and humane working conditions. Others view it as improving social relationships at workplace through autonomous workgroups. Finally, others take a broader view of changing the entire organizational climate by humanizing work, individualizing organizations and changing the structural and managerial systems.

In general terms, QWL, refers to the favourableness or unfavourableness of a job environment for people. It refers to the quality of relationship between employees and the to total working environment. According to Harrison, QWL is the degree to which work in an organization contributes to material and psychological well-being of its members. One expert defines quality of working life as "a process of joint decision making, collaboration and building mutual respect between management and employees". It is concerned with increasing labour management co-operatives to solve the problems of improving organizational performance and employee satisfaction. According to the American Society of Training and Development, it is "a process of work organization which enables its members at all levels to actively participate in shaping the organization's environment, methods and outcomes. This value based process is aimed towards meeting the twin goals of enhanced effectiveness of organization and improved quality of life at work for employees.

Broadly, the definition of quality of work life involves four major parts: safe work environment, occupational health care, suitable working time and appropriate salary. The safe work environment provides the basis for the person to enjoy working. The work should not pose a health hazard for the person. The employer and employee, aware of their risks and rights, could achieve a lot in their mutually beneficial dialogue. The working time has been established by the state according to legislation. The standard limits on overtime, rest days, and public holidays etc., have also been stipulated. The appropriate salary is agreed upon by the employee and the employer and fixed by the Pay Commission. The Government also establishes the rate of minimum wage; the employer should not pay less than that to the employee.

The concept of QWL is based on the assumption that a job is more than just a job. It is the centre of a person's life. In recent years there has been increasing concern for QWL due to several factors :

- increase in education level and consequently job aspirations of employees;
- association of workers;
- significance of human resource management;
- widespread industrial unrest;
- growing of knowledge in human behaviour , etc.

Objectives of QWL

The main objectives of the QWL programs are to ;

- Improve employee satisfaction;
- Improve physical and psychological health of employees which creates positive feelings;
- Enhance productivity of employees;
- Reinforce workplace learning;
- Improved management of the on-going change and transition; and
- Build the image of the company as best in recruitment, retention, and in general motivation of employees.

Definitions

Robbins (1989) has defined Quality of Work Life as process by which an organization responds to employee needs by developing mechanisms to allow them to share fully in making the decisions that design their lives at work.

Quality of Working Life is a generic term for a range of techniques and processes that are designed to give employees greater discretion and control over their work. The principle behind all Quality of Work Life initiatives is that greater participation and involvement in decision-making by employees will lead to increases in satisfaction, motivation, and commitment, which in turn, might lead to improvements in performance.

Johnson and Stephen (1999), have defined Quality of Work Life as "the favourable conditions and environments of a workplace that support and promote employee satisfaction by providing them with rewards, job security, and growth opportunities".

From the above definitions, it is clear that Quality of Work Life is not a distinct concept, but can be associated with aspects such as autonomy, opportunity for career growth, skills development, job satisfaction, job stress, and the overall well-being of the workers.

Workload is considered to be an important element of the Quality of Working Life. For many people having too much work to do and not enough time or resources to do it can be stressful. Surveys commonly identify workload as a major source of stress. Workload causes both psychological as well as physical outcomes that are reflected through factors like job satisfaction, job stress and burnout. Work overload exists when demands exceed the capacity of a worker to meet all of them adequately.

Job Satisfaction is central to the concept of Quality of Work Life. Job Satisfaction is concerned with expectations and outcomes. It is a measure of the degree to which valued and expected rewards, extrinsic or intrinsic, are realized on the job. The relationship between job satisfaction and performance is a complex one that still is largely unexplained by theory or research. While a positive correlation clearly exists between the two, the degree and direction of the interaction is unclear. (Ann Harriman, 1996)

According to P.C. Smith *et.al.*, (1960) 'Job Satisfaction is the persistent feeling towards discriminable aspects of the job situation.'

Locke (1976, p.1300), has defined job satisfaction as a "pleasurable or positive emotional state, resulting from the appraisal of one's job experiences."

Psychologists have identified a number of dimensions or sources of job satisfaction, including attitudes to pay, working conditions, co-workers and superiors, career prospects, and the intrinsic features of the tasks performed.

The Job Description Index (Smith, Kendall, and Hulin 1969), one of the commonly used scales for measuring job satisfaction, uses the following five constructs to measure job satisfaction *viz.*, satisfaction with pay, satisfaction with promotion policies, satisfaction with supervision and satisfaction with co-workers. An evaluation of all these dimensions of the job is a necessary pre-requisite for determining the Quality of Work Life.

Researchers working in the area of quality of work life use many scales to measure Quality of Work Life. Some of these are (1) Need Satisfaction Questionnaire (2) Job Description Index (3) Hassles and Uplifts Scale (4) McNabb and Sepic's Quality-of-Work Life Measure (5) Lewellyn and Wibker's Job Satisfaction Measure (6) Manz and Grothe's Quality-of-Work Life Measure and (7) Hart Quality of Work Life Measure. (Joseph Sirgy, 2001)

Thus, Quality of working life (QWL) refers to the favourableness or unfavourableness of a job environment for people. The basic objective is to develop jobs that are excellent for people as well as for production. QWL is a targe step forward from the traditional job design of scientific management which focused solely on specialisation and efficiency for the performance of narrow tasks, adopting division of labour, rigid hierarchy, and standardisation of labour to reach its objective of efficiency. The idea was to reduce cost by using unskilled, repetitive labour that could be trained easily to do a small part of the job. Job performance was controlled by a large hierarchy that strictly enforced the one best way of work as defined by technical experts.

The classical design gave inadequate attention to quality of worklife, leading to development of many difficulties. There was excessive division of labour and overdependence on rules, procedures and hierarchy. Specialised workers become socially isolated from their feNow workers because their highly specialised work weakened their community of interest in the whole product. Many workers were so deskilled that they lost pride in their work. The result was higher turnover and absenteeism. Quality declined and workers became alienated. Conflict arose as workers tried to improve their conditions.

Management responded to the situation by tightening controls, increasing supervision and organising more rigidly. These actions were expected to improve the situation but actually they made situation worse because they further dehumanised the work.

A factor contributing to the problem was that the workers themselves were changing. They are more educated, more affluent and more independent. They began reaching for higher-order needs, which is more than physiological needs. Classical design was best for poor and uneducated workers who lacked skills but was not appropriate for the new workforce. Design of jobs and organisations had failed to keep up with vast changes in workers' aspirations and attitudes. Employers now have to redesign jobs for a better QWL for two reasons:

1. Classical design gave inadequate attention to human needs and
2. Needs and aspirations of workers themselves are changing. Several options are available to the management for solving the problem.

3. Leave the job as it is and employ only those workers who like rigid environment and classical design.
4. Leave the job as it is but pay the workers more so that they will accept the situation.
5. Let machine do the routine job and terminate the unhappy workers.
6. Redesign jobs that have attributes desired by the people. This approach will help to improve the QWL.

QWL produces more humanised jobs. It seeks to serve the higher-order needs of workers as well as their basic needs. It seeks to bring out the higher skills of workers and provide an environment that encourages them to improve their skills. The basic assumption of humanised work is that it is most advantageous when it provides a "best fit" among workers, jobs, technology and the environment.

The relationship of man to work is the basic element of social life. Drastic change in this relationship has been termed as revolution. There have been two such revolutions in the past. The first one with the use of machine power (replacing muscle power with machines in the 19th century), the second one with the explosion of information technology (computer). The third revolution is now taking place —humanisation of work.

Humanisation Of Work

The term 'humanization of working life,' and 'industrial participative work' are interchangeably used for the same concept. The core of these concepts is the value of treating the worker as a human being and emphasising his development and involvement in work decisions. The concepts are very close to HRD concepts.

Herrick and Maccoby identified four basic principles which humanise the work. These principles are as follows:

1. **The Principle of Security** Humanisation of work implies freedom from anxiety, fear and loss of employment. The working conditions should be safe and there should be no fear of economic loss. This will ensure utmost development of skills and ideas.

2. **The Principle of Equity** The equity principle requires that there is a just way of evaluating the conditions of an employee. If work has to be humanised, equity also requires sharing in the profits of the organisation according to the individual contribution.

3. **The Principle of Individuation** Individuation refers to the work environment in which employees are encouraged to develop themselves to their fullest competence,

a system of work which facilitates the fullest possible development of individual potential. The precondition for this is the availability of freedom and autonomy in deciding their own pace of activity and design of operations.

4. **The Principle of Democracy** This principle implies greater authority and responsibility vested into the workforce. Increasing controls, over supervision and high degree of institutionalisation inhibit humanisation of work. Participation in decision-making also guarantees the 'right to citizenship.'

Some say improvement in working conditions would lead to better quality of life, while others feel a fair compensation and job security would lead to better quality of life. Walton mentioned the following eight principles that constitute the quality of working life:

1. **Adequate and fair compensation:** This implies a just and fair balance between effort and reward. It includes proper job evaluation, training to perform the job, ability of the organisation to pay and profit-sharing. In India, the Minimum Wages Act, 1948 was passed to prevent the exploitation of labour and the Payment of Wages Act, 1936 was passed to prevent unauthorised deduction of wages.
2. **Safe and healthy working conditions:** To improve the quality of working life, the work environment should be congenial and free from hazards detrimental to health and safety of workers. Reasonable working hours, zero-risk, physical conditions of work and age restrictions on lower side ensures good work environment. In India, in the Factories Act there is adequate provision for health, safety and welfare of workers.
3. **Immediate opportunity to use and develop human capacities:** The factory work today has become repetitive, fragmented and lifeless. The workers respond mechanically to the demands of machine without much control on them. Quality of working life will be improved if the job allows sufficient autonomy and control.

A job has five characteristics, (i) ***Skill variety:*** The degree to which a job requires a variety of different activities, so that one can use a number of different skills, (ii) ***Task identity:*** The degree to which the job requires completion of a whole and identifiable piece of work, (iii) ***Task significance:*** The degree to which the job has a substantial impact on the lives of other people, (iv) ***Autonomy:*** The degree to which the job provides substantial freedom, independence and discretion to the individual in scheduling the work and in determining the procedures to be used in carrying it out. (v) ***Feedback:*** The degree to which carrying out the work activities required by the job, results in the individual obtaining direct and clear information about the effectiveness of his performance.

The first three dimensions — skill variety, task identity and task significance — combine to create the work meaningful, important and worthwhile. Jobs that possess autonomy give the worker a feeling of personal responsibility for the results and if a job provides feedback, the worker will know how effectively he is performing.

4. **Opportunity for continued growth and security:** Here the focus is on career opportunities as against the job. What type of opportunities are available to develop new abilities and skills to avoid' obsolescence? The employee is eager to know whether the newly acquired skill could be put to some use and thereby lead to personal growth and security.

5. **Social integration in the work organisation:** One of the objectives of quality of working life is to generate satisfying identity with the organisation and develop a feeling of self-esteem. The factors which inculcate these feelings are openness and trust, opportunity for upward mobility, a sense of community feeling on the job and equal opportunity for all irrespective of caste, creed, sex and religion.

6. **Constitutionalisation in the work organisation:** The governance by the Rule of Law is necessary to improve the quality of working life.

7. **Work and the total life span:** The demands of the work life — late hours, frequent travel and transfers are socially very costly to the employee and his family. Such events definitely depress the quality of working life.

8. **The social relevance of work life:** The organisation's lack of concern for social responsibilities like low quality products, disregard for pollution, bad employment practices, make workers depreciate the value of work which in turn affects their self-esteem.

In the past, the traditional approach to human resources development had been through training of employees. But training of individuals play a limited role on developing people. People develop not only through better training but also through the way the organisation works. The job or the role the person has in the organisation also determines to what extent the person will be able to develop. HRD has to take both role and the job into account.

The concept of quality of working life thus includes — emphasis on extrinsic and intrinsic job factors and other aspects like individual power employee participation in the management process, fairness and equity, social support, use of one's present skills, self-development, a meaningful future at work and social relevance of the work.

Now we shall discuss different operational systems through which the concept of quality of working life manifests itself.

Job Enrichment

People were dissatisfied with the traditional approach to jobs. With the emphasis on the so-called scientific method of production there was a: tendency to break-up the job and assign a specific function to a person. An individual was given a very simple task on the assumption that by continuously doing that task, the individual would be able to work more efficiently and more would be produced in a given time.

But this division of work has some limitations. The person became bored as he performed the same job again and again. There was no sense of achievement when the person did the same work again and again like a machine. People realised that this was the process of dehumanisation. The main difference which Herzberg made between hygienes and motivators was that the hygienes were not directly related to work and therefore he called them 'job context factors' while the motivators were directly related to work and so he called them 'job content factors.' Herzberg proposed the need to look at the work itself and to analyse the factors which would make the work a satisfying experience. According to him, motivators contribute to the satisfaction of the people in the job and their development while they work in an organisation.

Herzberg's theory — the two factor theory of motivation led to a practical programme of using a job as a major medium of developing people and changing some organisational practices. The practical aspect of intervening in the organisation was called job enrichment. Herzberg also called this 'vertical loading of the job.' He used the term to indicate the need of providing more motivators in work. The process of enrichment is the process of providing valuable things to a person, if an employee's job is extended so that he has to do more work, then it is not vertical loading but horizontal loading. Vertical loading is an attempt to provide more and more motivators in a job.

Several experiments show how job enrichment helps in providing the motivational level amongst employees and contributes to their development. Job enrichment uses the job as the main medium of developing employee competence and the ability of the employees to share higher responsibility.

Job Rotation

Job rotation can be either horizontal or vertical. Vertical rotation is nothing more than promoting a worker into a new position. Job rotation represent an excellent method for broadening the manager and for turning specialists into generalists. In addition to increasing the employee's experience and allowing him to absorb new information, it can reduce boredom and stimulate the development of new ideas.

Job rotation offers a potential for dealing with the problem of general worker dissatisfaction caused by overstructuring. It allows the employees to diversify their activities and offset the occurrence of boredom. Job rotation can renew enthusiasm for learning and motivate workers to higher performance. This is particularly useful to 'plateau employees' (those who are not growing) as it provides them an opportunity to prove themselves.

Quality Circles

The concept of quality circles (QCs) is essentially Japanese. When Japan lost the Second World War, its economy suffered a major setback. In order to revive a shattered economy, Japan started to imitate the manufacture of several western goods. The strategy however did not work because the quality of most of these goods were poor. Despite price advantage, Japan found it difficult to face and survive global competition. It was then felt that a sustained effort to employ Statistical Quality Control (SQC) to manufacturing operations would be the only way to review the Japanese economy.

The Japanese Union of Scientists and Engineers (JUSE) was formed in 1946. One of the objectives of JUSE was to propagate and popularise the concept of SQC in a large number of Japanese industries. JUSE undertook the responsibility of educating the Japanese managers, supervisors and workers in SQC techniques through training programmes, seminars and dissemination of relevant information.

QCs in Japan were formalised in 1960 by K. Ishikawa. He succeeded in convincing the management about the potential of significant contribution from the large workforce to quality, productivity and several work-related issues. During the last two decades the number of these circles has increased at a phenomenal rate in Japan. In reputed Japanese companies, there is hardly a worker who is not a member of one quality circle or the other.

In the mid-60s, the West became aware of the success of QCs in Japan. Several European and American companies started forming these circles with encouraging results in areas of quality control, cost reduction, productivity, safety etc.

QCs have been defined as a small group between 3 and 12 people to do the same or similar work, voluntarily meeting together regularly for about an hour per week in paid time, usually under the leadership of their own supervisor and trained to identify, analyse and solve some of the problems in their work, presenting solutions to management and where possible implementing solutions themselves.

In simple words, a quality control circle is a participative management system in which a small group of employees, doing similar work, voluntarily meet together regularly to identify, analyse and resolve their quality problems and take corrective actions for better results and are collectively known as Quality Control Circles or Quality Circles in modern management parlance. The intention is to use knowledge that has earlier been transmitted to foremen. The central message of QC is a culture of participation of trained manpower to draw out their infinite possibility. It reflects an attitude of faith, understanding and respect between managers and the managed. The significance of QC lies in the fact that it helps the organisation to build upon the immense, hidden potential of human resources.

The following are the key elements that will describe the basic foundation of the QC programme. They are: (i) It is a people building philosophy; (ii) It is voluntary; (iii) Everyone participates; (iv) Members help to develop others; (v) Projects are circle efforts — not individual effort; (vi) Training is provided to worker and management; (vii) Creativity is encouraged; (viii) Projects are related to members' wont; (ix) Management has to be supportive; (x) Quality and improvement consciousness develop.

There is no hard and fast rule about the timing, duration and frequency of QC meetings. The members may meet during or after working hours. An hour's duration is usually quite adequate for a typical QC meeting. QC meetings are normally held once a week.

The potential benefits are mainly improved quality, cost savings, improved morale created by those achievements and the increased employee participation which is the essence of the process. In recent years QC movement started in Brazil, Mexico, Argentina, Taiwan, Korea, China and many other newly industrialised economics. In India— BHEL, SAIL, Indian Airlines and many others have introduced QC.

Need for QC: Frequently, even the most competent employees are dissatisfied with their effort to produce high quality work. Some reasons are poor communications, poor design and poor material. These conditions lead to disinterest in the job, poor quality, defective workmanship, waste and high absenteeism and low productivity. Many think that they are supposed to park their brains as well as their cars in the parking spot and only use their hands and sometimes legs to perform routine tasks. QCs allow the workers to participate, make ways and means to solve quality problems. As the product quality improves so does the company's reputation in the world and as a result, sales generally increase. These are the real reasons for having QCs and the effects are widespread. Employees enjoy the work in QC since their suggestions are accepted. Thus, cordial labour management relations are created within the company.

Participation is the key to successful QC programme: The basic philosophy of QC is to promote recognition of workers. Often people are neglected, this creates feelings of worthlessness among the workers. These feelings can be vanished slowly by instituting QCs. Thus, workers get chance to participate, to express their ideas to let everyone know that they know their jobs well. They get opportunity to discuss ideas with management, feel proud to show their achievements and feel free to ask for solutions to their problems on the job. Thus, motivation, participation and recognition are three major aspects of a successful QC programme.

Workers' Participation: Participation means an act of taking part. It may be defined as taking part in sharing of power and status between the managers and the workers. In a factory there are two different groups of people— managers and workers with two separate sets of functions to perform. Workers' participation has three basic features:

1. Power sharing between managers and the workers.
2. Reduction of conflict between labour and management by encouraging effective co-operation between workers and managers.
3. The personal involvement of workers in their tasks and work situations.

The basic objective is to provide workers a sense of importance, pride, freedom and opportunity for self-expression, a feeling of belongingness so as to create positive conditions for industrial relations and an environment of industrial peace.

The concept of workers' participation has its roots in the human relations movement in the field of industrial organisations. There was an acute social unrest in Western countries because labour was looked upon as a commodity of commerce. This unrest finally impelled industrialists to recognise that labour is not a commodity to be sold off at an arbitrary price, he is not a cog in the machine but a human being. Having recognised a capacity to grow and accept the responsibility of a citizen, a worker can participate in the affairs of the industry.

The workers' participation in India has not been able to show the kind of results it was expected to, due to the lack of interests shown by the employers.

Characteristics of QWL Improvement Programmes

The results, reported from a number of quality of work life improvement programmes, have some common characteristics. These are :

- Persistent commitment from management to the open non-defensive modus operandi of sincerely inviting collaborative inputs from the workforce regarding problem identification and suggestions for improving any aspect of the organization or the policies, practices and structure of work with incentives provided for such participation.
- Inviting involvement of members of tasks groups in recommending resolution of identified problem.
- Training of supervisors to prepare them to function effectively in a less authoritative style.
- Implementation of practicable suggestion and explanations for rejected ideas.
- Feedback arid recognition for good results achieved.
- Selection of personnel who can be motivated under appropriate conditions to strive for excellence in task performance.

- Evaluation and analysis of results, including failures, leading to renewed effort towards continual improvement in modus operandi.

Eight Practices Of QWL

Quality of working life though came into circulation in 1970s became popular only in 90s and organizations realised its potential to enhance the productivity in the new century. This works as a comprehensive model to those employers who want to ensure quality in working life of their employees. An ideal quality of work life programme will include practices in eight major areas as discussed below:

Adequate and Fair Compensation

This is fundamental to QWL. Human beings work for livelihood, mere tore success of rest of the initiatives depends upon fulfillment of this. However, important here is that compensation offered must be adequate, implying it must be proportionate to labour, and there should be internal consistency among salaries of employees.

Safe and Healthy Working Conditions

Unsafe and hazardous working conditions cause problems to both employers and employees. There may be little advantage to the employer in short-term but in medium and long-terms, it adversely affects the productivity. Therefore, adequate investment must be made to ensure safe and healthy working conditions.

Immediate opportunity of use and develop human capacities. The jobs have become routine, meaningless and too specialized, depriving the employees of fulfillment satisfaction. Therefore, efforts should be made to increase the autonomy, perspective and exposure to multiple skills.

Future opportunity for continued growth and security. This is related to career aspects of employees. Meaningful career paths must be laid down and career mapping of employees is to be followed. The provision of advancement opportunities play a central role in QWL.

Social integration in the work organization. Relationships between and among the employees is an indicator of healthy work organization. Therefore, opportunities must be provided for formal and informal interactions. All kind of classes, religions, races, crafts, and designations must be treated equally on a social platform. In other words, it creates egalitarian environment.

Constitutionalism in the Work Organization

This is related to organizational norms that affect the freedom of an individual employee. Efforts must be made to see right norms are formed in the organization. It means norms that accommodate the privacy of an individual employee, freedom of speech, equity and freedom to dissent on some aspects.

Work and the Total Life Space

Employees should not be allowed to continuously exert themselves. The continuous hard work causes psychological and physical strains. Therefore, there has to be a balance between personal and professional life. Organization must create proper work offs to enrich the life of employees.

The Social Relevance of Work Life

Employees must be given the perspective of how his/her work in the organization helps the society. This is essential to build relevance of the employee's existence to the society he/she lives in.

Techniques of Improving Quality of Work Life

The concept of quality of work life has been operationalized through various systems such as job enrichment, workers participation in management, organization development, quality circles, employee welfare, etc. While some of these schemes have been successful in improving the quality of work life, others are still to show results. The quality of work life movement is of recent origin and has a long way to go. Individuals as well as organized efforts are required to improve the quality of work life for millions of workers in the country.

In 1981 the National Productivity Council organized a national seminar on quality of work life. The seminar made several suggestions and pointed out the responsibilities of different groups in improving the quality of work life. These responsibilities are summarized below:

1. **Responsibilities of Employers:**

   (a) Provision of physical amenities at the work place. Health and safety and welfare provisions.

   (b) Involving workers in decision making on all matters.

   (c) Initiating suitable forms of work design.

   (d) Formalization of QWL experience for future use.

   (e) A re-examination of policies of work.

   (f) Developing an appreciation of changing environment.

2. **Responsibilities of unions and workers:**
   (a) Educating and making workers aware of QWL.
   (b) Search areas of collaboration with management.
   (c) Identifying ways and means to satisfy workers' needs through non-monetary alternatives.
   (d) Organizing labour in the unorganized sector and specially making them aware of QWL
   (c) Encouraging workers to participate in QWL activities.
3. **Responsibilities of professional organizations:**
   (a) Organize workshops and seminars to bring about greater awareness of QWL
   (b) Initiate specific research projects in this field.
   (c) Provide professional assistance to organizations to help generate internal competences.
   (d) Developing state-of-art profiles on QWL.
   (e) Developing special programmes for various classes of workers.
   (f) Developing a network for collection, storage and dissemination of information on QWL.
4. **Responsibilities of the Government:**
   (a) Legislating standards and norms in newer areas.
   (b) Change in policy to provide greater autonomy to experiment with QWL.
   (c) Executive action to ensure implementation of legislated facilities.
   (d) Encouragement and adoption of appropriate technology.
   (e) Finding projects on QWL.
   (f) Suitably modifying the structure and scope of education in the country.

Some of the techniques used to improve QWL of an average worker in India are given below:

1. **Job Redesign:** Narrow jobs need to be combined into large units of accomplishment. Jobs should be redesigned to enrich them. Job enrichment helps to satisfy higher order needs by providing interesting, stimulating and challenging work.

2. **Career Development:** Opportunity for career advancement and growth personality improve commitment. Career planning, counselling second careers, etc., help to meet expectations of achievement-oriented employees.

3. **Autonomous Work Groups:** In an autonomous work group, employees are given the freedom of decision making. In such a group the workers themselves plan, co-ordinate and control their activities. The group as a whole is accountable for success or failure. It is also called a self-managed work team.

4. **Flexible Work Schedules:** Flexible working hours (flexi time), staggered hours, reduced work weak, job sharing, part-time employment and other types of alternative work schedules provide freedom to employee in scheduling their work.

5. **Participative Management:** Employees want to participate in deciding matters which affect their lives. Therefore, quality circles, management by objectives, suggestion system and other forms of employees' participation in management help to improve QWL.

6. **Job Security:** Adequate security of job is a high priority of employees and should be provided.

7. **Administrative Justice:** The principles of justice, fair and quality should be applied in disciplinary procedure, grievance procedures, promotions, transfers, work assignment, leave, etc.

The Role of the Supervisor in QWL

The Supervisor is one key to the quality-of -work life. A study by University of Michigan which sought to relate a large number of characteristics of workers jobs to overall satisfaction illustrates the wide variety of ways by which supervisory behaviour affects subordinate satisfaction. The eight most closely related factors are listed below:

- Having a 'nurturant' supervisor
- Receiving adequate help, assistance, etc.
- Having a few 'labour standard problems' (such as safety hazards, non-availability of materials, or poor transportation)
- Fair promotional policies
- Supervisor not supervising too closely
- Having a technically competent supervisor
- Autonomy in matters affecting work
- A job with 'enriching' demands.

The supervisor influences the quality of work life directly or indirectly. He affects subordinates directly through his daily interaction with them. He can be supportive or disagreeable, friendly or distant, available to provide help or always busy. He influences the design of jobs, plays a key role in the administration of career and reward systems, and is also in a position to foster the development of social systems. Nonetheless, the vigilant supervisor can join together these factors so that quality of work life will be enhanced as well as organizational objectives will be accomplished.

The Role of the Management in QWL

Management has to play a very significant role in improving quality of life of employees. Management must strive to make the quality of employees work life as satisfying as possible. At the moment, employees are challenged as never before to balance work and personal responsibilities. Therefore, the management should continually addresses these challenges by utilizing personnel flexibilities and establishing programs that help employees meet their work and personal obligations.

The steps that should be taken by the management are :

(a) Establishing appropriate, reasonable and enforced work rules. Work rules can help to create and maintain an orderly atmosphere that is pleasant to work in where employees can work effectively. Work rules can help improve quality of work life by:

- creating an atmosphere where employees are treated with dignity and respect.
- helping to ensure that employees conduct themselves in a professional and safe manner.
- encouraging open communication between employees .
- ensuring that all employees are treated fairly and that they follow the same rules.

(b) Develop and implement a flexible work policy and procedure.

(c) Provide training to managers and supervisors on how to respond effectively to work life issues.

(d) Provide resiliency and personal accountability training for staff.

(e) Invest in organization-specific quality of work life programs in eldercare, childcare, diversity, etc.

(f) Encourage participative work teams to reinforce an environment of trust and help employees to work more effectively and efficiently in order to accomplish organization's mission.

(g) Provide employees assistance through the Employee Assistance Program (EAP), a free, confidential counselling and referral service to resolve personal problems.

(h) Actively support employee's health and welfare.

How to Measure QWL

The following indices may be used to judge the quality of work life in an organization:

- **Job Involvement:** It represents the degree of an individual's identification with or ego involvement in the job. The more central the job is to the individual's life, the greater is his involvement in it. Therefore, the individual spends more time and energy on the job. People with high job involvement are better motivated and more productive. Research reveals that skill variety, achievement and challenge help to improve job involvement.
- **Job Satisfaction:** It implies the worker's satisfaction with the environment of his job environment consisting of nature of work, quality of supervision, pay, co-workers, opportunities for promotion, etc. Job satisfaction is related to job involvement and people involved in their jobs are satisfied with their jobs and *vice versa*.
- **Sense of Competence:** It refers to the feelings of confidence that an individual has in his own competence. Sense of competence and job involvement reinforce each other. An individual acquires a greater sense of competence as he engages himself more and more in work activities. When he feels more competent he becomes more involved in his job and becomes better motivated.
- **Job Performance:** When an individual's job involvement, job satisfaction and sense of competence increase, there is a rise in job performance.
- **Productivity**, When, the level of job performance increases the output per unit of input up. Thus, match between job characteristics and productivity traits of employees generally result in higher productivity.

The Effect of Quality Work Life

The Positive Aspects of QWL are:

- Improved communication and co-ordination among the workers and organization helps to integrate different jobs resulting in better task performance.
- Better working condition enhances workers motivation to work in a healthy atmosphere resulting in motivation and increase in production.

- As QWL includes participation in group discussion and solving the problem, improving the skill, enhancing their capabilities and thus building confidence and increased output.
- QWL attracts talented employees and make them loyal towards the organization.
- Making employees feel valued.
- Increased productivity.
- Reduced absenteeism.
- Earn the reputation of being an employer of choice.
- Retaining valued employees.
- Help employees to have work-life balance .

The net result is — more satisfied and productive workers produce better and quality products.

Organisational Development and QWL

Organisational Development has contributed enormously to the improvement of quality of working life. OD represents change. The change of direction is usually towards such goals as (i) the better utilisation of human resources; (ii) the design of structures and procedures that facilitate communication flow and decisions being made closer to the information source; (iii) the development of reward systems that relate more directly and effectively to the so-called higher order needs in human motivation; (iv) the involvement of people in decisions that directly affect them and in general (v) the creation of more humanistic oriented work situations.

OD has been defined by Beckhard as an effort—(i) planned; (ii) organisation-wise; and (iii) managed from the top to (iv) increase organisation effectiveness and health through (v) planned interventions in the organisation's "process" using behaviourial science knowledge.

1. **It is a planned change effort:** An OD programme involves a systematic diagnosis of the organisation, the development of a strategic plan for improvement and the mobilisation of resources to carry out the effort.
2. **It involves the total system:** An organisation development effort is related to a total organisation change such as a change in the culture or reward'systems or the total managerial strategy.

3. **It is managed from the top:** In an organisational development effort, the top management of the system has a personal investment in the programme and its outcomes. They should actively participate in the management of the effort.
4. **It is designed to increase organisation effectiveness and health:** To understand the goals of the organisational development, it is necessary to have an idea of an effective organisation. An effective organisation is one in which form follows functions, decisions are made by and near the sources of information, communication is undistorted and the organisation and its parts interact with each other.

The following objectives clearly indicate how it improves the quality of working life:

1. To increase the level of trust and support among organizational members,
2. To increase the incidence of confrontation of organisational problems, both within groups and amongst groups,
3. To increase an environment in which authority of assigned role is augmented by authority based on knowledge and skill,
4. To increase the openness of communications laterally, vertically and diagonally,
5. To increase the level of personal enthusiasm and satisfaction in the organisation,
6. To find synergistic solutions to problems with greater frequency and through which all parties gain more through co-operation than through conflict.
7. To increase the level of self and group responsibility in planning and implementation.

Labour Welfare

The International Labour Organisation was set up in 1919 for improving working conditions in the factory. Welfare is a total concept. It is a desirable state of existence for a man involving the physical, mental, moral and emotional well-being.

Labour welfare has both positive and negative sides. On the positive side, it deals with the provisions of opportunities which enable the worker and his family to lead a good life, socially as well as personally. On the other side, labour welfare attempts to neutralise the negative effects of large scale industrialisation and provides a counterbalance to the undesirable social consequences. Labour welfare in the wider sense will promote the well-being of the workers. It is an effort to make life worth living for the worker.

The necessity of welfare activities in a modern welfare state can hardly be over-emphasized. Labour welfare has come to be known as Internal Social Responsibility of the organisation. While the ultimate aim of labour welfare is to increase productivity, it is assumed that quality of working life and productivity usually go hand in hand.

In India, there are two different types of labour welfare — statutory and voluntary. While statutory welfare is imposed by Govt. to guarantee the minimum facilities at work, voluntary welfare is the most significant contribution of the organisation to improve the quality of working life.

Human Engineering

Human Engineering is the study of people at work and of work methods. It includes the study of equipment design, pacing of work, hours of work and environmental conditions of work etc. In this age of machines, the question is how to fit the man to the machine. The real problem is rather how to fit the machine to man. The purpose of Human Engineering is to improve productivity, job satisfaction and quality of working life.

Work -life Balance

Alongside the basics of good employment practice—contracts of employment, regular reviews, training and development etc., companies are staring to look more closely at the issue of work -life balance . More than ever before, employers need a committed workforce, flexible to the rapidly changing needs of most business. At the same time, employees want new ways to balance work with the other dimensions of their lives. Therefore , part of the 'people plan' of an organization should include looking at what sort of work-life balance one would need to stay healthy as a business. In addition to meeting needs, own productivity, recruitment and skills retention needs, there are external influencing factors, such as changing customer expectations and new employment legislation to take into account too.

What Kinds of Changes are Emerging?

Some of the key trends with respect to work-life balance are talked about below:

Work-life is becoming more integrated and imbedded into HR. Employers have a better understanding of what work-life is not just flavour-of -the-month perks, but rather true benefits. Work-life is playing a critical role in recruitment and retention strategies. On-line services for resource and referring are becoming the norm and are increasingly expected by companies buying these services. Telecommuting still leads the way for flexible work arrangements. Work-at-home has arrived as a way of life. Companies with multiple locations are planning to develop several on-site childcare facilities. Companies want creative solutions to problems. New programs such as concierge services, reading / relaxing rooms, etc., are becoming popular. Time is considered a critical work-life benefit. This means that benefits need to go beyond helping employees balance work and personal life. Employees want control over their time.

There will be an increased focus on the "work" rather than on the "job". Employees are not being hired to fill a specific position (or job), but rather based on their overall ability to contribute to the company. Reports indicated that new workers (out of B School) stay in their first job roughly three to four years. So, employers Incamp.

However, if one looks at the increasing pace of business activity, especially over the last 50 years, and related global expansion, it seems that this will be the most difficult barrier to overcome. This hold especially true for the "knowledge worker" in industries such as software, consulting, investment banking etc. There seems to be a tacit logic that the "new economy" never stops, that you have to work 24 hours a day and 365 days a year. Look at today's stock traders; for them the markets never really close as businesses expand their reach across time zones- so the Tokyo, London, New York and Sydney stock exchanges ensure that the work these stock traders do is beyond the normal daily human routine of work, rest and recreation.

Despite the obvious benefits for employees, many organizations have yet to appreciate the value of supporting work-life balance and more importantly have taken little action to address the issues. The impact on employees is clear.

Organizations may do whatever they can, but today employees have as much of a responsibility to reorganize that work-life balance starts with their own personal decisions. about what they do with their lives.

In a 1999 survey of managers' changing experiences in relation to the Quality Working Life:

- 71 % reportd that working long hours had an adverse impact on health.
- 79 % reported an adverse impact on their relationship with spouse or partner.
- 86 % reported an adverse impact on their relationship with their children.
- 68 % reported an adverse impact on productivity. In the same survey:
- 58 % believed that long hours were expected by their employer.
- 37% believed long hours were unacceptable but they had no choice.
- 33 % believed long hours were a necessary sacrifice to get ahead in their careers.

(***Source:*** The Quality of Working Life: 1999 Survey of Managers; Changing Experience by Professor Les Worrall and Professor Cary Cooper.)

Work timings are one of the most significant factors impacting work-life balance today. However, if one looks into the factors impacting absenteeism at the work place, they comprise of several causal factors, as shown below:

Health & lifestyle factors	Workplace Factors
Genuine illeness / poor health smoking excessive use of alcohol lack of exercise body weight	working patterns health and safety concerns travel times excessive hours
Attitudinal & stress factors	**Domestic & Kinship factors**
Job satisfaction Career satisfaction intention to leave organisational commitment Stress absence "culture"	Gender No. of children under 16 lack of flexible working arrangements

Today, inflexible work schedules and restrictive family -leave policies are more the norm than the exception, and often such discrepancies affect both performance on the job as well as educational outcomes of employees' children. Employees today are unable to change either their starting or their quitting times for the purpose of accommodating family needs.

Work-life Balance -The Employers` Perspective

Organizations now-a-days need employees who are talented, committed and flexible at the same time. How to manage the employee? This question has undergone a significant change in the recent past. Increased focus on maintaining a balance between the work and personal life of the employees, is at the heart of any effective people management strategy.

Lack of concern for maintaining this balance results in various problems, ranging from the ill-health of workers, high levels of stress, family problems, decline in performance, problems in retaining employees and an unmotivated workforce. All these problems accrue to hit the business results of the company and finally, the bottom line.

Employers often feel that their employees sometimes have unrealistic expectations when it comes to work-life balance. Employers tend to ask questions like, "What exactly does that mean? How is that defined?" A lot of what it means, and what gets offered, is based on the business's needs, and individuals need to understand that. Can a receptionist be allowed to come and go as she pleases? Can a company accountant take extended time off during tax season? A lot of unrealistic employees get unhappy because their requests are not met, as often, it's a decision based on business.

There's also the reality of many people feeling uncomfortable about even asking for time off. They don't want to show up as being needy," think some of the employers. This is especially true for people who work for workaholics. Employers may talk a lot about the need for a work-life balance, but often they don't practice it themselves, especially the senior management. They work crazy hours. So, in order to feel with the in-crowded, employees decide that, that's what they have to do as well.

How are Corporations Responding?

"I employ talented individuals and don't discriminate because of personal circumstances. If did, I would be denying my company access to extraordinary people who help me to achieve fantastic success."

-Lin Arlgo, MD Aricot Vert Design,
winner of 2000 Parents at Work/Lloyds
TSB Best Boss Award

Some of the trends followed worldwide while implementing work-life policies are:

1. **Flexible hours:** Arrangements for flexible hours working can be of particular benefits for parents with younger children, who need taking to / from school, or people with other caring requirements. There is a wide range of models of flexible hours arrangement, which allow employees greater or lesser autonomy, if the tension of having to reach office at 9 is removed, it relieves a person a great deal. In metropolitan cities, flexible hours also take away the tension related to travel during rush hours.
2. **Term-time working:** It is one of the most family friendly policies initiated by companies in pursuance of work-life balance policies. Many people are allowed to take their leave/vacation breaks from work around school holidays so that the whole family can be free at the same time.
3. **Job share:** It is a form of collective part time arrangement. In this an individual employee can be insured that his job is being carried on by some one else when he is not around. This is one of the most effective ways by which companies retain the best talent.
4. **Part-time work:** Sometimes, full-time work may cause conflicts for the other, engagements of the employees. It has been implemented by companies especially for people who have special needs like caring for young children after work etc.

5. **Home-working:** This arrangement has been found useful for employees having excessive domestic responsibilities.

6. **Telecentre working:** This not only enables the employees to work from closer to their places of residence but it also ensures that services reach nearer to the customers.

7. **Virtual organization:** Many organizations are creating their virtual forums, with the advancement of media and communication techniques. The employees may work from home/local offices managing business of another locational area. This again provides greater commitment and motivation to the employees.

Organizations such as IBM and AT & T have pioneered the 'alternative workplace', where the combination of non-traditional work practices, settings and locations are beginning to supplement traditional ways of working. Some of the 'alternative' work practices include:

Reduced working arragement	• Part - time working • Job sharing • Term - tine working
Flexible time arrangements	• Flexitime • Compressed hours • Annualised hours • Shift working • Shift – swapping • Self - rostering
Alternative locations	• Home working • Teleworking • Hotdesking
Others	• Stress management centres • Recreational facilities • Counselling • Parental leave

Whilst these initiatives will differ according to the needs of each organization, there are some generic proven benefits:

- Increase productivity and greater business efficiency.
- Improved levels of customer satisfaction.

- Reduced stress amongst employees leading to reduced turnover.
- Reduced absenteeism.
- Improved staff moral, motivation, enthusiasm and loyalty.
- Keeping experienced staff who need to alter working hours at different stage of the life cycle.
- Providing opportunities for junior staff to gain work experience deputizing for senior absent staff.

Increased attractiveness as an employer, with the ability to attract a wider pool of potential recruits who may not be available to work full-time.

Work-life Balance—The Indian Perspective

The stress and strain of modern day working life is no longer something thas is alien to the Indian setup. With more and more transnational companies landing on Indian shores, the work culture has undergone a dramatic change. This change is not limited to foreign companies but has percolated deep into the Indian working psyche. Indian companies, in order to meet the challenge of competition, have had to imbibe this culture. Even the much tarnished image of Public Sector Undertakings has undergone a dramatic change. More and more management bosses are now implementing work schedules, which extend far beyond the usual 9-6 affair. Although Indian laws and even those in the rest of the world do not permit work beyond certain number of hours, it is no longer the statutory requirement to stay at office, but the increased pressure to confirm with work standards is that what causes problems. The Indian work environment has a typical set of drivers, which are not prevalent in the West. Although most of the companies in India have imbibed a working, pattern alike to the Western business model, but the basic psyche of the employee remains different.

Consider Factors Such as

- Regional differences contributing to factors like differences in social and cultural mindsets, working ethics, work styles and personality types.
- Diverse workforce emanating from different social backgrounds, educational institutions and age profiles.
- Diverse work place cultures: work places like public sectors, family business houses, traditional Indian organizations and the new multinational corporations would have extremities when it comes to working style, culture and nature of relationships between subordinates and supervisors.

Add to this the phenomenon of surplus labour markets (both at the skilled and unskilled levels) particularly on Indian soil, and greater emphasis on hierarchy within Indian organizations.

This implies that Indians are more susceptible to staying late even if there is no work in the office but if their boss or supervisor is there. It also implies that Indian subordinates would typically not question being called to work on weekends on a sustained basis.

A friend of mine who works for a multinational bank recounted his experience when he had gone on a short assignment to London and was shocked that his British manager there was actually apologetic for asking him to stay back to work on weekend something that was taken for granted in India.

All these factors have to be taken into account, because Indian work scenario has certain conditions, which are unique.

- Restrictions on women working especially after marriage
- Social customs, festivals, rituals etc.
- Preference of particular job in one particular region
- Mindset of working by the clock rather than the job at hand
- Prevalence of a strong hierarchy in the work set up of any organization
- Loyalty towards one job.

While all these trends have undergone a major change in the recent past, this change has been limited to the metropolitan cities. The introduction of any work-life balance policy comes as culture shock to many.

In July 2001, Human Capital, Andersen conducted a telephonic cum e-mail based survey across various companies in Mumbai and Delhi primarily. The main purpose of the survey was to assess the percentage of firms who actually follow work-life balance policies.

The survey covered 27 companies across various sectors like information technology, FMCG, Diversified groups, banking and manufacturing.

The survey covered the following aspects:

- Existence of WLB policies.
- Key driving factors behind introduction of such policies.
- Key considerations/ changes for effective implementation of these policies.
- Descriptors of WLB policies practiced within the organization.
- Custodian of WLB policies.

- Measurement of effectiveness of WLB policies
- Linkage of WLB policies introduce to type of industry.
- Change management initiatives.

The range of work-life balance policies covered in the survey included:

- Housing
- Concierge Services
- Flexitiming
- Medical facilities
- Leave/Part time work
- Recreational facilities
- Stress Management / Training

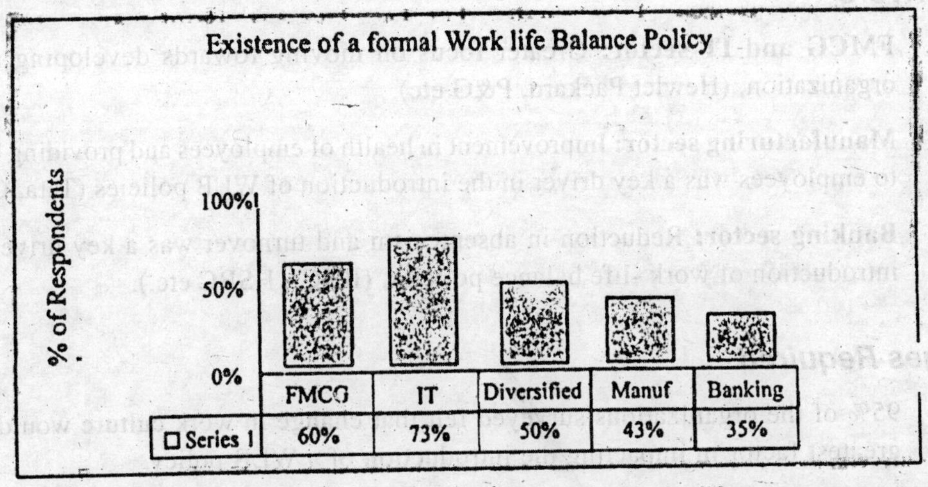

- **FMCG sector:** Though 40% did not have a formal work-life balance ('WLB') policy, there were various schemes that could be seen as WLB policies.
- **IT sector:** While 73% of the IT companies had formalized WLB policies in India (e.g. NUT, WIPRO, SAP Labs), almost all companies surveyed had WLB policies in their foreign offices, that had not been implemented in India. Among banking , HSBC also had a formal WLB policy.
- **Manufacturing sector:** Nature of employee benefits provided differ from IT and other industries, primarily because of the difference between the key drivers and employee age profile.

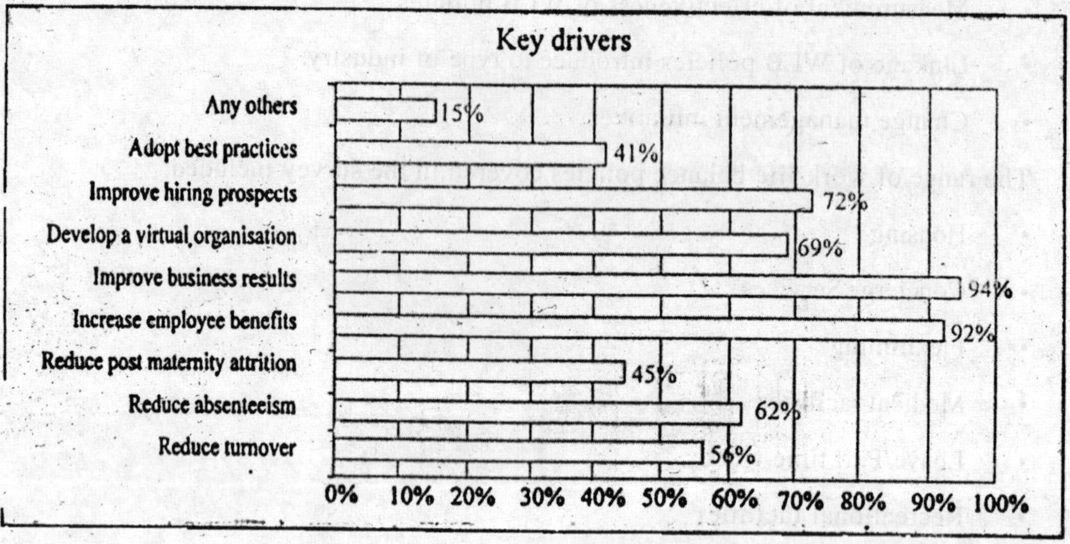

Key Drivers

- **FMCG and IT sector:** Greater focus on moving towards developing a vitual organization, (Hewlet Packard, P&G etc).
- **Manufacturing sector:** Improvement in health of employees and providing benefits to employees was a key driver in the introduction of WLB policies (Tata, GE etc.)
- **Banking sector:** Reduction in absenteeism and turnover was a key driver in the introduction of work -life balance policies, (ICICI, HSBC etc.).

Changes Required

- 95% of the organizations surveyed felt that change in work culture would be the greatest factor in impacting the introduction of a WLB policy.
- 73 % felt that the introduction of flexible work practices could be a starting point for introduction of a full -fleged WLB policy.
- Only 15% felt the change in organization structure was required to ensure the continued success of a WLB policy.

Based on the survey, the most popular amongst the 'Indian' work-life balance techniques were:

- **Flexitiming:** in IT firms (85% in the IT industry reffered to this as the most popular initiative)
- **Housing /Medical benefits:** Manufacturing diversified (75% in this sector preferred this initiative)

- **Recreational** activities also achieved high scores in IT firms (Rated the second best by 72 %.of the respondents in this sector)

In traditional organisations workers preferred free housing as the most important of all the work-life benefits. In IT concerns it was the freedom to be flexible, casual (in attire) and creative which assumed maximum importance.

How to Get Yourself Ready for it?

Different companies will use different work practices and arrangements depending on their needs and environment. To some, alternative working may mean 'hot-desking' where people share desks and office equipment depending on when they are in the office. At Arthur Andersen we have developed an approach to offering flexible work options that help employees balance their personal and professional lives. This begins with evaluating an organisation's suitability to adopt and align different work practices and arrangements, using a range of diagnostics. The diagnosis would enable an organisation to consider.

Are you committed to new ways of working? For example, are you committed to change performance measures to align them with the individual's new ways of working?

Are you prepared to examine your incentives and reward policies in light of the different ways of working?

Is the nature of your business and your culture conducive to new working practices? For example, does your organization have an open culture? Do you have proactive managers that will actively support the new ways of working and champion the culture transformation?

To what extent are your organisation's systems and processes designed for face to face working, or do you operate through voice and data communication channels?

Are you prepared to invest in tools and training to equip people with new skills and behaviours to handle new work practices? For example, are you willing to invest in computer equipment new phone lines for home makers?

Are you prepared for resistance? New working arrangenments tend to involve a culture shift for an organization and therefore require people to change their behaviour and attitudes. This can be met with resistance and at all levels and should be expected.

Flexible work options, such as home working , help to increase job satisfaction and reduce stress among employees. They also help to reduce absenteeism, as employees are better able to manage personal and professional demands . Other benefits include improved employee retention, improved impact on customer service, lower commuting and other work related costs for employees and potentially reduced facilities costs for employees.

The only way to ensure that flexible work options benefit both company and employee is to evaluate employees based on productivity results achieved, work quality and overall effectiveness. Measuring results requires managers and employees to work together to set goals for a specific period. Managers evaluate employees at regular intervals to ensure employees are meeting preset goals. Implementing an appropriate performance management process enables individuals to meet work goals through alternative work practices.

6 easy steps to developing flexible work options recommended by Andersen (Human Capital) include:

1. ***Explore use of the most common work options:*** Flexible work options generally consist of flexible hours (Flexi time), telecommuting, compresed work-weeks, part time work and job sharing. Not all options are right for all companies and jobs. To determine which programmes are most feasible, we weigh up the needs and concerns of the company along with information obtained about employee needs. For example, we have found that at some companies the corporate culture and pervasive management style may be too rigid to accept telecommuting as a work option. However, compresed work weeks or flexi time might achieve corporate goals in addition to satisfying employees.

2. ***Identify and addess management concerns regarding flexible work options:*** Although flexible work options are common in today's workplace, introducing them into a company is sometimes met with resistance by managers who typically have some of the following concerns:

   — Employees's flexible schedules will make them hard to supervise.

   — Productivity will decrease because managers cannot directly supervise all workers.

   — Employees using flexible or part-time options will lack commitment.

   — People who are not eligible for programmes will resent those who are.

   — People will abuse the system.

3. ***Formalise flexible work options and make them broadly available where appropriate:*** Although some companies offer flexible work options on a case by case basis, this is not the prefered approach to flexibility in the workplace. When employees strike their own informal arrangements with managers, other employees often perceive the arrangements as special situations available only to a select few. This can breed confusion and resentment among other employees and are often troublesome for employees using them too, because they may not feel accepted by others in the work place . It is therefore advisable for companies to formalize flexible work options and make them broadly available to employees working in jobs that lend themselves to flexibility.

4. ***Pilot programmes before full scale implementation:*** Any new flexible work options programme may present some unforeseen problems. Therefore, it is prudent to pilot programmes first. In this way, companies are able to identify and address problems before implementing programmes on a broad scale. Pilot tests also-help companies quantity the true costs of programmes, measure their likely benefits and detect procedural problems.

5. ***Ensure accountuing and information systems allow for workplace flexibility:*** A company's accounting procedures and information systems must facilitate, not impede, flexible work options. Often a company's accounting systems makes flexible work options almost impossible to implement. Counting every employee as one headcount or having a payroll system that automatically triggers overtime after an eight hour-work-day both present problems for flexible work options. Using a fulltime equivalent head-counting method, which counts hours instead of employees allows for job sharing and part-time work without each employee being categorised as a full time employee.

6. ***Manage by results, not time:*** Flexible work options, such as telecommuting, require many managers to change their management style to one that de-emphasizes supervision and emphasizes results. Managers must abandon "line-of-sight" or face -time" management styles- the idea that as long as employees are in the office and can be seen, they must be working . Telecommuting, in particular, requires trust on an employer's part. Employees must be worthy of that trust, however, and not all employees perform well in telecommuting arrangements. It is found that employees who are highly organized and disciplined tend to be the best candidates.

Review Questions

1. What do you mean by quality of working life? What are the different approaches to it?
2. What are the different principles of quality of working life? Explain them.
3. What are the different techniques of quality of working life? Explain them.
4. Highlight the needs for quality circles. Explain the concept.
5. What do you mean by job enrichment? How does it differ from job enlargement?

✿ ✿ ✿

Chapter 12

LEARNING ORGANIZATIONS

Learning Objectives

1. *Learning Organizations*
2. *Knowledge-sharing Culture*
3. *Human Networks*
4. *Harnessing Tacit Knowledge in Organisations*
5. *Knowledge Base - Source of Competitive Advantage*
6. *Two Dimensions of Organisational Knowledge*

Learning Organizations

There is a growing awareness for promoting learning environment on workplaces, which could be called "learning organization". Corporates are increasingly becoming aware that knowledge is a vital asset and that the companies excel or decline on the basis of what they know and how well they create new knowledge to improve performance. The implementation of this learning organization is designed to produce a better sharing of information and knowledge in order to improve productivity and innovation. The learning organizations follow certain parameters under the able guidance of HR professionals:

- Learning from their past history,
- Learning from the best practice of others,

- A systematic problem solving,
- Experimenting with new approaches to getting things done,
- Transferring what is learned quickly and accurately throughout the organization.

Companies such as Xerox, Motorola, Honda, Coming, and General Electric have all acted on the premise that organizational learning yields a more competitive advantage in the changing business environment.

Knowledge-sharing Culture

There is also the need to translate the "knowledge-sharing" philosophy into action, through effective management of HR, for resolving the crisis situations and thereby bringing in "professionalism" into work atmosphere. For this, the HR policies and principles that govern the companies, have to be modified. Emphasis should be laid on adoption of latest technologies that will enable sharing of knowledge systems from across the globe.

The emergence of various "knowledge parks" in India is a milestone in this direction. The ICICI Knowledge Park, Genome Valley located at Hyderabad is a classic example for this knowledge-sharing concept facilitating qualitative research in the "pharma" and "biotechnology" sectors.

The HR policies should mandate fairness and equity for employees. More systematic career guidance and planning programs have to be adopted. Outreach programs, such as internship programs, scholarships, targeting recruitment in the community, and lectures at business schools have to be given priority as part of managing diverse cultures on work place. This creates a common wavelength among the employees that enables them to strive for the fulfillment of organizational goals and objectives.

Human Networks

The HRD of an organization should essentially implement certain management principles for the development of "human networks". This is required for effective "knowledge management". The fundamental combination of Knowledge, Innovation and Competitiveness, required for corporate progress, emanates from the development of human networks. The HR policies should be able to fill the gap between the requirement and availability of knowledge workers who are perceived to be innovative and enterprising. This can be bridged through human networks. These networks typically comprise of colleagues who share their insights on topics they care deeply about. Knowledge-sharing through "social networks" is found to be very useful in project-based organizations wherein the impact is on the team performance. Any organization that follows this blended system of "learning management" will increase its return on investment, and have an edge over its competitors. Thus, the concept of "continuous learning" is the shifting paradigm in HR management policies.

Harnessing Tacit Knowledge in Organizations

The success of any organization greatly depends on management of knowledge. Such knowledge should be shared among the members of the organization. In this perspective, explicit knowledge is easy to transmit than tacit knowledge. Harnessing tacit knowledge calls for suitable HR interventions in organizations.

The eminent management thinker Peter F. Drucker predicted that in the 21st century, companies would compete with each other by using their knowledge and the major challenge before the managers would be in managing the collective knowledge of the organization effectively. The knowledge base should be managed in such a way that it develops at a pace to match the current challenges of business environment, encourage all the members to contribute to it as well as to benefit from it, and above all, that cannot be easily utilized by the competitors. Each person should make use of the best and most current knowledge. In order to support such knowledge sharing systematically, many companies have adopted knowledge management practices and implemented worldwide knowledge management systems by utilizing global communication networks and groupware technology. This article first discusses knowledge base as a source of competitive advantage followed by the issues of harnessing tacit knowledge.

Knowledge Base - Source of Competitive Advantage

All businesses sell their knowledge on the selected line of business in the market for a price. For example, a mutual fund company sells its knowledge (expertise) on financial management and a pharmaceutical company sells its drug formula. The knowledge manifests itself into an innovative product, efficient production process, and better utilization of human resource or market intelligence in manufacturing organizations.

The vast size of modern global enterprises, the speed with which the markets move, the increased knowledge of clients, customers, and competitors, and increased demands for personalization and specialization in products and services, come together to demand that organizations be smarter than ever before. Moreover, organizations today operate in an increasingly complex world that require them to apply large amounts of knowledge to their activities. Managing knowledge is a key to organizational success. Earlier, knowledge management itself was not that important in an organization; in the information era, knowledge needs to be managed overtly. In the global economy, knowledge is a company's greatest advantage.

In the prevailing competitive landscape, traditional sources of advantage have become less relevant. Organizational advantages are rarely derived from superior technologies, distribution efficiencies, or from other value—chain activities. Rather competitive advantages are mere. In order to achieve sustainable competitive advantage; the strategy should be based on the organization's knowledge base.

The organization's ability to acquire, integrate, maintain, develop and use the knowledge base is important to build sustainable competitive advantage. Effective management of knowledge base is possible only when members of the organization create new knowledge and share it with other members rapidly and widely within the organization.

Two Dimensions of Organizational Knowledge

Organizational knowledge—the ability to accomplish tasks that will create value to the stakeholders of the organization, has two dimensions - Tacit Knowledge *vs.* Explicit Knowledge.

"Explicit" or codified knowledge refers to knowledge that is recordable and transmittable by using systematic means. Explicit knowledge is structured and is much easier to comprehend. Organization's explicit knowledge is found in engineering drawing, procedure manuals, patents, and computer databases. Modern advancements in information and communication technology is capitalized in capturing and sharing explicit knowledge in organizations. For instance, information about market size regulations in an overseas market can be concretely transferred to a report that too within the organization. By drawing analogy between knowledge base of an organization and an iceberg, we can say that the explicit form of knowledge is only the tip of the iceberg but tacit knowledge is largely hidden and huge in size and potential.

"Tacit" or implicit knowledge, on the other hand, is individual-oriented and difficult share. Tacit knowledge includes judgement, intuition, deep understanding and feelings of members of the organization. Tacit knowledge is an essential part of "knowing how" and "knowing why" and is essential in making knowledge useful to the organization. Tacit knowledge is generally not easy to structure and explain. Consider, for instance, a quality control engineer, through years of experience, can identify the quality of a newly manufactured engine by its very sound and vibrations. Such knowledge cannot be transferred through a written document but is of great importance to the organization.

Issues in Sharing Tacit Knowledge

Knowledge is of no use to anyone unless it is shared. As explicit knowledge is easier to transfer and share, tacit knowledge is more valuable and the issue of "how to harness tacit knowledge in an organization" becomes an important one. Two pertinent questions come to one's mind when the issue of sharing tacit knowledge crops up. First is, how employees can be induced to share inherent knowledge and the second is, how a knowledge sharing culture can be built in the organizations. Both the issues have to be seen in the light of the inherent human, tendency to hoard rather than share knowledge and the fact that knowledge, many times, is used as a base of power in organizations.

Encouraging Employees to Share Knowledge

One of the sources of power for an individual is "Expertise" knowledge that he/she possesses. As such, sharing the knowledge may be perceived as losing some amount of power. Therefore, the very idea of knowledge sharing may be frowned upon. So, such activities must be coupled with appropriate incentives, rewards and above all an organization culture that encourages sharing.

Building Knowledge Sharing Culture

Having the right tools and systems in place will not be of much help in an organization if such efforts are not backed by the culture that encourages knowledge transfer. Tacit knowledge, by its very nature is complex, subtle, internalized and very difficult to externalize. An individual who possess tacit knowledge will often find it difficult, if not impossible to part with such knowledge. Tacit knowledge transfers generally require extensive personal contacts. Therefore, the kind of culture that will encourage knowledge transfer can be built

Building Knowledge Map

The greater the size of an organization, the more the probability that the knowledge we need exists within the company, but it simultaneously decreases the chances of our knowing who possess it, how and where to find it. One way to overcome the difficulty in locating knowledge source is to build knowledge maps. Knowledge maps, point to sources where knowledge is available in the organization. Knowledge seekers can refer to knowledge maps to locate the knowledge sellers who know best about the concerned issue. But building such maps require an organized effort throughout the organization.

Capturing Tacit Knowledge

Organizations should try to capture, codify and document tacit knowledge so that it will be available to the organization forever. Another way is to transfer as much knowledge as possible to other people through mentoring or apprenticeship. Multimedia computing can also be used for this purpose.

Just Talk

One of the simplest ways in which tacit knowledge can be harnessed in organizations is to let their employees interact freely in an informal atmosphere. Social interactions are the most effective way of harnessing tacit knowledge. Since, casual atmosphere created during social interactions put people at ease, effective articulation and listening result in the process of tacit knowledge sharing. Organizations can find innovative ways to create such occasions and encourage employees to interact with one another. From formal meetings to casual talks in the cafeteria, from knowledge fairs to open forums, each of these methods is a sure fire way to transfer knowledge in organizations. This apart, appropriate infrastructure should be created with adequate techno-support in the form of intranets and hobby groups.

Managing Inhibitors

A number of cultural factors inhibit knowledge transfer. These inhibitors delay or prevent the transfer of knowledge. The following are some of the common inhibitors that a company needs to overcome in order to nurture a culture of knowledge transfer.

1. Lack of trust
2. Different cultures
3. Lack of time and meeting places
4. Status and rewards go to knowledge owners
5. Lack of absorptive capacity among recipients
6. Use of jargon
7. Intolerance for mistakes.

By building the right organization culture and encouraging employees to share their knowledge, a company can transform itself into an organization that generates and uses knowledge, one that interacts with the environment, absorbs information, turns it into knowledge and takes action based on it in combination with their experience, values and internal rules—a knowledge organization.

Conclusion

Today, on an average about 75% of companies' market value stems from their knowledge assets, in the form of intellectual capital-patents, copyrights, trade secrets, financial records, business strategies and overall know-how. Thus, the companies need to manage their knowledge base effectively in order to achieve sustainable competitive advantage in the market. Companies which are agile in continuously creating, disseminating new knowledge and transforming the knowledge into improved products, processes, strategies will definitely have a cutting edge over others in competitive scenario.

Harnessing tacit knowledge in organizations calls for suitable HR interventions. HR programs and policies can be strategically aligned to the goal of harnessing tacit knowledge of the employees. One such powerful HRM tool is compensation system and it should be designed in a way to motivate employees to share their knowledge freely with others. HR interventions should be aimed at creating a learning organisation where people should feel no hesitation in sharing their knowledge with others as well as seeking knowledge from others. Any successful initiatives to harness tacit knowledge need to break psychological barriers rather than organizational ones.

Knowledge Management and Role of HR

Peter Drucker once said that organizations of the future would be knowledge-based and would essentially employ specialists who direct and discipline their own performance through organized feedback from colleagues, customers and corporate headquarters. Knowledge management as a concept with people at the centre stage has, thus, emerged as a new management tool in the corporate world, which this article proposes to discuss.

In the recent past, knowledge and knowledge management have generated a lot of interest among corporate leaders. It is of course the advent of information society and its move towards "knowledge economy" that has brought knowledge and the importance of its management within organizations into the forefront. But this doesn't mean that there was no knowledge earlier and that people were not concerned about its management. Knowledge has been with us since mankind came into existence. Indeed, it is the accumulation and application of knowledge over centuries that transformed the agrarian society into industrial society and ultimately into information society. The only difference from the past is that today knowledge has become one of the key factors of production. In fact, many are now considering knowledge as the only economic resource in the knowledge society. The very fact that we consider today's economy to be knowledge economy places "knowledge" at the centre-stage. Against this background, this article attempts to define what is knowledge, and what for and how knowledge management, is accomplished, and the key role of human resources in effective knowledge management.

Knowledge and its Varied Facets

Knowledge creation is a process of value addition to the existing knowledge through innovation. It means the more of it we have, the more we are likely to generate and that is what we have been witnessing all along. Simply put, knowledge creates knowledge and in the process it bestows competitive advantage on its owners leading to wealth creation. According to Davenport and Prusak, "Knowledge is a fluid mix of framed experience, values, contextual information, and expert insight that provides a frame work for evaluating and incorporating new experiences and information. It originates and is applied in the minds of the knower. In organizations, it often becomes embedded not only in documents or repositories but also in organizational routines, processes, practices, and norms."

There are two approaches to manage knowledge in organizations, namely, the management of people and their behaviour, and management of explicit knowledge or information.

While implicit knowledge can be captured and codified as information for future use , explicit knowledge merits different treatment. For instance, a computer servicing company can list probable failures that can be anticipated based on past experiences and also record plausible remedies for all such problems and make it available for it. Once knowledge is transformed from an activity status to an servicing workforce as an operating guide.. "Know how" that resulted from the conversion of tacit knowledge into explicit knowledge can be transferred to others through a well-structured learning process.

Why and How of Knowledge Management

Knowledge management is basically concerned with explicit knowledge, know-how or implicit knowledge and tacit knowledge. These three are quite interrelated and in fact can — not be segmented, as knowledge management is an outcome of people's interaction with other people, Juki and information and the environment in which they function. We should, therefore, treat knowledge as an activity and not as an object. Once knowledge is transformed from an activity status to an object status, it becomes a piece of information, and then it becomes pretty easy to manage it through information management systems. That is where technology comes handy in effectively managing knowledge. Technology facilitates quick transmission and exchange of information by cataloguing the knowledge created by the organizational members and makes it accessible to the right people, paving way for enhanced knowledge sharing.

Most of the knowledge management activities undertaken by organizations are found to be a mix of knowledge and information management. Knowledge management essentially aims at value addition to users. It leads not only to improvement and innovations in the existing operations, but also adds value to the existing pool of organisational knowledge by filtering, synthesizing and interpreting knowledge by making use of the feedback from the users. Unless it goes beyond mere search and acquisition of knowledge, it cannot play a significant role in 'achieving organizational efficiency. In this context, it is "collaborative technology" rather than the information management tools that are found to be more competent to handle knowledge management.

In a globalized economy, companies face stiff competition as consumers are enjoying an unprecedented array of choices for goods and services across the globe. It is the agile responsiveness with which businesses can deliver services to customers that has become the key determinant of survival. It is often found that intelligence gathering and market intelligence have enabled many Japanese companies to succeed. That is how knowledge management has taken centre stage in collecting bits and pieces of information relating to customers and competition in the market and synthesizing it into ready-to-use information to race competition.

There is yet another fear among the organizations: A fat lot of tacit knowledge that exits only in the minds of people often found walking away from the organizations as people left them for one reason or the other. Similarly, "downsizing" resorted to by companies as a cost reduction exercise has also resulted in "knowledge scarcity". It is to capture and retain such a critical knowledge within the organization that knowledge management has become a must. The importance of knowledge management in organizations has been well captured by Stewart in his statement: Knowledge has become the primary ingredient of what we make, do, buy and sell. As a result, managing it—finding and growing intellectual capital, storing it, selling it, sharing it—has become the most important economic task of individuals, business and nations.

Role of HR in Knowledge Management.

We have seen that knowledge management essentially deals with acquisition, construction and transfer or sharing of knowledge among the members of the organization, so as to facilitate better accomplishment of organizational goals. Research findings also indicate that the organizational 'culture and the communication strategy adopted free dialogue among the team members are the two critical factors for effective knowledge sharing. The very tact that knowledge is collected from and in turn shared among the members of an organization and the culture of an organization that facilitates smooth sharing of knowledge highlights the criticality of human resources in the management of knowledge.

Learning in the organizations mostly occurs within groups. Social learning may be defined as the process by which knowledge and practices built in the system are transmitted across different work situations and across time and the procedures that facilitate generative learning, which enables an organization to react creatively to sudden and unanticipated developments. Research findings indicate that effective social learning in the organizations calls for empowerment of staff to seek and experiment with new knowledge; trust and mutual respect among the members; a culture that encourage employees to take risks; forgiving culture of mistakes — that encourages knowledge construction based on the lessons learnt; cohesion development can be among the team members that encourages sharing of knowledge related from the goals; and transparent decision-making across the organization. The scope for social learning is found to be in next generation of new enhanced with the use of "dialog" which involves going beyond individual consciousness into mutual communing to perceive reality knowledge development can be appreciated from the fact that it facilitates generation of new meanings through collaborative thinking and mutual communing. All this only highlights the importance of human resources in the entire gamut of knowledge management.

What HRMD Should do for a Better Knowledge Management?

Research findings indicate that HRMD must strive to create essential social learning enablers in an organization to ensure effective knowledge management. Some such critical enablers are:

- Positive communication climate - having a workplace where people can freely approach the manager and say, "Hi! 1 don't understand this. It might be stupid, but would you please help me figure it out?".
- Effective leadership - workplace that depicts accessibility to their staff, non-judgemental approach to the staff and the issues that they bring to the manager.
- Goal alignment - ensuring cohesiveness between the leaders and team and within the team members enabling everyone to know where the other is heading, listening to everyone's problems and making everyone understand what and why changes are happening.
- Constructive performance management - setting realistic goals before every member and rightly recording and measuring the performance.
- Valuing skills and reward and recognition strategies - the very fact of being valued makes an individual willing to engage in a dialog with team-mates, learn and share knowledge with others resulting in team cohesiveness; in short, it is simply practicing the common axiom "praise is better than money".
- Enabling workplace design - having a workplace design that fosters physical proximity ensures better communication among team members resulting in good engagement in dialog.
- Team-based morale - learning in the organizations is basically a social process of interaction which is facilitated by dialog, and unless high morale prevails among the team members, dialoguing cannot take place freely.

- Socializing- feeling good about the colleagues in the team is a great motivating factor to generate a sense of belonging to the group; such identity results in awareness about the expertise possessed by team members; healthy social relations build trust, make people learn faster and make them more creative and productive; informal socialization leads to better and easy sharing of knowledge.
- Timely induction programs - induction programs conducted for new recruits well in time provides "foundation knowledge" to the new members; such programs minimize the scope for misunderstandings and pave for better working relationships by reducing anxiety and improve the efficiency of members by letting them know as to what is expected of them.

These enablers are likely to develop a suitable architecture for effective management of knowledge in the organization, but if not effectively used, they also have the potential to pose challenges to knowledge management.

Conclusion

To be is to learn; to learn is to know and to know is to win. Today, by offering wide range of choices to consumers across the globe at the mere click of a mouse, the Internet world has made consumers a highly knowledgeable lot. To survive in such a competitive world, organizations have to necessarily build knowledge, replenish it, and distribute it among the organizational members, so that the accumulated knowledge can be put to use for accomplishing organizational goals. In building up knowledge bases, organizations must be conscious of what is and is not knowledge for the organization and only collect, interpret, synthesize and distribute such knowledge among its members which has a bearing on its performance. It is worth bearing in mind here that it is only an enabler of knowledge management. Human resources are the key deciders of the effectiveness of knowledge management for it is they who are instrumental in generating knowledge, learning from new knowledge and using it for the good of the organization. It is the leadership and its style of managing the human resources and the enabling culture that they create in the organizations which ultimately defines the effectiveness of knowledge.

Review Questions

1. Define learning organizations.
2. What do you understand by knowledge sharing ?
3. What is knowledge management ? Explain with a suitable real life example.
4. What steps are to be taken to build a knowledge sharing culture in an organization?

5. Enlist the factors that inhibit the process of knowledge management.

6. Discuss the role of HR in knowledge management.

References

1. Manish Pharasi, Nihar Pradhan, Knowledge Management, Quality Circle Forum of India, May, 2000.

2. Chun Wei Choo, Nick Bontis, The Strategic Management of Intellectual Capital and Organizational Knowledge, Oxford University Press, 2002.

3. Daniel Ashish & S.Senthil Kumar - The ICFA1 Business School, Hyderabad.

✿ ✿ ✿

Chapter 13

ORGANISATIONAL EFFECTIVENESS

Learning Objectives

1. *Organisational Effectiveness*
2. *Management of People*
3. *Less Effective Chief Executives*
4. *Effective Communication*

Organisational Effectiveness

As the pace of change quickens, and as organisations become flatter, organisational effectiveness has become a competitive weapon. While possession of it is a major strategic advantage; the lack of it is a potentially career-ending weakness. In spite of this, high performance organisations are rare. Only 11% of business leaders believe their organisation is highly effective (see chart below). Many more believe their organisation holds them back. The ailments, whatever they are, are clearly widespread.

A recent survey of business leaders indicates that they are convinced about the 'why' of organisational effectiveness. What is needed is guidance on the 'what' and the 'how'.

70% agreed with the statement 'culture is the true source of competitive advantage'. 91% agreed that 'culture erodes if not actively nurtured'.

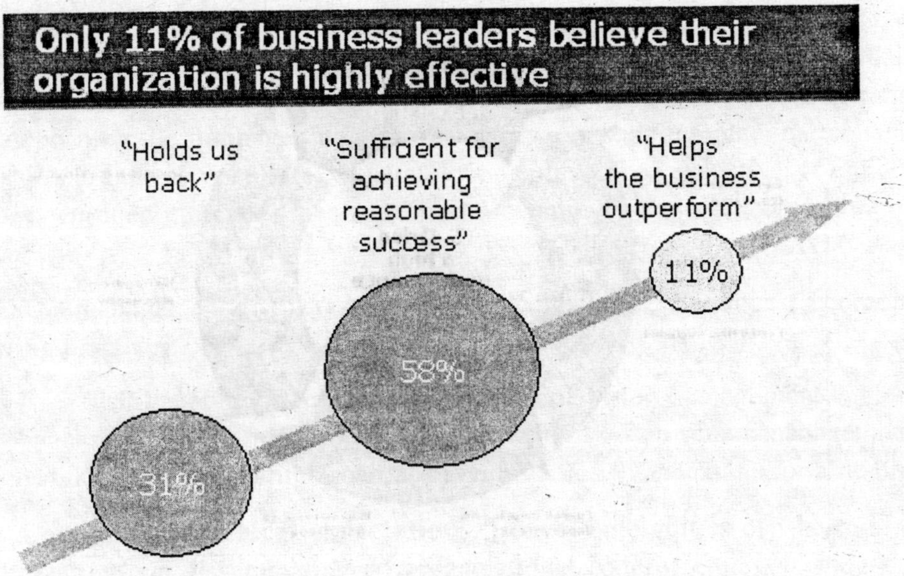

(*Source:* EIU survey of business leaders [n = 202])

The paradox of organisational effectiveness, simply stated, is this — everyone knows the principles of effective organisation, yet few consistently put them into practice.

- A high performance organisation is enormously valuable, yet few achieve it and many don't even try .
- Everyone knows that organisation is complicated and multi-dimensional, yet few have identified the culture they need and actively manage towards it.
- Even high performance organisations must evolve, yet few rigorously assess organisational health over time.

Seven common ailments that undermine organisational health have been identified.

1. Integrated Approach is Essential

Organisations are living organisms with an ecosystem all of their own. Every element of the organisation, whether positive or negative, has evolved for a purpose and plays a role. Changes must be thought through from the perspective of the overall system.

Solving for one element of an organisation is rarely effective. An example of this would be Ford's recent attempt to introduce forced ratings and rankings of its people, as part of its drive to develop a high performance culture. It ran into well-publicised difficulties in implementing this policy. An integrated framework and approach are essential. There are five things to get right, and organisational effectiveness is as strong as the weakest link.

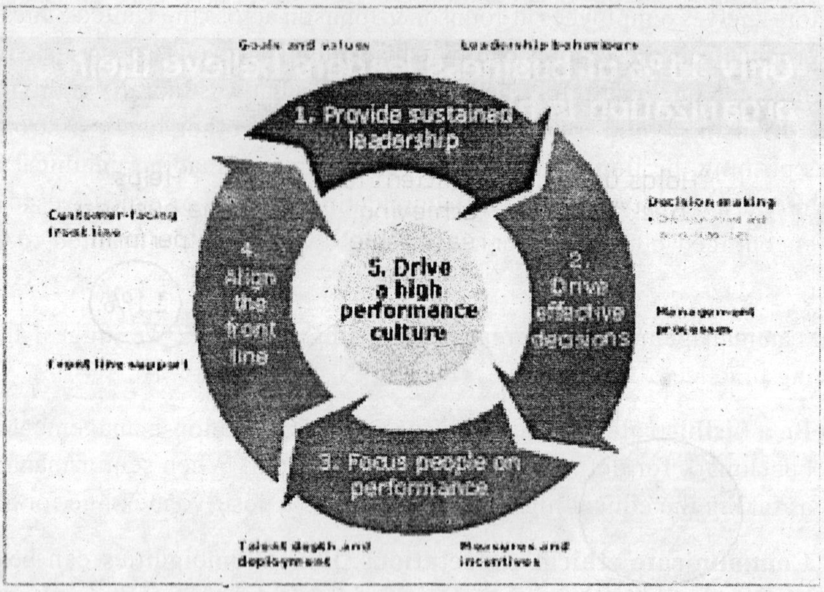

2. Beacon-on-the-Hill

As with all complex issues, it helps to have a clear picture in mind from the outset of what success looks like. Call this the Beacon-on-the-Hill.

Beacon-on-the-Hill

	From	To
Values and goals	• Blurred	• Clear
Leadership behaviours	• Uncoordinated	• Cohesive
Decision making	• Confused	• Crisp
Management processes	• Bureaucratic	• Value-adding
Talent	• Deficient	• Deep and well deployed
Measures and incentives	• Mediocracy	• Meritocracy
Customer-facing front line	• Execution blockage	• Consistent high quality execution
Front line support	• Obese	• Fit
Performance culture	• Low performance pressure and accountability	• Think and act like owners
Capacity to change	• Behind the game	• Continuous evolution

3. Nobody's perfect and nothing lasts forever

Based on our research, high performance organisations are not perfect, just a little bit better on each dimension.

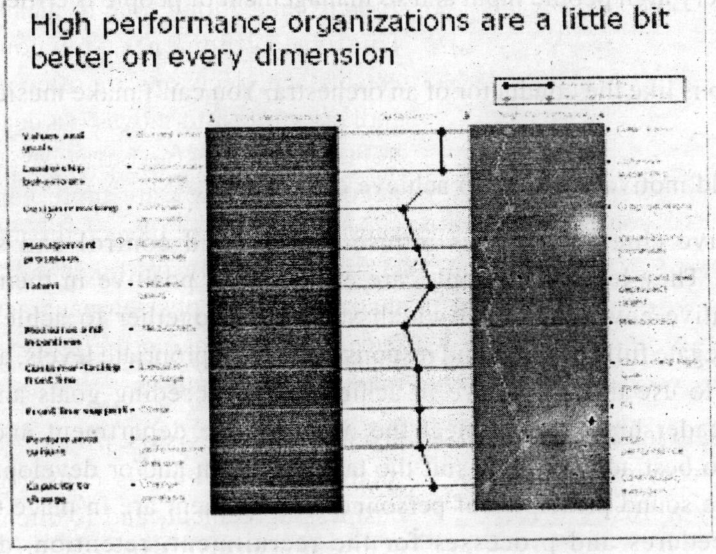

General Management Competencies

Management of People, Managerial Expertise and Effective Communication – play an important role in achieving effectiveness.

This group of competencies focuses on the capability of chief executives to ensure their departments operate efficiently and effectively. Demonstration of these competencies would reveal the ability to:

- organise, develop and motivate staff and manage their performance to enhance their contribution towards achieving the department's current and future goals and objectives;
- adapt highly effective management practices to organise and integrate a wide range of production and support and long-term and short-term functions and activities, and manage the resources of the department to achieve identified goals and results; and
- use oral and written communication skills to establish a dialogue with and inform, persuade and influence a range of people to create an environment in which the organisation operates effectively.

Management of People

Concerned with maximising the quality and contributions of staff to achieve the department's goals and objectives, now and in the future.

"...we have a very high people input and so management of people is critically important ..."

"...the CE's job is like the conductor of an orchestra. You can't make music on your own as a conductor ..."

"...the CE could motivate people to achieve excellence ..."

Highly effective chief executives arouse interest and control and sustain work performance levels. They lead by example, are enthusiastic, positive in their attitude and develop a co-operative environment in which staff work together to achieve goals and objectives. They delegate full authority and responsibility to appropriate levels, and encourage and empower staff to use their initiative in achieving or exceeding goals and objectives. They tailor their leadership style to meet the needs of the department and adapt their management style to best advantage to suit the task, situation and/or developmental levels of staff. They ensure sound principles of personnel management are in place to ensure fair and equitable procedures and processes for the recruitment, retention, development, deployment and redeployment of staff.

Less effective chief executives pay inadequate attention to ensuring appropriate human resource management systems are in place and to ensuring these structures and systems contribute to corporate goals. They maintain an inappropriate leadership style and do not adapt their management style as necessary. They either overmanage and lead through threat and/or imposition of their own views or undermanage when staff need direction and support. They pay lip service to merit and equity principles and do little to promote a friendly climate of good morale and co-operation. They either do not delegate or require responsibility without allowing autonomy and in general permit little or no freedom or independence to others in making decisions and determining direction. They tend to be office bound or work behind closed doors.

Indicators of highly effective behaviour are:

- Provides a clear sense of direction and purpose to others.
- Inspires others, communicates a shared view, which generates motivation, enthusiasm and commitment to the department's mission.
- Is "visible" and models exemplary leadership qualities and behaviours.
- Delegates full authority, responsibility and accountability to appropriate levels.

- Empowers staff and encourages autonomous action.
- Recognises the importance of having overall managerial strength, and builds a strong corporate management team.
- Ensures appropriate human resource management systems and procedures are in place for motivating, directing and sustaining optimal levels of work performance.
- Displays an appropriate sense of humour and fun.
- Aligns human resource policies and practices with the strategic direction of the organisation.
- Ensures all human resource management practices, incorporate equal employment opportunity principles.
- Confronts and deals with others openly and directly about performance problems.

Indicators of ineffective behaviour are:

- Fails to identify, describe and establish an appropriate culture within the organisation.
- Unable to stimulate a high level of productive and focused performance and consistently fails to deal with people in a way which satisfies their needs.
- Acts in a manner that is inconsistent with generally accepted leadership qualities and behaviours.
- Exhibits an approach based on control, direction and derived authority rather than involvement and earned authority.
- Delegates reluctantly or delegates inappropriately in relation to position in organisation, abilities and skills.
- Tends towards controlling others and provides little opportunity for self directed performance or development.
- Uses inappropriate styles and methods in managing, guiding, advising or directing others towards task accomplishment.
- Unable to secure the co-operation and commitment from subordinates and from others within and outside the department.
- Adopts a serious task orientated approach and/or uses humour and fun inappropriately.

Managerial Expertise

Concerned with a sound understanding and application of the most effective management practices to achieve organisational goals and objectives.

"... knowledge of the way the real business world out there works ..."

"... they run a tidy ship and people liked being part of it ..."

"... top quality is a benchmark - everything is top class. The way the phone is answered, the way they treat you when you go into the office ..."

Highly effective chief executives are well informed about management techniques and the trends and issues in the business world. They run their department with a business orientation, analysing stakeholder and customer needs and developing and implementing operational plans which deliver bottom line results. They recognise the need to balance available resources against competing demands within the context of the corporate plan and objectives and in relation to both short and long term requirements. They develop practices designed to use resources in a manner which will achieve organisational goals and objectives. They have a balanced view of service delivery and policy advice, giving due consideration to both input and output factors. They develop and implement quality management systems, measure and evaluate performance against objectives, review risks and adjust plans and strategies as necessary.

Less Effective Chief Executives

"... overspends, runs into bottlenecks, key people and assets under used ..."

"... managers from that department once said that their agenda was determined by listening to the radio news in the morning.

Less effective chief executives demonstrate limited knowledge of management practices and tend to lose sight of the fact that they are running a business. They show limited understanding of broad financial management requirements and display little or no recognition of the importance or relevance of resource planning and management. They demonstrate an inadequate level of understanding of what is required of a particular situation, to develop the solution and apply it. They experience difficulty in resolving competing resource requirements and/or in reallocating resources in response to shifts in priorities and/or unexpected changes in available resources. They are unlikely to manage the setting and monitoring of performance targets, or to develop strategies for improvement in efficiency and/or effectiveness with which results are achieved. Alternatively they over-focus on inward-looking activities, such as planning, quality management, etc., at the expense of serving the Minister, customers and the community.

Indicators of highly effective behaviour are:

- Demonstrates knowledge and understanding of the breadth and diversity of general management principles and commercial activities.
- Structures and positions the organisation to meet Government priorities.
- Establishes and accepts personal and collective accountability.
- Adopts an approach focused on the identification of, and response to, user/interest group and stakeholder needs.
- Uses financial, physical and human resources efficiently and effectively to achieve required outcomes.
- Identifies and manages areas of risk.
- Manages change so as to achieve positive outcomes.
- Recognises and creates new business opportunities.
- Ensures systems and procedures are in place to achieve optimal utilisation of resources.
- Creates systems and a culture to ensure continuous improvement in quality.

Indicators of ineffective behaviour are:

- Displays insufficient or no recognition of the importance or relevance of financial, physical and human resources in planning activities.
- Makes decisions, or sets priorities based on inadequate consideration of potential benefit, return-on-investment of resources, or cost-benefit analysis.
- Displays little evidence of accepting either individual or collective responsibility.
- Fails to respond to key environmental trends and/or user/interest group and stakeholders' needs.
- Shows insufficient evidence of translating broad corporate direction and objectives into planning, resource allocation and organisation of his/her own area of responsibility.
- Ignorant of possible risks involved in a course of action.
- Adopts a management approach, in an environment of change, that prevents positive change occurring or impedes its progress.

Effective Communication

Concerned with clear and effective two-way communication with a wide range of people and in all situations, in order to explain, persuade, convince and influence others.

Highly effective chief executives communicate, both orally and in writing, with a wide range of people, either individually or collectively, in a clear purposeful manner. They are easy to talk to and listen actively, asking open questions and encouraging involvement. People's concerns are reflected and responded to as appropriate, which may, on occasions, necessitate altering one's own viewpoint and/or behaviour. They use negotiation skills to achieve a win/win outcome and assist in resolving real or potential conflict situations in a constructive manner. When addressing a larger group, they get the attention of the audience and hold it by using interesting and appropriate language and other non-verbal communication techniques.

The expression of less effective chief executives, both oral and written, lacks clarity, fluency and impact. Their form of presentation is often tense, argumentative or aggressive. Alternatively they may be unduly expansive and/or overly conciliatory. Presentation of ideas is disjointed, unstructured, and lacks balance and logical order. They are unable to gain or hold the attention of an audience, and unable to demonstrate any awareness and/or appropriate response to audience reaction. Their listening skills are inadequate and they respond inappropriately to others, either having not heard what is being said or failing to be receptive and/or accommodate alternative viewpoints. At times this results in people not keeping them informed as they do not expect to be heard. They have difficulty in negotiating situations and conflict is unlikely to be resolved to the satisfaction of all parties concerned.

Indicators of highly effective behaviour are:

- Achieves desired impact through the use of convincing expression in individual, group and public speaking situations, using appropriate language and other non-verbal communication techniques.
- Written and oral communication has clarity, fluency, impact and conciseness.
- Uses the full range of communication media and judges how and when to use them.
- Brings conflict into the open and encourages and/or facilitates a beneficial resolution of conflict.
- Negotiates mutually acceptable (win/win) solutions with all parties involved.
- Ensures the provision of thoroughly researched, constructed and targeted written documents which are clear and concise.

- Listens well, is receptive and encourages participation and mutual understanding.
- Actively seeks feedback on communication style(s).

Indicators of ineffective behaviour are:

- Avoids difficult people and/or (communication) situations.
- Presentation of ideas both orally and in writing, is disjointed, unstructured, lacks balance and logical order.
- Does not gain or hold the attention of an audience and generally has difficulty in persuading, convincing and/or informing others.
- Uses exclusive (biased) language and communication is inappropriate in tone, language and/or content for the listener(s).
- Creates win/lose situations either by going after a win at all costs or by making unnecessary concessions.
- Avoids situations which require conflict resolution and/or escalates an already tense situation.
- Does not listen to the message/information conveyed, responds inappropriately to other(s), and/or leaves the other party feeling they have not been heard/understood.
- Non-verbal language and signals convey an inappropriate lack of interest.
- Communicates in a way that shuts down dialogue.

Review Questions

1. What is Organisational effectiveness? How does it help to counter competition?
2. Describe the competencies that are essential to achieve Organisational effectiveness.
3. Link management of people and Organisational effectiveness.
4. How does managerial expertise help achieve Organisational effectiveness.
5. What is the role played by communication in achieving Organisational effectiveness?

✿ ✿ ✿

Chapter 14

ORGANISATIONAL CULTURE

Learning Objectives

1. *Meaning of Organisational Culture*
2. *Strong vs Weak Culture*
3. *Role of Organisational Culture*
4. *Culture Creation*
5. *Ethical Organisational Culture*
6. *Culture & Nations*

Organisational Culture

Culture may be defined as, "... the integrated pattern of human behaviour that includes: thought, speech, action and artefacts, and depends on a person's capacity for learning and transmitting knowledge to succeeding generations."

Culture also influences behaviour in a group and that leads to sub-culture. Culture and sub-culture mould employees' values and values influence employees' perceptions and decisions. Values represent stable, long lasting beliefs about what is important. They are evaluative standards that help us define what is right or wrong, good or bad, in the world (Sagie & Elizur 1996). In each country there are different work values because of the dominant and subordinate cultures, which co-exist in that country.

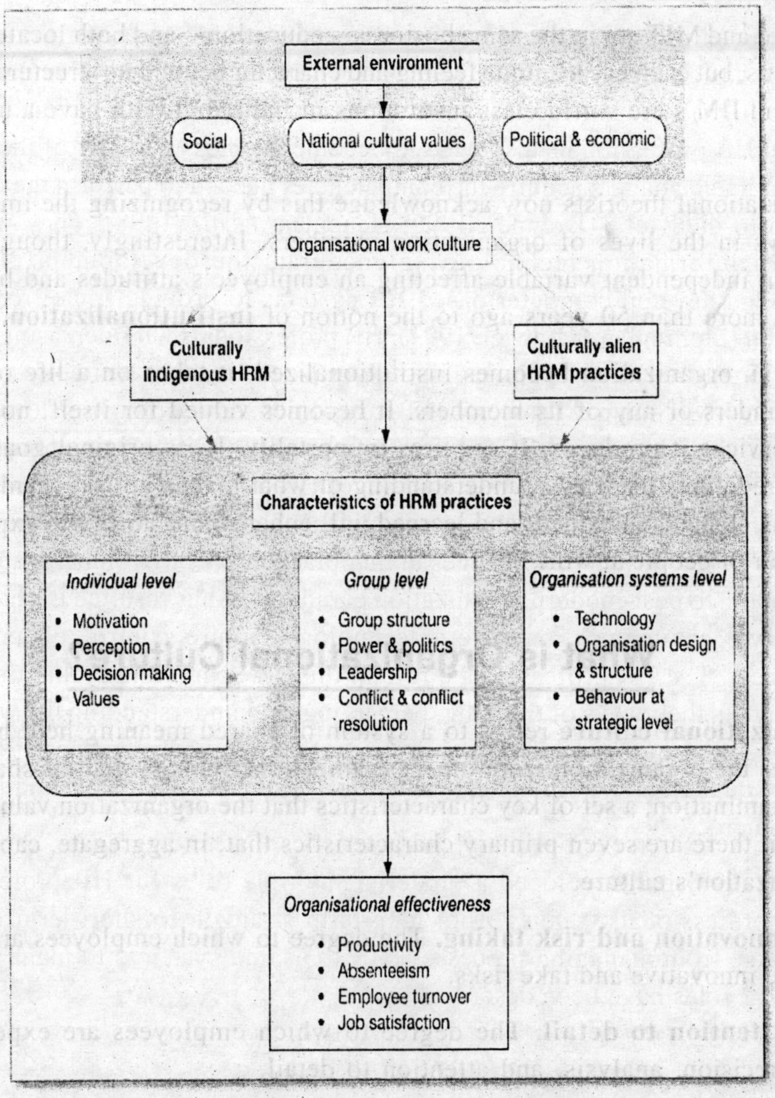

Culturally Indigenous and Alien HRM Practices Model

The idea of viewing organizations as cultures—in which there is a system of shared meaning among members—is a relatively recent phenomenon. Until the mid-1980s, organizations were, for the most part, thought of simply as rational means by which to co-ordinate and control a group of people. They had vertical levels, departments, authority relationships, and so forth. But organizations are more, they have personalities too, just like individuals. They can be rigid or flexible, unfriendly or supportive, innovative or conservative. General Electric offices and people are different from the offices and people at General Mills.

Harvard and MIT are in the same business—education—and both located in Cambridge, Massachusetts, but each has a unique feeling and character beyond its structural characteristics. The IIT's and IIM's are world class institutions in India, but both have a unique culture of their own.

Organizational theorists now acknowledge this by recognizing the important role that culture plays in the lives of organization members. Interestingly, though, the origin of culture as an independent variable affecting an employee's attitudes and behaviour can be traced back more than 50 years ago to the notion of **institutionalization.**

When an organization becomes institutionalized, it takes on a life of its own, apart from its founders or any of its members. It becomes valued for itself, not merely for the goods or services it produces. It acquires immortality. If its original goals are no longer relevant, it redefines itself. An understanding of what makes up an organization's culture, and how it is created, sustained, and learned will enhance our ability to explain and predict the behaviour of people at work.

What is Organizational Culture?

Organizational culture refers to a system of shared meaning held by members that distinguishes the organization from other organizations. This system of shared meaning is, on closer examination, a set of key characteristics that the organization values. The research suggests that there are seven primary characteristics that, in aggregate, capture the essence of an organization's culture.

1. **Innovation and risk taking.** The degree to which employees are encouraged to be innovative and take risks.
2. **Attention to detail**. The degree to which employees are expected to exhibit precision, analysis, and attention to detail.
3. **Outcome orientation.** The degree to which management focuses on results or outcomes rather than on the techniques and processes used to achieve those outcomes.
4. **People orientation**. The degree to which management decisions take into consideration the effect of outcomes on people within the organization.
5. **Team orientation**. The degree to which work activities are organized around teams rather than individuals.
6. **Aggressiveness**. The degree to which people are aggressive and competitive rather than easy going.

7. **Stability**. The degree to which organizational activities emphasize maintaining the status quo in contrast to growth.

Each of these characteristics exists on a continuum from low to high. Appraising the organization on these seven characteristics, then, gives a composite picture of the organization's culture. This picture becomes the basis for feelings of shared understanding that members have about the organization, how things are done in it, and the way members are supposed to behave.

Do Organizations have Uniform Cultures?

Organizational culture represents a common perception held by the organization's members. Acknowledgment that organizational culture has common properties does not mean, however, that there cannot be sub-cultures within any given culture. Most large organizations have a dominant culture and numerous sets of sub-cultures.

A **dominant culture** expresses the core values that are shared by a majority of the organization's members. When we talk about an organization's culture, we are referring to its dominant culture. It is this macro view of culture that gives an organization its distinct personality.

Subcultures tend to develop in large organizations to reflect common problems, situations, or experiences that members face. These sub-cultures are likely to be defined by department designations and geographical separation.

The purchasing department, for example, can have a sub-culture that is uniquely shared by members of that department. It will include the **core values** of the dominant culture plus additional values unique to members of the purchasing department. Similarly, an office or unit of the organization that is physically separated from the organization's main operations may take on a different personality. Again, the core values are essentially retained, but they are modified to reflect the separated unit's distinct situation.

If organizations had no dominant culture and were composed only of numerous sub-cultures, the value of organizational culture as an independent variable would be significantly lessened because there would be no uniform interpretation of what represented appropriate and inappropriate behaviour. It is the "shared meaning" aspect of culture that makes it such a potent device for guiding and shaping behaviour.

Strong Versus Weak Cultures

It has become increasingly popular to differentiate between strong and weak cultures. The argument here is that strong cultures have a greater impact on employee behaviour and are more directly related to reduced turnover.

In a **strong culture,** the organization's core values are both intensely held and widely shared. The more members who accept the core values and the greater their commitment to those values is, the stronger the culture is. Consistent with this definition, a strong culture will have a great influence on the behaviour of its members because the high degree of sharedness and intensity creates an internal climate of high behavioural control. For example, Seattle based Nordstrom has developed one of the strongest service cultures in the retailing industry. Nordstrom employees know in no uncertain terms what is expected of them, and these expectations go a long way in shaping their behaviour.

One specific result of a strong culture should be lower employee turnover. A strong culture demonstrates high agreement among members about what the organization stands for. Such unanimity of purpose builds cohesiveness, loyalty, and organizational commitment. These qualities, in turn, lessen employees' propensity to leave the organization.

Culture`s Functions

Culture performs a number of functions within an organization. First, it has a boundary-defining role, that is, it creates distinctions between one organization and others. Second, it conveys a sense of identity for organization members. Third, culture facilitates the generation of commitment to something larger than one's individual self-interest. Fourth, it enhances the stability of the social system. Culture is the social glue that helps hold the organization together by providing appropriate standards for what employees should say and do. Finally, culture serves as a sense-making and control mechanism that guides and shapes the attitudes and behaviour of employees. It is this last function that is of particular interest to us. As the following quote makes clear, culture defines the rules of the game.

Culture by definition is elusive, intangible, implicit, and taken for granted. But every organization develops a core set of assumptions, understandings, and implicit rules that govern day-to-day behaviour in the workplace. Until newcomers learn the rules, they are not accepted as full-fledged members of the organization. Transgressions of the rules on the part of high-level executives or front-line employees result in universal disapproval and powerful penalties. Conformity to the rules becomes the primary basis for reward and upward mobility.

The role of culture in influencing employee behaviour appears to be increasingly important in today's workplace. As organizations have widened spans of control, flattened structures, introduced teams, reduced formalization, and empowered employees, the shared meaning provided by a strong culture ensures that everyone is pointed in the same direction.

Barriers to Change Culture is a liability when the shared values are not in agreement with those that will further the organization's effectiveness. This is most likely to occur when an organization's environment is dynamic. When an environment is undergoing rapid change, an organization's entrenched culture may no longer be appropriate. So consistency of behaviour is an asset to an organization when it faces a stable environment. It may, however, burden the organization and make it difficult to respond to changes in the environment. This helps to explain the challenges that executives at organizations like Mitsubishi, Eastman Kodak, Xerox, Boeing, U.S. Federal Bureau of Investigation, have had in recent years in adapting to upheavals in their environment. These organizations have strong cultures that worked well for them in the past. But these strong cultures become barriers to change when "business as usual" is no longer effective.

Strong cultures put considerable pressure on employees to conform. They limit the range of values and styles that are acceptable. Organizations seek out and hire diverse individuals because of the alternative strengths these people bring to the workplace. Yet these diverse behaviours and strengths are likely to diminish in strong cultures as people attempt to fit in. Strong cultures, therefore, can be liabilities when they effectively eliminate the unique strengths that people of different backgrounds bring to the organization. Moreover, strong cultures can also be liabilities when they support institutional bias or become insensitive to people who are different.

Culture Creation

Culture creation occurs in three ways. First, founders hire and keep only employees who think and feel the same way they do. Second, they indoctrinate and socialize these employees to their way of thinking and feeling. And finally, the founders' own behaviour acts as a role model that encourages employees to identify with them and thereby internalize their beliefs, values, and assumptions. When the organization succeeds, the founders' vision becomes seen as a primary determinant of that success. At this point, the founders' entire personality becomes embedded in the culture of the organization.

The culture at Hyundai, the giant Korean conglomerate, is largely a reflection of its founder Chung Ju Yung, Hyundai's fierce, competitive style, and its disciplined, authoritarian nature are the same characteristics often used to describe Chung. Other contemporary examples of founders who have had an immeasurable impact on their organization's culture would include Bill Gates at Microsoft.

Once a culture is in place, there are practices within the organization that act to maintain it by giving employees a set of similar experiences. For example, many of the human resource practices we discuss in the next chapter reinforce the organization's culture. The selection process, performance evaluation criteria, training and development activities, and promotion procedures ensure that those hired fit in with the culture, reward those who support it, and penalize (and even expel) those who challenge it. Three forces play a particularly important part in sustaining a culture, selection practices, the actions of top management, and socialization methods.

Selection: The explicit goal of the selection process is to identify and hire individuals who have the knowledge, skills, and abilities to perform the jobs within the organization successfully. Typically, more than one candidate will be identified who meets any given job's requirements, When that point is reached, it would be naive to ignore that the final decision as to who is hired will be significantly influenced by the decision maker's judgement of how well the candidates will fit into the organization. This attempt to ensure a proper match, whether purposely or inadvertently, results in the luring of people who have values essentially consistent with those of the organization, or at least a good portion of those values. In addition, the selection process provides information to applicants about the organization.

Candidates learn about the organization and, if they perceive a conflict between their values and those of the organization, they can self-select themselves out of the applicant pool. Selection, therefore, becomes a two-way street, allowing employer or applicant to abrogate a marriage if there appears to be a mismatch. In this way, the selection process sustains an organization's culture by selecting out those individuals who might attack or undermine its core values.

Top Management: The actions of top management also have a major impact on the organization's culture. Through what they say and how they behave, senior executives establish norms that filter down through the organization as to whether risk taking is desirable; how much freedom managers should give their employees; what is appropriate dress; what actions will pay off in terms of pay-raises, promotions, and other rewards and the like.

Organizations, over time, often develop unique terms to describe equipment, offices, key personnel, suppliers, customers, or products that relate to its business. New employees are frequently overwhelmed with acronyms and jargon that, after six months on the job, have become fully part of their language. Once assimilated, this terminology acts as a common denominator that unites members of a given culture or sub-culture.

Creating an Ethical Organizational Culture

The content and strength of a culture influences an organization's ethical climate and the ethical behaviour of its members.

An organizational culture most likely to shape high ethical standards is one that's high in risk tolerance, low to moderate in aggressiveness, and focuses on means as well as outcomes. Managers in such a culture are supported for taking risks and innovating, are discouraged from engaging in unbridled competition, and will pay attention to *how* goals are achieved, as well as to *what* goals are achieved.

A strong organizational culture will exert more influence on employees than a weak one. If the culture is strong and supports high ethical standards, it should have a very powerful and positive influence on employee behaviour. Johnson & Johnson, for example, has a strong culture that has long stressed corporate obligations to customers, employees, the community, and shareholders, in that order. When poisoned Tylenol (a Johnson &Johnson product) was found on store shelves, employees at Johnson& Johnson across the United States independently pulled the product from these stores before management had even issued a statement concerning the tamperings. No one had to tell these individuals what was morally right; they knew what Johnson & Johnson would expect them to do. On the other hand, a strong culture that encourages pushing the limits can be a powerful force in shaping unethical behaviour. For instance, Enron's aggressive culture, with unrelenting pressure on executives to rapidly expand earnings, encouraged ethical corner-cutting and eventually contributed to the company's collapse.

What can management do to create a more ethical culture? We suggest a combination of the following practices:

- **Be a visible role model.** Employees will look to top-management behaviour as a benchmark for defining appropriate behaviour. When senior management is seen as taking the ethical high road, it provides a positive message for all employees.
- **Communicate ethical expectations**. Ethical ambiguities can be minimized by creating and disseminating an organizational code of ethics. It should state the organization's primary values and the ethical rules that employees are expected to follow.
- **Provide ethical training**. Set up seminars, workshops, and similar ethical training programs. Use these training sessions to reinforce the organization's standards of conduct; to clarify what practices are and are not permissible; and to address possible ethical dilemmas. Visibly reward ethical acts and punish unethical ones. Performance appraisals of managers should include a point-by-point evaluation of how his or her decisions measure up against the organization's code of ethics. Appraisals must include the means taken to achieve goals as well as the ends themselves. People who act ethically should be visibly rewarded for their behaviour. Just as importantly, unethical acts should be conspicuously punished.
- **Provide protective mechanisms**. The organization needs to provide formal mechanisms so that employees can discuss ethical dilemmas and report unethical behaviour without fear of reprimand. This might include creation of ethical counsellors, ombudsmen, or ethical officers.

Creating a Customer-Responsive Culture

French retailers have a well-established reputation for indifference to customers. Salespeople, for instance, routinely make it clear to customers that their phone conversations should not be interrupted. Just getting any help at all from a salesperson can be a challenge.

And no one in France finds it particularly surprising that the owner of a Paris store should complain that he was unable to work on his books all morning because he kept being bothered *by customers.*

Most organizations today are trying very hard to be un-French-like. They are attempting to create a customer-responsive culture because they recognize that this is the path to customer loyalty and long-term profitability. Companies that have created such cultures—like Southwest Airlines, FedEx, Johnson & Johnson, Nordstrom, Olive Garden, Walt Disney theme parks, Enterprise-Rent-A-Car, Whole Foods, and L.L. Bean—have built a strong and loyal customer base and have generally outperformed their competitors in revenue growth and financial performance. In this section, we will briefly identify the variables that shape customer-responsive cultures and offer some suggestions that management can follow for creating such cultures.

Managerial Action

Based on the previously identified characteristics, we can suggest a number of actions that management can take if it wants to make its culture more customer-responsive. These actions are designed to create employees with the competence, ability, and willingness to solve customer problems as they arise.

Selection: The place to start in building a customer-responsive culture is hiring service-contact people with personality and attitudes consistent with a high service orientation. Southwest Air is a shining example of a company that has focused ill hiring process on selecting out job candidates whose personalities aren't people-friendly. Job applicants go through an extensive interview process at Southwest in which company employees and executives carefully assess whether candidates have the outgoing and fun-loving personality that it wants in all its employees.

Studies show that friendliness, enthusiasm, and attentiveness in service employees positively affect customers' perceptions of service quality.' So managers should look for these qualities in applicants. In addition, job candidates should be screened so new hires have the patience, concern about others, and listening skills that are associated with customer-oriented employees.

Training and Socialization: Organizations that are trying to become more customer-responsive don't always have the option of hiring all new employees. More typically, management is faced with the challenge of making its current employees more customer-focused. In such cases, the emphasis will be on training rather than hiring. This describes the dilemma that senior executives at companies such as General Motors, Shell, and J.P.Morgan Chase have faced in the past decade as they have attempted to move away from their product focus. The content of these training programs will vary widely but should focus on improving product knowledge, active listening, showing patience, and displaying emotions.

In addition, even new employees who have a customer-friendly attitude may need to understand management's expectations. So all new service-contact people should be socialized into the organization's goals and values. Lastly, even the most customer-focused employees can lose direction every once in a while. This should be addressed with regular training updates in which the organization's customer-focused values are restated and reinforced.

Culture and Nations

As business gets global, the culture of a country becomes an important determinant of peoples' behaviour. Stories, rituals, language, traditions etc., of the country impacts the culture of the organization of that country. For instance, cultures differ widely in terms of their concept of time. Besides the obvious implications for punctuality, the difference also lies in how people from different cultures use their time. Many Western cultures (e.g. U.S., Germany, Switzerland etc.) are highly 'mono-chronic', i.e., people from these cultures prefer to deal with one task at a time. Thus, it is normal that a German would plan out every activity in a step-by-step manner. On the other hand, many Latin and Asian countries (e.g. India, Brazil, Spain, Arab Countries etc.) have a 'polychrome' orientation, i.e., it is quite normal for people to deal with more than one activity' at the same time, (it would not be unusual for an Italian or Latin American to interrupt a meeting to make a personal call).

People from polychrome cultures find monochronic cultures too mechanical, compartmentalized, and rigid. On the other hand, people from a monochronic background find polychronism to be an evidence of lack of focus and sincerity.

Similarly, in more individualistic countries (e.g., U.S., Australia, U.K. etc.), it is culturally acceptable to speak one's mind and express disagreements. For a person coming from a collective culture (e.g., Mexico, Indonesia, Japan, China etc.), such expressions would be perceived as discourteous, and even aggressive. On the other hand, in collective cultures, disagreements are expressed (if at all) in more subtle manner, which to a person coming from individualistic culture, would look as dishonest and lacking in trustworthiness.

Social Institutions

Countries differ considerably in the kind of social institutions they have - e.g., the way their education system functions, the way financial system works, the structures of governance etc., — which have a direct impact on how business is conducted in that country. While often not recognized as such, these social institutions are important repositories of a country's culture, and often embody its basic values and assumptions. The educational system in Germany has a heavy emphasis on technical and apprenticeship training. It is quite common for the CEO of a German company to have grown through the Meister system of apprenticeship training, while the MBA education is quite unknown.

CANADA	INDIA
The process of doing business moves fast. Decision making is fast.	The process is more time consuming—long lead times and expanded time frames are required. Indians take a long time to make decisions or finalize agreements, but once trust is established, decisions are often made quickly. Indians are fast to move to a deal or agree on common interests, but slow to complete negotiations. They are more concerned with substantive issues like credit and reliability. Decisions are always taken by the top-level management. Local bureaucracy also slows pace, thereby making the process of decision making very lengthy.
Attitude is 'business to business'; efficiency, quality, accountability, and time, are the key words.	Greater emphasis is placed on personal relationships, which is considered key to a business agreement, and is often regarded as a prerequisite to efficiency, quality, and accountability.
Partnership is more legal or is a contractual agreement.	Partnership is built on long-term, personal relationships, through the establishment of trust. Good rapport is considered more important than a signed agreement.
Personal connections are not as important as the business itself.	Business partners who are well connected are generally considered very important for a successful business venture, as business is generally conducted through connections and personal contacts. Nepotism is high; each layer of the society has its own old boy network.
Direct style of communication is preferred.	Indirect style of communication is generally the norm; sometimes negotiated through a third party for the sake of harmony, essential for maintaining business relationships. Prefer to say what the other party wants to hear, to avoid disharmony.

Monochronic People	Polychronic People
Do one thing at a time.	Do many things simultaneously.
Concentrate on the job.	Are highly distractible and subject to interruptions.
Take time commitments (deadlines, schedules) seriously.	Consider time commitments an objective to be achieved, if possible.
Are low-context and need information.	Are high-context and already have information.
Are committed to the job. Adhere religiously to plans.	Are committed to people and human relationships. Change plans often and easily.
Are concerned about not disturbing others; follow rules of privacy and consideration.	Are more concerned with those who are closely related (family, friends, close business associates) than with privacy.
Show great respect for private property; seldom borrow or lend.	Borrow and lend things often and easily.
Emphasize promptness.	Base promptness on the relationship.
Are accustomed to short-term relationships.	Have strong tendency to build lifetime relationships.

Review Questions

1. What is organizational culture ? Are cultures the same across organizations? Explain with suitable examples.
2. Explain the relationship between culture and ethics or values.
3. How is a responsive culture created ?
4. What are the implications of different cultures on managers?

✿ ✿ ✿

Chapter 15

HR AND OTHER SUBJECTS AND RECENT TRENDS IN HR

Learning Objectives

1. *HR and Other Subjects*
2. *Recent Trends in HR*
3. *Emerging Challenges*
4. *Need to Redesign and Reinvent*
5. *Myths and Realities about HR Profession*
6. *HRM in India*
7. *The Role of HR Professionals*

HR AND OTHER SUBJECTS

A growing acceptance of behavioural science, especially aspects related to needs, motivation, satisfaction, and expectancy, has played a major role in promoting the new theory of management. Most organizations have become increasingly aware of the significance of human hopes and aspirations and are now willing to consider them while decision-making; they are also reconsidering and restructuring their training and management development programmes accordingly. A comparison of the old and current brochures and training manuals of several organizations clearly indicates new inputs in the training contents. A number of sessions are devoted to human resources management in each functional programme.

Sensitivity training, interpersonal relations, superior-subordinate relations, and communication are some areas that are added and/or emphasised in these programmes. This is in addition to specific full length programmes on human relations in industry. The number of executives sponsored by organizations to attend programmes offered by the three Indian Institutes of Management, the Indian Society for Applied Behavioural Science, the National Productivity Council, and the All-India Management Association, their local bodies and other agencies, is increasing. In future, human factors will have to be taken into greater account in running organizations.

There is an element of interdependency as organizations need people as much as people need organizations. In fact, HR integrates social sciences as well as other disciplines that can contribute to the subject. Moreover, HR is developmental. It is concerned with the growth and development of people toward higher levels of competency, creativity and fulfillment because it is the central resource in any organization and society.

HRM has its links with Business Management today but not in the traditional sense. It is more of a Supportive approach that it follows. HRM believes that better treated people achieve better results. The focus therefore is on people orientation rather than task or process orientation in organizations today.

HRM also has its links with Psychology, as people are a different commodity altogether unlike materials and money. Study of nature of the people, individual differences, value of the person and functioning as a team help to improve the management of Human resources. Use of Emotional Quotient and the services of a counsellor to obviate stress, all necessitate a knowledge of Psychology. Thus, the two subjects are brought closer and for better results studied in conjunction with each other rather than in isolation.

Recent Trends in Human Resource Profession Challenges and Opportunities

Introduction

Organisations are exposed to the challenges and opportunities posed by the increasing change and complexities in the business environment. The emergence of globalisation, technical advancements, telecommunication revolution, growth of knowledge based workforce and intense competition, mandate the transformation of Human Resource Management (HRM) in organizations.

Emerging Challenges

The challenges produced by today's rapidly changing environment global competitiveness, workforce diversity, ethical issues, rapid advances in technology and communication, shift away from an exploitative approach to an ecologically sensitive approach to the natural environment. The growing expectations from employees for meaningful work along with opportunities for personal and professional growth — all these require different responses from HR professionals. In the new paradigm of post modern organizations, there is a major shift in the approach to work.

In the post modern world of today, the environment is anything but stable. The organization recognizes the chaotic and unpredictable nature of the world. where organizational boundaries have been diffused and the primary form of capital is not money but information. In this environment, only change is constant. To cope with this chaos, organizations need a decentralized structure that emphasises horizontal co-operation. The trend has shifted from highly structured bureaucratic approaches to more flexible management systems that empower employees to make decisions and provide intrinsic job satisfaction. The older form of management is inadequate to cope with the new problems of the present day world. Equality, empowerment, horizontal relationship and consensus building are important in the post-modern organisation (Daft,1997).

Similarly, traditional concepts of the nature of work itself have also been eroded (Minehan,1996). Increasingly, organizations are pursuing workplace initiatives, combining non-traditional work practices, settings and locations to supplement : conventional offices(Apgar,1998). Attention is being paid to the manner in which work is organized in order to take advantage of flexible labour deployment. High performance work practices have been introduced to build employee advantage (Whitfield commitment. These practices can provide a source of competitive Poole, 1997).

The major competitive challenges faced by executives include:

- Globalization
- Building and operating customer responsive organizations
- Profitability through cost and growth
- Redefining organizational capabilities for sustained and integrated individual competencies
- Focusing on transformation to create fundamental and enduring change, making technology a viable and productive part of work setting
- Attracting, retaining as well as measuring intellectual competence.

These challenges and changes in organizational structure and work place practices; necessitate changes in style of human resource management. Human resource management is referred as the systems and processes within a firm (for example; staffing, compensation, and communication), that govern people and how, their work is done (Ulrich, 1997). These processes must be judged by the extent to which they enhance competitiveness.

The new competitive reality described above, calls for a new agenda focused on championing competitiveness for both, HR practices and HR professionals. The HR professional's role includes the development of individual and organizational capability, developing HR strategies for better organizational performance, making change happen, and developing intellectual capital (Hathcock, 1996: Heneman *et al.*,1998). Ulrich (1997) suggested that HR holds the key to success in overcoming the challenges facing today's executives. These challenges required that HR practices add value and the HR functions deliver business results. Response to these challenges should focus on organizational capabilities such as speed, responsiveness, relationships, agility, learning, and employee competence. Organisations have to learn, move and act faster than those of their competitors and HR practices should be seen as a source of competitive advantage. HR professionals should focus on quality of the deliverables of their work in terms of value than doing or completing and articulate their role creation (Ulrich, 1997). Weiss (1997) presents an interesting metaphor:

Need to Redesign and Reinvent

"Human resources as profession, must redesign itself into an active business partner, totally integrated into business ethos. If it does not do this soon, under enlightened leadership, it will become the vacuum tube of the 21st century-occasionally used, narrowly specialized, nostalgically remembered and wholly irrelevant."

HR professionals must reinvent their role as strategic business partners in shaping and directing strategic outcomes to ensure their viability. There is a need to restructure HR function by reorganizing the HR department, its systems and process. HR professionals must be prepared to adopt contemporary dimensions to their roles to meet the challenges posed by emerging organizational realities. They must be able to identify the capabilities critical to business success and design and deliver human resource management practices that can create these capabilities. The major concern of HR managers will be to figure out how to build organizational capacity to maximize the potential of business.

Myths and Realities about HR Profession

There are a number of myths and misconceptions about the HR profession. Line managers have propagated these myths, and this needs to. be overcome. HR professionals should ensure that such myths are not perpetuated and people in the organisation understand the realities of HR. They have to be practice, perform their sole to build competencies and art in a professional manner. Ulrich (1997) has presented these myths and realities (see figure 1)

Old Myths	*New Realities*
People go into HR because they like people.	HR departments are not designed to provide corporate therapy or as social and health and happiness retreats. HR professionals must create the practices that make employees more competitive, not more comfortable.
Anyone can do HR.	HR activities are based on theory and research. HR professionals must master both theory and practice.
HR deals with the soft side of a business and therefore is not accountable.	The impact of HR practice on business results can be measured. HR professionals must learn how to translate their work into financial performance.
HR focuses on costs, which must be controlled.	HR practices must create value by increasing the intellectual capital within a firm. HR professionals must add value, not reduce costs.
HRs job is to be the policy police and the health and happiness patrol.	The HR function does not own compliance managers do HR practices do not exist to make employees happy to help them to become committed. HR professionals but must help managers commit employees and administer policies.
HR is full of fads.	HR practices have evolved over time. HR professionals must see their current work as part of an evolutionary chain and explain their work with less jargon and more authority.
HR is staffed by nice people.	At times, HR practices should force vigorous debates. HR professionals should be confirmative and challenging as well as supportive.
HRs is HR job.	HR work is as important to line managers, as are finances, strategy and other business domains.

Myths that keep HR from being a Profession

HR professional's role and responsibilities in any organization is influenced by number of factors including the environment of the organization; business goals and strategy, organizational structure, culture, technology, and employment system. While there are certain generic or "culture-free factors" that shape the role of HR globally, it should also be recognized that "culture bound" factors exist and these will determine the focus of HR practice in any country. The factors, which influence the HR profession are given in the figure below.

HRM in India

In India, there have been some changes happening in HRM systems and the role of HR professionals in the context of changing business environment, but the progress has not always been dramatic. Many organizations have changed the name of personnel department into HRD/M department, but the focus on HR is still lacking barring few exceptions. There is little support from the top management, as they feel that HRD/M has not lived up to their expectations.

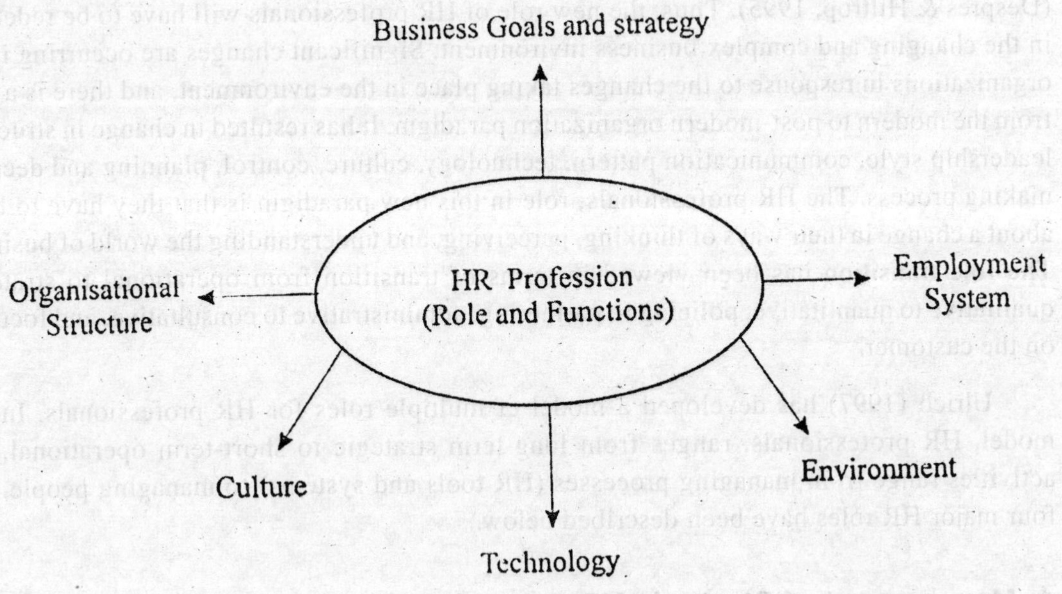

Tactors Influencing HR Profession

THE ROLE OF HR PROFESSIONALS

Many commentators agree that the role of HR professionals in the future would be pivotal as business strategists. This will require considerable business acumen and the ability to contribute effectively to strategic decision-making (James, 1997;McNerny,1996).HR professionals also act as change agents by developing competence in managing and implementing change (Micolo, 1996; Mohrman, & Lawler, 1997). Wilhelm (1995) suggested that change management competencies, in conjunction with business competence and HR craft, competence, comprise a model of a complete human resource professional for the foreseeable future.

A number of other important roles will become characteristic of the HR professional. The ability to design high value added agendas within the organization and to ensure that HR practices are aligned and unified around these agendas is critical (Brockbank, 1997; Heneman, *et al.,* 1998). HR professionals also need to become business partners of the line managers - ensuring that line managers acquire the competencies needed to perform the HR tasks that are being added to their jobs (Brenner, 1996; Heneman, *et al.,* 1998). They will need to take advantage of information technology to encourate the development of organizational capabilities and develop computer based HR systems to provide some freedom from daily administration (Mohraman & Lawler, 1997). HR professionals will increasingly need to utilize outsourcers to reduce HR costs and tap into expertise not readily available in the organization (McNerny, 1996, Mohrman & Lawler, 1998). In addition, developing high levels of competence in designing and implementing HR systems is essential in knowledge intensive organizations (Despres & Hiltrop, 1995). Thus, the new role of HR professionals will have to be redefined in the changing and complex business invironment. Significant changes are occurring in the organizations in response to the changes taking place in the environment, and there is a shift from the modern to post-modern organization paradigm. It has resulted in change in structure, leadership style, communication pattern, technology, culture, control, planning and decision making process. The HR professionals; role in this new paradigm is that they have to bring about a change in their ways of thinking, perceiving, and understanding the world of business. The role transition has been viewed in terms of transition from operational to strategic, qualitative to quantitative, policing to partnering, administrative to consultative, and focusing on the customer.

Ulrich (1997) has developed a model cf multiple roles for HR professionals. In this model, HR professionals, ranges from long-term strategic to short-term operational, and activities range from managing processes (HR tools and systems) to managing people. The four major HR roles have been described below.

1. Management of Strategic HR

The focus of strategic HR manager is to translate business strategies into HR priorities through organizational diagnosis. The have to act as "strategic partners by participating in the process of defining business strategies, and help executives to accomplish business objectives by aligning HR practices with business strategy.

2. Management of Firm Infrastructure

HR professionals should design and deliver efficient HR processes for staffing, training, appraising, rewarding, promoting and managing the flow of employees in the organization. They should work as efficient administrators by reengineering HR processes and reward those who are efficient. They should engage themselves in those activities, which lead to continued reengineering of work processes.

3. Management of Employee Contribution

HR professionals should involve themselves in day-to-day problems, concerns, and needs of the employees. They should try to develop intellectual capital so that they become competent and committed.

4. Management of Transformation and Change

HR professionals should add value to a firm to manage transformation and change by altering the culture. They should act like change agents by identifying and framing problems, building relationships based on trust, solving problems and creating and fulfilling action plans. Thus, the importance of HR (systems, and processes), and HR professionals (implementer of these systems and processes) has grown after the realization that the 'people' aspect really matters and it can make a difference. With shifting priorities, HR professionals are moving to leadership positions, and organizations depend on them to improve their performance (Kemske, 1998). HR professionals have to look for opportunities to acquire influence within the world of organizations, and to make top management understand the importance of HR. An analysis of some of the Indian HRD award winning companies indicates that excellent performers do follow good HR practices. Rao (2000) has presented an interesting analysis of HRD award winning companies and found that most of them continue to grow and expand despite a turbulent environment. These companies consciously built internal competencies and acquired sustaining capability. They also coped well with the challenges of liberalization and exploited opportunities by becoming customer oriented and quality conscious. They changed the structure and culture of the organization and benchmarked their HR system. They have been continuously improving them in order to become learning organizations. The role of HR department to initiate these changes through their HR managers is praiseworthy, as their involvement spanned strategic planning, quality programs and restructuring exercises.

Total Quality Implementation in Managing Human Resources

Introduction

The total quality approach is changing the role of HR manager by changing the expectations of the stakeholders, within and outside the profession, with regard to HRM responsibilities. Thus, while HR professionals reflect the organisational culture within which they are working, they also are expected to influence and shape it. A preview of these changing expectations and the difference total quality makes is indicated in the following table in which a comparison of traditional and total quality HRM approaches is provided.

Basis of Distinction	*Traditional HRM Approach*	*Total Quality HRM Approach*
1. Philosophy	A fair day's work for a fair day's pay.	Shared responsibility commitment, and rewards.
2. Business Objectives	Increased productivity, profitability, quality is secondary, focus on labour.	Increased quality, productivity, customer satisfaction, employee satisfaction and loyalty.
3. Quality Objectives	Adequate quality to remain in business; staff driven approaches to quality improvements.	Total quality management and continuous improvement across every level.
4. Business Information Sharing	Limited to information on an as-needed basis for job performance.	Open books, share broad information on profits, productivity, quality, costs, and capital spending plans.
5. Major Constituencies	Managers, stockholders, customers, and employees.	Customers, all employees, and stockholders.
6. Employee Involvement	Programmes, suggestions, plans, individual employees awards; usually no formal system.	Extensive within and between levels and functions; "way of life" pattern.
7. Education and Training	On the job training, feedback on job performance.	Quality and economic education, multiple skill training, problem solving and group process.
8. Reward Structure	Management designed and administered.	Designed and adjusted by management-employee committee; formal, and early union movement.
9. Job Security	Labour as a variable cost, layoffs common during business turnarounds.	Formal commitment — a key consideration in all decisions.

Implementing TQ HRM

This concentrates mainly on three areas as:

1. Theoretical models for Implementing Total Quality.
2. Total Quality Integrated Implementation plan for managing Human Resources.
3. Probable pitfalls in Implementation of TQ HRM.

They are discussed as follows:

1. Theoretical Models

There are at least six different theoretical models for implementing total quality. They are:

(i) Total Quality Element Approach: Uses elements of quality improvements program rather than full implementation of a total quality system, such as quality circles, statistical process control and quality function deployment used in isolation.

(ii) Guru Approach: Uses the writings of Devicing, Juran and Crosby for analysis and implementation. Deming's 14 point model is an example.

(iii) Japanese Model Approach: Uses the writings of such Japanese writers as Kqoru Ishikawa and the educational guideliness of the Union of Japanese Scientist and Engineers.

(iv) Industrial Company Model Approach: Leaders from one organisation visit another organisation using total quality, identify its system and integrate this information with their own or European Quality Award ideas to create a customized approach.

(v) Hoshin Planning Approach: Focuses on successful planning, deployment and execution of monthly diagnosis, developed by the Japanese firm Bridgestone and used successfully by HP.

(vi) Prize-Award Criteria Approach: Uses the criteria for Deming Prize, the Baldrize Award, European Quality Awards etc., to identify areas of improvement and follow criteria guidelines for a system change.

The most useful Total Quality implementation plan would be an integrated blend of all approaches mentioned above.

Total Quality Integrated Implementation Plan for Managing Human Resources

An integrated plan for implementing total quality HRM must meet a number of criteria to incorporate the system throughout the organisation and be operationally useful.

(i) It must identify activities, indicators and timeliness to adopting total quality HR improvements efforts at distant phases in the total quality HR implementation process.

(ii) It must recognise the need for completing institutional assessment efforts and ethical work culture diagnoses at critical phases in the development process.

(iii) It must identify four levels at which total quality HR improvement efforts may be initiated. They are:

(a) Strategic Implementation.

(b) Process Implementation.

(c) Project Implementation.

(d) Individual Performance Evaluation.

(iv) It must recognise the need for continual evaluation and control of the HR area and its quality improvement efforts with the evaluation and control based on facts.

The Total Quality integrated implementation plan meets the above criteria and presents a flow of seven operational steps for systematic implementation. This integrated approach to implementation is necessary if the situational feasibility of every organisation is to be considered. The seven operational steps for systematic implementation are:

1. Goal Setting Implementation.
2. Assessment Implementation.
3. Strategy Implementation.
4. Process Implementation.
5. Project Implementation.
6. Individual Performance Implementation.
7. Evaluation and Control Implementation.

A total quality integrated implementation plan consists of actions required to achieve each stage. Each action in turn, specifies what should be done, who should be doing it, why this particular action is necessary, how the action should be carried out, when it should be done and what indicators are required to ensure that it has been completed.

Probable Pitfalls in Application of TQ HRM

The following are the three reasons why TQ HRM seems to languish.

(i) Programmatic Overexpectation: Unrealistic expectation for success.

(ii) Conceptual Failure: The theories about causation and the relationships underlying the policies and programmes are inaccurate and incomplete.

(iii) Implementation Failure: The failure to carry out policy and programmes as designed.

1. Enhanced workplace portals and intranets: As enterprise portals evolve into worker productivity tools, several HR domains will benefit from new online solutions, including e-health tools, defined contribution health care models, compensation systems and performance management tools.

Other personalization features will continue to expand, with a new emphasis on web services that provide data that organizations and their employees need.

2. Increased technology access to more workforce segments: Companies will continue initiatives to get more employees web-connected, allowing greater access to corporate systems and HR information from home or travel.

3. Greater reliance on ROI (return on investment) Tools: Top management will exert more pressure on HR to justify investments in HR technology through ROI analysis and business case development.

4. Growing focus on optimizing current HR systems: Sensibility will be the key factor as companies seek system optimization and integration solutions. Optimization trends will include improving legacy systems and connecting existing disparate systems.

5. Increased use of virtual workplaces: With an eye toward increasing worker productivity, approaches such as online meetings, project team workspaces, web conferences and video conferencing will continue to gain popularity, with the added benefits of controlling costs, employee safety and time commitments.

6. Decision support tools: Traditionally the province of financial departments, HR departments will begin using analytical tools to measure the success of their HR practices and to predict future results.

7. Business continuance planning: The 2001 terrorist attacks spurred a new understanding of HR's critical role in helping companies get their people back to work by providing space, systems and support that employees need to be productive. Look for sharpened HR involvement in employee communications and disaster recovery plans.

8. Increased standardization of XML (extensible mark-up language) data schemes and structure: Growing co-operation between organizations will continue the trend of standards that are usable for HR domains. The HR-XML consortium (www.hr-xml.org) has already completed schemes supporting recruiting, benefits enrollment, and time and expense reporting, and plans more in 2002.

9. Attention to small cost-saving measures that add up: Following the substantial cost-cutting measures many companies implemented in 2001. HR will focus on the cumulative effect of additional process improvements and cost-saving initiatives, such as technologies that improve data accuracy and easy data access.

10. Demand for better integration and collaboration between vendors: HR will carefully select technologies to meet overall business needs and examine how vendor services can be bundled. Vendor performance measurement and ease of integration with other solutions will be critical factors.

Emerging Trends in Managing Human Resources

If we trace back the history of business environment, in the early years, trading patterns and markets were stable, technology was static, customers were passive, speed in getting to market was secondary, competition was limited to sectors and regions, and hierarchies were generally accepted in all walks of life. No more, since 1960s, America and much of the rest of the world has been almost continually buffeted by change. Customers demand that businesses do it better, faster, cheaper and employees want to control more than the "Stop" button on the assembly line. The twentieth century saw nations around the world become part of the global village, with trade barriers between them reduced or removed completely. Globalization of trade and economy are taking deep roots in India. The holistic paradigm shift to a single global company has opened up new economic opportunities. Events of the last five years of the previous century have focused our attention on knowledge industries. Quality human resources have therefore become an important base with which to respond to the emerging environment. The knowledge workforce in particular has a vital role to play in the emergence of the digital economy.

A look at the trends in managing people in this dynamic industry reflects that Attracting, Managing, Nurturing talent and Retaining people has emerged to be the single most critical issue in lieu of the enormous opportunities spun off by the market. The new avatar of talent is the knowledge professional who is innovative, business savvy, quick on the uptake, has an instinctive ability to network, and possessing unbridled ambition. They are propelled by an urge to experiment, scan new avenues that can spur their creativity. The knowledge professional will gravitate to an organization that is flexible, has strong values, a robust performance ethic and provides challenging work on latest technology. This has led to companies proactively taking measures on three fronts. First, companies create an organizational ambience where talent can bloom. Second, they put in place systems that help unleash their potential and third, they build a reward and recognition mechanism that provides value for people.

Profound systemic changes have been seen in the way companies are structured. The concepts of leadership and managing people gave undergone a radical rethink. Cubicles, hierarchies and rigid organization structures of the past, have now given way to open work environment, flat structure with informality being a general rule and empowerment of individuals. Today work itself is centred around projects, which have virtual teams working on them. This work structure has led to a culture of flexi time, round the clock accessibility to the workplace. Also catching up fast is the trend of workstations at home, remote access, video-conferencing and reporting by exception. To stay one step ahead of the aspirations of their people, companies are continuously striving to provide an intellectually stimulating — environment. Few examples being, in-house libraries, continuous upgradation of knowledge and skills, knowledge sharing, building relationships with academia, thus, enabling knowledge workers to pursue multiple careers within a single company. Coming times will see sabbaticals forming part of the organization culture, corporate universities dotting the new horizon, competing companies bunching together to setup knowledge networks.

Companies today are constantly striving towards enhancing the quality of work life and also the personal life of its employees and this does not stop with the employee but gets extended to his/her family as well. In-house health clubs, yoga and meditation centres to relieve stress, sports and cultural activities, employees get-togethers with invitations to come over with families, day care centres and many of the like are being provided by companies.

With the increasing size of the companies, the top down communication model of yesteryears has been replaced by bottom up, cross level communication thereby encouraging people to voice their opinions and feelings. Open house sessions, mentoring, online chats on the intranet have emerged to be the communication enablers.

The new economy has given rise to a culture of working in teams. Today no job in the knowledge industry can be performed in isolation. Since working in teams is not a passing fad, companies are now designing compensation structures, which rewards team performance in addition to individual performance.

To conclude, change is here to stay, and we need to understand that all the practices that are working today may not necessarily work tomorrow. Customers' expectations, market changes and strategic decisions will drive the tools to managing the human assets.

Reference

http://www.humanlinks.com/manres/articles/trends hr.htm

http://www.careerindia.com/careerhub/workplacewatch/ingoodco/2912ehr.htm/

Review Questions

1. Explain recent trends in HR profession.
2. What are the challenges and opportunities of HR profession.
3. Explain the role of HR professionals.

✿ ✿ ✿

CASE STUDIES

Case Let : 1

GROWING PAIN`S OF THE PENNATHUR TYRE COMPANY

The Pennathur Tyre Company (PTC) was incorporated as a partnership firm in 1986. According to Mr.Mani, who had worked with the foreign tyre company nearly 15 years, there was no company that really had for its major aim the production of tyres at the minimum cost and their sale to the customer at the affordable price. Mr.Mani started PTC in partnership with close friends. Mr.Mani was actively involved in the business.

As business began to expand, more customer services was added and the company attained excellent reputation for its wheel balancing service. In 1998, the company had to expand its premises, operation and personnel. Mr.Mani described them to me as follows: "Sometimes I wish we had never expanded our business. At first, it was exciting to expand the business and services to our customers. But because of our increased staff size, we are beginning to lose control. The personal touch that they established with our customers seems to be slowly slipping away. Employees must be more customer oriented, but they seem to be more concerned about their interdepartmental problems. For instance, last week, while a customer was waiting patiently, the mechanic who was to have changed the oil and filter in his car was arguing with the clerk. Customers are serviced without delays bother me."

"Another potential problem lies in the way some employees come across to others in the company. For instance, young brash Engineer who is knowledgeable and productive has serious looks and talks very abrupt and in other extreme people who are just opposite, laughing and joking all time."

"Ultimately, I would like to see each service department as individual profit centres and share the additional profits with the workers. I am thinking that if employees have stake profits they will work harder and no supervising is required. But they should work well together so there is more collaboration and joint problem solving rather than competition and dysfunctional conflicts. I was wondering if you have advice for me on how to handle these issues".

Discussion Questions

1. Do you think Mr.Mani should increase the price of the tyres?
2. Should Mr.Mani and his partners go in for expansion?
3. What steps should Mr.Mani and his partners take to make employees more customer oriented?
4. How should the Interdepartmental conflict be solved?
5. How should the stress levels be decreased among the employees?

Case Let : 2

COPING WITH JOB STRESS

Shivakumar, a manager with KL Technologies, has coped well with his outplacement because he has never relied solely on his job to provide him with a sense of self-esteem. He realised that, when Mass System Private Ltd., acquired KL Technologies in 1989, a Mass System Manager would be replaced as soon as the merger was completed. But after 18 years of working for KL Technologies, he still found the layoff hard to take. His typical day begins with a visit to the office of an outplacement firm in Adyar, Chennai. He makes a few calls and dictates a letter or two to a staff secretary. He has inquired about 50 jobs and pursued about 6. He received an offer from one corporation in Karnataka, but he didn't want to move that far. Shivakumar insists that he is flexible and open to jobs in organisations much smaller than KL Technologies and to jobs that probably cannot match his former six-figure salary. He maintains his active involvement in the Red Cross of Chennai because it enables him a feeling of self-worth. He understands that losing a job is an emotional blow, but it doesn't have to be a career disaster. He consulted a major human resources consulting firm, which indicated him about several steps to make the period of unemployment shorter.

- Stay clam. The worst mistake that you can make is to reach out frantically for the first job you can find.
- Save your network of contacts and friends until you are ready to move.
- Be flexible. The more broadly you define your skills, the greater are your options.
- Maintain a daily routine. Visit the outplacement firm regularly, eat well, exercise and take time to relax.
- Try to avoid emotional highs and lows.

Discussion Questions

1. Why do you think Shivakumar found if difficult to manage the layoff?
2. Discuss the work behaviour of Shivakumar.

Case Let : 3

PLANNED CHANGE AT THE PIEDMONT CORPORATION

The Piedmont Corporation produces and markets variety computer products for the global market. In order to compete in this industry firms need to introduce new products which requires co-ordination among different functional departments. For major products Piedmont creates task forces for co-ordination, the different co-ordination needed to develop, produce and sell the product. Stan Ledford headed omega task-force for introducing the new omega word processor. Task held for four half day meetings, but Stan felt frustrated by the progress of meeting and attributed these feelings to members, inability to work well together. Stan explained his problem to his close friend who then advised to meet the members of division of HR department. Stan met Sue Serbia an internal consultant for Piedmont who specialised in OD and he explained ideas about task force's problem. Sue then suggested about team-building strategy and she would facilitate this process by interviewing team members about their perceptions of the problem and feeding the data back to members at special meeting. Sue suggested Stan to take active leadership role in team-building and whether to use her as their consultant.

Stan agreed and at team, next meeting he described with Sue and outlined team building proposal, members were interactive and agreed to try team building. Sue conducted one hour interview with each member and they were aimed at 3 major areas things team did well, things that impeded task performance and suggestion for improvement. Interview data was placed on a large sheet of newsprint. In feedback options and save suggestions she provided input about the role of group norms in determining members, behaviours. Members thanked Sue for solving the problem and group were able to handle the problems. Next few months Stan and his team implemented most of the suggestions from the feedback session. Omega team was judged by Piedmont executives to be one of its most affective new product task-force.

Discussion Questions

1. Describe the readiness for change that seems to be exhibited by individuals in this case?
2. Would you describe the change approach in use as action research? Why or why not?
3. Using the force field analysis techniques discussed in the chapter, analyse this case. Be specific about the pressures for change and the resistance to change that seem to be operating in this situation. Identify which types of pressure and resistance are likely to be the strongest?
4. Use the systems model of change to identify key variables that might be changed in order to increase the overall effectiveness of Piedmont Corporation?

Case Let : 4

SPOOKED BY COMPUTERS

The New Delhi Arts project has its headquarters in South Delhi. The project has five full time employees, but during festive season, they hire as many as six part-time workers to type, address envelopes and send out mailings. Samantha, for instance was the executive director, head of the office, but she would be found doing the same job like the part-timers.

Despite a constant sense of being a month behind, the office ran relatively smoothly. The office would be stacked with people sometimes but that would not put down the workers. The office had started to spend more on part-time workers. Hence, Mr.Vivek, the office co-ordinator suggested to get a Computer. Vivek was fresh out of college and to him computer was a tool to make job easier. But his belief was not shared by others in the office, they felt the computer would eat the project's mailing list, send wrong things to wrong people, convincing them that the project was a faceless organisation that did not care.

Samantha began to wonder if they should get a computer or not? So, did the others. They consulted Samantha regarding this issue after the office hours. They began to feel that they will have to look out for other job. They feared that they will have to learn the computer language along with the English Vocabulary which they are still struggling to improvise.

One time morning, Samantha called Vivek into the office and asked him if he could recommend any computer consultants. Samantha had read an article about computers that had changed her mind. Vivek was pleased because Samantha had evidently accepted the idea of a computer in the office. But at the same time, Vivek realised that he has a lot of work to do henceforth.

Discussion Questions

1. Is organisation development appropriate in this situation? Why or why not?
2. What kinds of resistance to change have the employees of the project displayed?
3. What can Vivek do to overcome the resistance?

Case Let : 5

RISING UP FROM THE LOWS

Twenty seven year old Rita was diagnosed and treated with depression as a teenager. But after a move to Delhi, and at the time of accepting a demanding job as an account manager, she felt healthy and ready for the challenge. The trigger for a relapse came in the form of a relationship break-up, combined with dealing with a demanding work client. Things started to spin out of control. "I would come to work and turn on my computer, but just couldn't cope. I was just going through the motions," she says.

Within three months Rita was on the verge of suicide and sought help from a doctor, she was soon on antidepressants. "This helped me to stop and think about things in a rational and relaxed way, and enabled me to finally address the problem with my manager."

"I don't blame the employer or employees for not noticing. But if there was more awareness and less stigma in the workplace, it might have not got to the point it did and perhaps reduced the effect it had just on me but my work environment too."

Rahul is a director of marketing communications companies 360, the Glasshouse and Determine. His experiences with employee depression including Rita has taught him to take a proactive approach to creating a positive and open workplace for employees and he is a strong advocate for other organisations to actively create opportunities for people to open up about their difficulties in a safe and comfortable way. "It is definitely becoming more and more prevalent than in years gone by," says Rahul. "Employees who are usually bright, bubbly and intelligent may suddenly go through increased mood swings, a changed work ethic and find it hard to get through the day."

Rahul says he is now quicker to respond to such cases and develop ways of moving forward, "in hindsight, with Rita, I was too slow to put the pieces together." He recommends creating an environment promoting understanding and honesty. "Have a weekly one-to-one session; outline your expectations for the week. Check that your employees are comfortable with that; encourage them to let you know if they think it might be too much, or if they are having a bad day."

Discussion Questions

1. What should be done to clear up employees' grievances?
2. How does mood swings affect the work environment?
3. Rita should be made to come out of the depression. Justify.

Case Let : 6

MURUGAN CLEANING CENTERS

Currently, the Murugan Cleaning Centers have no formal orientation and training policies or procedures, and Swetha believes, this is one of the reason the expected standards thought by her and her father are not followed by the employees. They preferred certain level of practices and procedures for dealing with customers at the front counters. For example, all customers should be treated "Big Wear", where at time of billing, the garments should be inspected for damages and stains and told to the customers when they notice one and be replaced even before the customers come over to complain about the store. Then the garments should be immediately replaced and a ticket with the customers name and telephone number should be noted clearly and precisely on all the copies. And they are also made to give the customers other services so that they return to the store. Finally, as the customers leave, the counter person is supposed to make a courteous comment like "have a nice day" and "drive safely". Each other jobs in the stores like pressing, ironing etc., should be done in a certain procedure and maintain the standard which Shwetha and her father prefers.

Shwetha feels the company has other problems because of a lack of adequate employee training and orientation. For example, two employees got very upset last month when they were not paid on the Friday, but instead were paid only on next Tuesday. The owners use the extra two days in part to give them to me to obtain everyone's hours and compute their pay. According to Shwetha, the reason why they do this is because, they have found psychologically that they seem to be less likely to just walk out on them on Friday evening and not to show on the Monday morning if they were paid. Many new strategies were also made by the owners so that the employees can be taught of ethical values and the customers can be satisfied.

Discussion Questions

1. What sort of training do you think the employees of Murugan Cleaning Centers require?
2. How would you go about determining what the specific training objectives should be?
3. What are the strategies followed to satisfy the customers of Murugan Cleaning Centers?

Case Let : 7

INDIAN BAKER COMPANY

As a result of rapid growth in sales, the Indian Baker Company had to double the size of the central secretarial pool. Many of the current secretaries, ages 35 to 55, had been with the company since its inception. None had more than high school education. The group had previously been given the assignment of hiring new secretaries; it was felt that the doubling of staff required addition of persons with advanced data processing skills. Eight secretaries were hired by the management. Several had education beyond high school, and all were in their 20s. Unexpectedly, the performance level of the pool fell off drastically even though doubled in size. The manager interviewed a few of the old staff and they told him that the secretaries just didn't fit in. They were hard to work with, wouldn't listen, and would not take that direction. When their mistakes were corrected, they got offended. In interviewing the few of the secretaries, they told him that the older secretaries refused to listen to new and more efficient ideas, They complained they were unable to use their training and the older secretaries would not socialize with them.

Discussion Questions

1. Why do you think the productivity of the group has fallen?
2. What would you recommend doing about this problem?

Case Let : 8

TYPES OF TRAINING

Organization with over 20,000 employees. We are working with a newly established Project Management Office responsible for providing services across the various departments.

There is a directive in place to establish common learning priorities for staff across the organization. One of the areas where they need to enhance in order to accomplish their aggressive business plan is in Project Management. The challenge facing by this client were establishing a new PMO and wanted all their newly hired project managers to have a common level of advanced understanding in project management. They had decided to hire novice to intermediate project managers and to provide for them a development path to get them a more advanced level.

Senior management felt that they need a programme designed and delivered by instructors. By having an in-house programme, they would be able to save costs in the long-term as well as use this training as a team-building opportunity.

With the input and collaboration of this organization's management, we designed a customized curriculum for a 'Maters of Project Management' certificate programme. This four week programme was scheduled to coincide with the start of these newly hired project managers. The curriculum was approved and forwarded to create training material. The curriculum included extensive training workshops in communication skills, change management skills, facilitation skills, and team building skills and the course included marked exam at each module.

We provided two instructors, they were able to assess the students, strengths and weaknesses areas for further improvement.

We graduated all fifteen students, who were ecstatic about the training and felt that the instructors were top notch. They are already working on projects and demonstrating excellent competencies. Due to the success of initial offering, the client is planning to offer this programme regularly for project managers across the organization.

Discussion Questions

1. What are the types of training they received?

2. How effective was the training and useful for the managers in the organization?

Case Let : 9

The Continuation With Case 8

One division was about to undertake a program aimed at improving several of its business processes. The program comprised of several sub-projects, senior management wanted to have each project managed by one of their functional managers in order to give them a professional development opportunity, also wanted to ensure success of these critical organizational projects.

They determined sending managers on traditional training will not be sufficient to mitigate risks if projects were not managed properly. Also they understood the benefit of not reinventing the wheel by seeking some best practices for managing these projects.

Key goals were to find an external partner that could:

- Provide an experienced and PMP certified project managers who would take on the role and bring expertise in training and development as well as executing.
- Bring an established project manager methodology equipped with customizable processes, guiding steps and templates.
- Take on a mentoring role for project managers, at the same time remaining hands-on in terms of problem solving, executive reporting and change management.

Bay 3000 matches client's needs with one of senior consultant who brought past expertise in the public sector. The consultant felt that it would be essential to give team a common level of understanding the frame work of project management. She conducted training sessions, which proved extremely valuable and a proactive way to ensure understanding as well as set expectations.

With the Bay 3000 methodology as a guide, the consultant worked with project managers and the sponsors through the planning processes for each of the sub-projects. Once project plans were fully developed and appropriate resources allocated, the consultant was to mentor the project manager as they executed the project plan. Mentorship included problem solving, facilitating, sessions, progress tracking and sponsor, the consultant provided program-level status and performance reports, issue management, program bulletins and resource management.

The organization delivered all four sub-projects on time and obtained approval to proceed additional projects. The functional managers, who had no experience in managing projects, are capable of managing independently. Finally, the organization now set consistent templates and processes that they can reuse in future projects.

Discussion Questions

1. What is the type of training given to the managers?
2. How was the training helpful to them in solving the problem?

Case Let : 10

WORK-LIFE BALANCE

A good employer is differentiated from any other employer through the feeling of 'well-being' that is generated at the workplace by the employees. A balance between work and personal goals, and wants of an employee contributes positively to the retention of employees. Although compensation given, employees long for an employer who understands the importance of the employee's work as well as his/her personal requirements. Flexi-timing is one of the popular initiatives that IT company has implemented to bring in work-life balance. Employees are allowed to put in an average of nine hours of work a day according to their convenience. Working mothers were offered a choice to work half days and allowed to complete their work from home. Telecommuting was another facility allowing greater flexibility; here, employees could work from their homes using new technologies such as broadband for conferencing. The importance of employees' families began to be recognized and efforts were made to build strong bond between the company and the entire family of each employee. Sometimes, they give a day off on the employee's birthday or on an anniversary or organizing annual events, parties and picnics for employees and their families or providing easy educational loans to benefit the children of the employees or initiating school drop and pick-up services for them. In 2002, the compnay started the 'Maitree' initiative. The idea was to build a sense of extended family among the families associated with the company. The programme was targeted at the wives of employees who were asked to volunteer a few hours a day for a social cause in association with NGOs. In addition to this programme, maitree.com, an employee portal was also established simultaneously to help employees in relocation, children's education, etc.

Discussion Questions

1. Will flexi-time be effective in this company?

Case Let : 11

LEADERSHIP

Poor leadership was identified as one of the reason for employee attrition through surveys. It is observed that leaders incapable of motivating and guiding employees to change jobs frequently. Wipro initiated the 'Wipro Leaders', 'Quality Survey' in 1992. The programme was end-to-end in nature with a 360 degrees survey process. In this plan, each leader would eventually prepare a 'Personal Development Plan' depending on the feedback he/she got. Wipro also incorporated 'Life Cycle Leadership Programmes' that included different leadership programmes for employees at various levels of management. For instance, the 'Entry-Level Programme' (ELP) was targeted at campus hires and lateral hires at the junior level, and aimed at developing managerial qualities within the employee. Similarly, the 'New Leaders' Programme' (NLP) and 'Wipro Leaders' Programme' (WLP) were aimed at developing potential managers and middle-level employees. The 'Business Leaders' Programme' (BLP) was for senior leaders with business responsibility. The BLP programme covered commercial orientation, client relationship development, and team building and performance management responsibilities among other things. The 'Strategic Leaders' Programme' (SLP) covered the top management employees with a focus and building star performers. Wipro conducted the SLP in association with leading business schools of international repute. Satyam incorporated a 'Leadership Development Programme' which enabled associates to realistically manage lateral and vertical growth in business, technical and delivery streams. The company initiated leadership training programmes such as the 'Harvard Global Leadership Programme' which included lectures from professors of Harvard University. Leadership forums were also initiated at Satyam; these comprised a leader and a number of team members who strove to enhance the maturity levels of processes and service offerings in order to delight stakeholders. In 2001, Infosys established the Infosys Leadership Institute to identify and groom future Infosys leaders. The prime objective was to equip employees with leadership qualities so that the company would have leaders working with leaders for the success of the organization.

Discussion Questions

1. What is leadership? What are the ways to improve qualities of a leader?

Case Let : 12

R.David Thomas, founder and senior chairman of Bonevista International Inc., is known as a great communicator by his franchisees. Some may even recognize him as the lonely boy from his autobiography, Dave's Way. But Samuel, Bonevista's chairman and CEO sees him as "Bonevista's Dad". According to him "no other chain has an active founder like him leading the way".

In fact, after ten years of virtually non-stop building the Bonevista's name, Thomas retired from day-to-day management in the early 1980s. "I felt the company people smarter than me to run" he expliained. His charming modesty proved to be a liability, however, after his departure in a short time franchise problems arose on heels. Many of Bonevista's original franchise owners had sold their stores to owners who were not interested in Thomas' standard of excellence, which had become integral to restaurant chain. Other owners assuming the business could run itself, simply left their franchises stranded. Some of them even decided to go public.

Aware that something had to be done, Thomas attempted to leave the situation to Samuel, who had been drafted in 1986 to become president and CEO of the company. Thomas hoped he had found his savior in Samuel, a board member since 1981 and one of Bonevista's most successful franchise owners, but he was less enthusiastic. But Thomas persisted and eventually Samuel agreed to take over. As a condition of accepting the position, though, Samuel insisted that Thomas become an active Bonevista's spokesperson and ambassador.

Although Thomas may have been initially reluctant, he has thrown himself wholeheartedly into the role of Bonevista's figure head. Maintaining an office next to Samuel's. Thomas tours the country regularly for market visits, promotional appearances, and television spots. Thomas's spots have scored consistently high in audience recognition and he has become a favourite of critics.

The "Bonevista's wildest tie contest" illustrates how well Thomas has learned to play his audience. Such visibility has not only made Thomas a well known figure, but it has also helped to shoot Bonevista's profitability and popularity back up and make it one of Wall Street's favourite restaurant. Many people attribute Bonevista's astonishing comeback to the enthusiasm was by their appointed leader. For Thomas himself, however, the success of the restaurant belongs to those who helped bring it about — his employees.

Discussion Questions

1. Is Thomas an effective leader? If so, what makes him effective? If not, why?
2. Do you consider Thomas charismatic? Why?
3. Are there styles of business in which Thomas' style might be less effective? More effective?

Case Let : 13

INXS Technologies is a well known IT company. Many of the company's clients were rapidly growing embedded solutions provider. Their solutions range from designing small micro-controller based systems and large real-time, multi-tasking software systems to developing board support packages and device drivers.

The business challenge facing this client was that many implementation projects were late and over budget. A key driver for improving their project management was that they had aggressive growth plans and the number of projects as well as the complexity of them would be increasing significantly. In addition, the functional managers and the senior executives were not obtaining the performance reporting that they needed during each engagement for resource and revenue planning.

At the same time as they were reevaluating their corporate strategic plans, they determined that they needed to assess their ability to deliver to the client, and to enhance the profitability of the project engagements. Key goals were to find an external partner that could: assess the current competencies of the project managers and propose a training and development plan appropriate to the organization's needs. Deliver a customized training programme for the project managers based upon the competencies assessment conducted and based on the unique needs for their types of projects.

Discussion Questions

1. Is a training programme necessary for project managers?
2. Suggest a solution to improve client deliver process?
3. Propose a training and development plan appropriate to organizational needs?

Case Let : 14

WORK BEHAVIOUR

Maya Sharma, a recent MBA Graduate, starts her first workday at the Bank of India This is a suburban bank which is experiencing steady but not phenomenal, growth for the pas three years. Its, located in area of expensive homes, shopping centers and two private Golc courses. Maya was hired as bank economist and assistant to the president. Her previous experience was as research economist with a small business administration for five years while she worked on her MBA degree in the evening. In Bank of India, she was a full-time employee, professional job in a private firm.

First few days of Maya's job was orientation to bank's operations and meeting other employee's. Amir Sani, bank president, chief executive officer, invited her to accompany him on new customer calls. He rarely drew her into banking and lending discussions with customers She silently took notes and listened. He never discussed any of the customers meeting with her.

Orientation and customer contacts happened for nearly three weeks, Maya started to doubt her decision on the accept of Mr.Sani's employment offer. His expectations were different. Mr.Sani promised her some special projects, including market analysis, cost studies of bank operations and evaluation of credit model for the bank's different categories of customers.

Four weeks has gone, but Maya was not given any special projects. She has met all the bank employees and many of the commercial borrowers. She knew she has the knowledge and skill to perform special projects. But she did know how to inform Sani to give her something.

One fine day Maya decided to talk to Sani's Secretary to do something for her. So she enquired about Sani, she found that Mr.Sani founded the bank ten years ago. Prior to that, he had been Vice-President and loan officer for larger regional bank. Maya was told that the bank never had anyone with an advance degree in Business Administration. The next morning after a sleepless night, Maya confronted to Sani 'saying' either you give me something meaningful to do or I am resigning.

Discussion Questions

1. What barriers to effective communication exist between Maya and Sani.

Case Let : 15

PALACE OF THE WEST EMPRESS

Koshy Mathew, 53 years old and 30% holder of "the Palace of the West Empress Restaurant Chain" was about to enter one of his 60th restaurant. This unit is recently opened in Madurai. He had a practice of giving surprise visit to each newly opened restaurant within the first few months of operation. His purpose of visit was to check on whether the employees were following the company's practice and policy. Even though he was the largest stockholder and clearly the most influential member of the board of directors, he was not actively engaged in day-to-day operations. All the 60 units were located in the mid-southern and south eastern areas. "Palace of the West Empress" was known for its cleanliness, food quality and customer service. Two years ago, Mr.Mathew relinquished the position of chief executive and chairman of the board of directors because of his moderately serious health condition and also of his repeated conflicts with several board members over his joke about Hindu-Muslim rivals and his opposition to Hindu-Muslim in restaurant management position. Mr.Mathew with his discriminatory treatment cost the firm to be under investigation by the state and federal civil right's agencies. Mr.Durai Swami the current CEO was hired 2 years back to negotiate the settlement of EEOC (equal employment opportunity commission). About 20 Hindu and Muslim claimed that they have been denied promotion because of racial discrimination. Mr.Mathew had entered the "the Palace of the West Empress" where he was treated by a Muslim hostess, two days after the visit of Mathew, Durai Swami was asked to resign along with 3 other top corporate official, including the female hostess who had welcomed Mr.Mathew.

Discussion Questions

1. Apply force field analysis to this situation and identify forces pushing for changes and forced resisting changes.
2. How could Lewin's change model be applied to "Palace of the West Empress" and key participants?
3. Outline an organization development and change program for "Palace of the West Empress". What do you hope to accomplish through such an effort?

Case Let : 16

RESISTANCE TO CHANGE

One of a General Manager of XYZ Company's concerns was that the organisation's way of doing things was causing health problems for its employees - especially its Managers. He'd read several newspaper and magazine articles about executive burnouts. There had been complaints about overloads, tight deadlines and confusion in assignments, but he tended to regard them as normal for any high-tech organization. If too much stress led to burnout, ill-health and poor performance, it might be cost-effective to do something about the problem.

The very next week the corporate newsletter carried a story on Quality of Work Life (QWL) programs of the company. It ended with an invitation to call and ask questions. That Manager did so and had a conversation with the Director of Human Resource Development of that company. The Manager explained his concerns and then the Director suggested that explicit attention could be paid to wellness within the framework of quality of work life and productivity. They discussed a specific proposal and the Manager invited all of his project directors to the meeting in that organisation's conference room and the Director started the presentation by outlining the purpose of QWL Programs, which are:

- To develop an attitude that company goals and personal goals can be mutually achieved.
- To promote mutual respect and trust among all personnel.
- To improve recognition of the individuals contributions and responsibilities.
- To improve employee morâle on and off the job.
- To promote physical and mental health and effective stress management.

And he continued that he wanted to be more sensitive to people's needs at work and ensure that people have control over their own work and are involved in making decisions and develop an atmosphere of respect and trust by sharing information with all employees.

He explained how the wellness program could be part of the QWL programme based on the concept of holism. A healthy lifestyle is outlined as individual's need for nutrition, exercise and relaxation. He also emphasized that people take health risks when they combine stress, physical inactivity and poor diets. He also highlighted some specific fundamental premises like physical fitness, nutrition, stress management etc. He said that it can be thought of as an employee assistance program and providing counselling also. The results would provide information to design improvement endeavours.

Then the Manager expressed his interest in taking the next step. He asked for reactions from his subordinates, the project managers. All was quick to respond that all this sounds good, but they don't have time to spend on helping people stay healthy and relaxed. If they had the rightstuff, they would thrive on this environment.

Responses from the others were mixed — several echoed his comments, a few expressed excitement about the prospects of e-wellness programmes that would be part of improving the quality of work life in the organization. Given the mixed reactions the Manager was unclear in his mind about what to do next.

Discussion Questions

1. Do you think pressure and stress are positively correlated with performance in organisations? Why or why not?
2. What is the connection between stress, health and performance in work organizations?
3. How much responsibility do the companies like this have for the mental and physical well-being of their employees?
4. Assume that the General Manager has asked you for advice, what would you tell him?

Case Let : 17

360-DEGREE FEEDBACK ON THE INTERNET

Performance appraisal system serve many purposes, such as providing formal feedback to employees on how to stack up with respect to the organization's standards, compensation decision, promotional decision, termination decision etc. Performance appraisal is one of the fundamental activities in human resource.

Traditionally, performance appraisal system was not able to provide good assessment for managers. To be more precise, it did not provide accurate evaluation for opportunistic managers.

With this background in mind there is much to be learned from experience of Shankarlal's company. The company had concerns that its old paper-based performance appraisal system was too slow and cumbersome, raters were not assured of the confidentiality of their rating and therefore they wanted a better appraisal system. It also wanted to enhance manager's project management and project team leadership skills. Given these concerns, Shankarlal decided to develop 360 degree feedback system. The innovative aspect was that the company decided to base the system to internet and its own intranet. An independent contractor, E-group developed the system and handles the collation and analysis of feedback information.

- It chose a 75-item survey called LEPAS, which measures 7 dimensions of leadership, for 360-degree instrument.
- It was available on web, so raters can pull all information with complete appraisals in 20 mins. After completion of appraisal the result was e-mailed to E-group to process.
- As the system was encrypted, it provided greater confidentiality for raters when compared to previous system.
- E-group was able to provide appraisal profile for the managers within 3 days after the evaluators e-mailed their input for the managers.
- Rating of managers also included leadership profile developed by Shankarlal's executives.
- By comparing the actual ratings with ideal profile, managers can identify areas for future development.
- Shankarlal chose this system only for development purpose, although recently it began to consider other purpose for the system.

Discussion Questions

1. What problems do you think Shankarlal experienced once the 360-degree system was successfully implemented on the internet?
2. What else is necessary to help ensure that performance appraisal system will be successful? How would you determine if the system affects the firm's performance?
3. Aside from the advantage of instantaneous transmission of information, what other advantages do you see with this type of performance appraisal system on the internet?

Case Let : 18

Career Planning

Sree Nidhi was a telephone operator at the headquarters in a large corporation. A high school graduate, she had no other skills other than a pleasing voice and personality. Nevertheless, Sree Nidhi wanted very much to improve her economic position. Recognizing her educational limitations, she began to take accounting courses on a random basis in an evening adult education programme. Unfortunately she did not have any particular plan for career development.

Sree Nidhi also took advantage of the corporation's bidding system by applying for openings that were posted, even though in many instances she did not meet the specifications listed for them after being rejected for several times, she became discouraged. Mrs. Sushma, one of the department managers in the corporation, observed her depressed spirits. Mrs. Sushma invited Sree Nidhi to come to her office for a talk about the problems she was having. Sree Nidhi took full advantage of the opportunity to express her frustrations and disappointments. As she unburdened herself, it became apparent that, besides lacking special skills and career objectives, during interviews she tended to apologize for having "only a high school education". This made it difficult for the interviewers to select her over the other candidates who were putting their foot forward. Mrs.Sushma suggested that Sree Nidhi might try taking a positive approach during her interviews. For example she could stress her self-improvement efforts at night school and the fact she was dependable and co-operative person who was willing to work hard to succeed in the job for which she was applying.

Following Mrs.Sushma's advice, Sree Nidhi selected a job for which she felt she could qualify. She made a very forceful and positive presentation during her interview, stressing, the favourable qualities that she possessed. As a result of this approach, she was selected for the job of invoice clerk. While this job did not pay much than that of a telephone operator, it did offer an avenue for possible advancement into the accounting field where the accounting courses she was taken could be of value.

Discussion Questions

1. What are some of the possible reasons why Mrs.Sushma did not seek or receive advice from his immediate supervisor.

2. Suggest all possible ways that Sree Nidhi can prepare herself for career advancement.

Case Let : 19

ORGANISATION STRUCTURE

Restructuring of Rexico

Rexico commenced a business unit of a large private sector organization. The organization had operations in a number of information technology applications. In mid 1990s, senior manager decided to undertake a programme of internal rationalization because management control was inadequate and it was exposed to wide range operations. Senior managers decided to engineer a buy out having raised the finance largely through an investment company and started an independent company in its own right. As a business unit of the original parent organization, Rexico had operated with a fairly simple, functionally arranged organizational structure. General Manager of the unit, who became the Managing Director of Rexico, had undertaken the over all co-ordinating role but with specific responsibility of the financial management of the business unit. Two other central business unit managers had specific functional responsibilities. One was responsible for arranging contacts and co-ordinating the parent organization. The HR department was aware of its image as being a cost. Rexico was able to draw on the central HR function whenever it required support in this area. The transformation of Rexico to an independent organization therefore heralded further change for this business who worked for it. The old parent organizations are the financial backing and the support of its corporate service provision. The strategy of out sourcing was seen as corporate service provision and the opportunity to test the market place to a greater extent had been in the case. The exposure to market focuses led to a number of structural changes. These were driven by a desire to cut cost, maximize utilization of work for Rexico and increase the level of managerial control. The strategy of the new organization was now focused towards their market place and competitors rather than the old parent organization for which they had traditionally worked. HR issues of almost any nature had been referred up to the personal function of the old parent organization.

Discussion Questions

1. How do you think Rexico's will react to its changing organisational structures and the strategies used to implement these changes.
2. How do you think these reactions will affect Rexico's ability to realise its intended strategy?
3. What recommendations would you make to the senior management of Rexico in relation to the scope and nature of HR strategies of the organisation?

Case Let : 20

10'O CLOCK's TOTAL QUALITY CULTURE

10'O Clock means "razor blade" in India. When we utter the word 10'O Clock even a child in India says its a Razor Blade for men and women. 10'O Clock dominates the 'wet shaving' market and has been for several generations. For example, in 1923, 10'O Clock was the market share leader and remained so till 1994.

10'O Clock has about two-thirds of the Indian market and its share of the world market is even higher. In North West India its market share is over 80 per cent.

Over the years, 10'O Clock has been faced with numerous competitive challenges, yet has always responded with improved products. This type of success doesn't just happen. It is the result of relentless quest for improvements in shaving technology and high levels of commitment and teamwork from employees. The CEO of 10'O Clock shaves half of his face with his product and half with a competitor's to compare the closeness of the shaves. Therefore, his employees also did the same everyday and every week each competitor is tested and analysed and improves his product. And even women comes with unshaven legs and do the same. This is the culture followed in 10'O Clock 'wet shaving' organisation. The VP in charge of 10'O Clock shaving technology lab is Mrs.Sherin she says we test the blade edge, the blade guard, the angles of the blades, the balance of the Razor's..... Finally she says "We own the face". We know about shaving than anybody.

Discussion Questions

1. Will the 10'O Clock Razor Blades retain their market share positions?
2. Can you suggest some ideas wherein they can improve their market share even in South India?

Case Let : 21

"HURRY UP AND SUCCEED" FADING RATES OF PROMOTION

Jain and Co., engaged in the business of manufacturing is headed by Mr.Sai an MBA from XLRI Jamshedpur. Over the years, the conventional managerial practices has made the company to experience growth and expansion. The product portfolio comprised of Cosmetics, Food and Beverage products. Initially, the company made greater revenues and was able to satisfy the targeted consumers. Later, the greater industrial growth brought in stiff market competition. Currently, the company faces challenges on (i) Meeting ever changing customer needs, (ii) To bring a change in organisational culture, (iii) To enhance employees' performance and satisfaction.

From the time of inception, the company is operating in a flattened organisational structure. Though Sai was able to manage the performance effectively, expansion urged delegation of authority at functional levels.

Initially employees had greater job satisfaction. But the current demands of changing technology, need to develop self managed teams, focus on quality in products and services has made workers feel fatigue and frustrations at work place.

Primarily, technological change has resulted in lower job security, increased demand on meritorious performance and their related rewards and promotion. Hence, many employees are worried about their career advancements, job fitness and monetary rewards.

Mr.Sai felt that he should bring an OD consultant to study the existing organisational culture, feasibility of introducing change and ways to enhance employee performance.

Discussion Questions

1. If you are an OD consultant, suggest the interventions to be used in Jain & Co.
2. Does the flattened organisational structure pose a threat for change in organisational culture?

Case Let : 22

(ORGANISATION CULTURE): BANK OF RAJASTHAN

Bank of Rajasthan has rediscovered its original culture. Mr.R.Mukesh Singh founded the bank to provide banking services for the immigrants of Sri Lanka. In its early years, the bank pioneered many services to make banking more customer friendly. It attracted thousands of small personal accounts by offering convenient branch banking, clever advertising and well-designed, "inviting" offices. At the same time, Mukesh took large risks, including backing projects as diverse as the Golden Gate Bridge.

The Bank of Rajasthan discovered great many things that worked well and institutionalized them, becoming both efficient and predictable. This success gave rise to a new set of assumptions that characterized its organizational culture for some years: Don't risk failure; take a short-term view; don't be frank when evaluating products or programmes; seniority is more important than performance; study every new idea to death. In the 1980s, a loss of market share and the resources used in fending of a hostile takeover attempt left Bank of Rajasthan in a weakened position. In addition, just when needed to respond to increased competition in the market its culture resisted the needed changes and the banks ways of doing business no longer worked.

Rather than responding with the new rules and regulations Bank of Rajasthan chose to reemphasize its core values and promote change by focusing on its original company culture. Core values included putting the customer in ease and respecting and rewarding both the customers and the employees. The bank communicated the new (original culture throughout the organization by means of meetings, publications and the training programmes. The new culture came up with a changed business strategy, including aggressive acquisition programme, returned the Bank of Rajasthan to profitability and preeminence.

Discussion Question

1. If you are a HRD Consultant, how will you help "Bank of Rajasthan" rediscover its culture?

Case Let : 23

THIS IS NOT AN EVOLUTION ITS A REVOLUTION

The $18 billion company under CEO James reflects how a big company can adapt to rapidly changing technology and competition. Its old organisation design made Xerox a classic American Corporation in which the chairman and top executives made all significant decisions.

This company had been organised in a Monolithic approach to Management. About 12 years ago Xerox was near collapse. It was bogged down by bureaucracy, slow to market its acting edge products, and lost sales to Japanese competitors such as Canon and Sharp. Management and Union were bitter foes.

Under the old structure the Chairman was at the top and factory workers at the bottom. Xerox operations were grouped into four gigantic units based on functions. Today, Xerox's new divisions resembles independent business with each performing nearly all functions. The company has no longer one all powerful President, but a six-person corporate office headed by James. Three separate geographic units sell and service all Xerox products.

A simple decision like the colour of the buttons on a copier used to climb the hierarchy nearly to corporate headquarters. Now such decisions are made by the respective divisions and they are accountable for the same.

On the manufacturing side Xerox needs to ensure that divisions don't monopolise cost-effective practices. Also, sales people remain accountable to all Divisions because Xerox's is not breaking up its salesforce. Thus, customers don't have to meet with a variety of representatives from different divisions.

Discussion Question

1. Comment on the Organisational Design of Xerox.